Youth, Identity, and Digital Media

This book was made possible by grants from the John D. and Catherine T. MacArthur Foundation in connection with its grant making initiative on Digital Media and Learning. For more information on the initiative visit www.macfound.org.

The John D. and Catherine T. MacArthur Foundation Series on Digital Media and Learning

Civic Life Online: Learning How Digital Media Can Engage Youth, edited by W. Lance Bennett
Digital Media, Youth, and Credibility, edited by Miriam J. Metzger and Andrew J. Flanagin
The Ecology of Games: Connecting Youth, Games, and Learning, edited by Katie Salen
Digital Youth, Innovation, and the Unexpected, edited by Tara McPherson
Learning Race and Ethnicity: Youth and Digital Media, edited by Anna Everett
Youth, Identity, and Digital Media, edited by David Buckingham

Youth, Identity, and Digital Media

Edited by David Buckingham

The MIT Press
Cambridge, Massachusetts
London, England

For information about special quantity discounts, please email special_sales@mitpress.mit.edu.

This book was set in Stone sans and Stone serif by Aptara, Inc.

Printed and bound in the United States of America.

Library of Congress Cataloging-in-Publication Data

Youth, identity, and digital media / edited by David Buckingham.
p. cm.—(The John D. and Catherine T. Macarthur Foundation series on digital media and learning)
Includes bibliographical references.
ISBN 978-0-262-02635-2 (hardcover : alk. paper)—ISBN 978-0-262-52483-4 (pbk. : alk. paper)
1. Internet and teenagers. 2. Identity (Psychology) in adolescence.
3. Teenagers—Computer network resources. 4. Digital media—Social aspects.
5. Internet—Social aspects. I. Buckingham, David, 1954–
HQ799.2.I5Y67 2008
302.23'10835—dc22 2007029791

10 9 8 7 6 5 4 3 2 1

CONTENTS

Foreword

In recent years, digital media and networks have become embedded in our everyday lives, and are part of broad-based changes to how we engage in knowledge production, communication, and creative expression. Unlike the early years in the development of computers and computer-based media, digital media are now *commonplace* and *pervasive*, having been taken up by a wide range of individuals and institutions in all walks of life. Digital media have escaped the boundaries of professional and formal practice, and the academic, governmental, and industry homes that initially fostered their development. Now they have been taken up by diverse populations and non-institutionalized practices, including the peer activities of youth. Although specific forms of technology uptake are highly diverse, a generation is growing up in an era where digital media are part of the taken-for-granted social and cultural fabric of learning, play, and social communication.

In 2005, The John D. and Catherine T. MacArthur Foundation began a new grant-making initiative in the area of digital media and learning. An initial set of exploratory grants in the study of youth practices and the development of digital literacy programs has expanded into a major initiative spanning research, educational reform, and technology development. One component of this effort is the support of this book series. As part of the broader MacArthur Foundation initiative, this series is aimed at timely dissemination of new scholarship, fostering an interdisciplinary conversation, and archiving the best research in this emerging field. Through the course of producing the six initial volumes, the foundation convened a set of meetings to discuss the framing issues for this book series. As a result of these discussions we identified a set of shared commitments and areas of focus. Although we recognize that the terrain is being reshaped even as we seek to identify it, we see these as initial frames for the ongoing work to be put forward by this series.

This book series is founded upon the working hypothesis that those immersed in new digital tools and networks are engaged in an unprecedented exploration of language, games, social interaction, problem solving, and self-directed activity that leads to diverse forms of learning. These diverse forms of learning are reflected in expressions of identity, how individuals express independence and creativity, and in their ability to learn, exercise judgment, and think systematically.

The defining frame for this series is not a particular theoretical or disciplinary approach, nor is it a fixed set of topics. Rather, the series revolves around a constellation of topics investigated from multiple disciplinary and practical frames. The series as a whole looks at the relation between youth, learning, and digital media, but each book or essay might deal with only a subset of this constellation. Erecting strict topical boundaries can exclude some of the most important work in the field. For example, restricting the content of the series only to people of a certain age means artificially reifying an age boundary when the phenomenon demands otherwise. This becomes particularly problematic with new forms of online participation where one important outcome is the mixing of participants of different ages. The same goes for digital media, which are increasingly inseparable from analog and earlier media forms.

In the case of learning, digital media are part of the redefinition and broadening of existing boundaries of practice and our understanding of what learning means. The term *learning* was chosen rather than *education* in order to flag an interest in settings both within and outside the classroom. Many of the more radical challenges to existing learning agendas are happening in domains such as gaming, online networks, and amateur production that usually occur in informal and non-institutional settings. This does not mean we are prejudiced against learning as it happens in the classroom or other formal educational settings. Rather, we hope to initiate a dialog about learning as it spans settings that are more explicitly educational and those that are not.

The series and the MacArthur Foundation initiative respond to certain changes in our media ecology that have important implications for learning. Specifically, these are new forms of media *literacy* and changes in the modes of media *participation*. Digital media are part of a convergence between interactive media (most notably gaming), online networks, and existing media forms. Navigating this media ecology involves a palette of literacies that are being defined through practice but require more scholarly scrutiny before they can be fully incorporated pervasively into educational initiatives. Media literacy involves not only ways of understanding, interpreting, and critiquing media, but also the means for creative and social expression, online search and navigation, and a host of new technical skills. The potential gap in literacies and participation skills creates new challenges for educators who struggle to bridge media engagement inside and outside the classroom.

The shift toward interactive media, peer-to-peer forms of media communication, and many-to-many forms of distribution relate to types of participation that are more bottom-up and driven by the "user" or "consumer" of media. Audiences have always had the opportunity to "talk back" to corporate media or to create their own local media forms. However, the growing dominance of gaming as a media format, the advent of low-cost digital production tools, and online distribution means a much more dynamic range in who participates and how they participate in the production and distribution of media. Gamers expect that media are subject to player control. Add to this the fact that all forms of media are increasingly being contextualized in an online communication ecology where creative production and expression is inseparable from social communication. Finally, new low-cost digital production tools mean that amateur and casual media creators can author, edit, and distribute video and other rich media forms that were once prohibitively expensive to produce and share with others.

We value the term *participation* for the ways in which it draws attention to situated learning theory, social media literacies, and mobilized forms of media engagement. Digital media networks support existing forms of mass media distribution as well as smaller publics and collectivities that might center on peer groups or specialized niche interests. The presence of social communication, professional media, and amateur niche media in shared online spaces introduces a kind of leveling effect, where small media players gain new visibility and the position of previously authoritative media is challenged. The clash between more socially driven or niche publics and the publics defined by professional forms of media is playing out in high-profile battles in domains such as intellectual property law, journalism, entertainment, and government. For our purposes, the questions surrounding knowledge and credibility and young people's use of digital media to circumvent adult authority are particularly salient.

The emerging power shift, where smaller and edge players are gaining more visibility and voice, is particularly important to children and youth. If we look at children and youth through the lens of digital media, we have a population that has been historically subject to a high degree of systematic and institutional control in the kinds of information and social communication to which they have access. This is one reason why the alchemy between youth and digital media has been distinctive; it disrupts the existing set of power relations between adult authority and youth voice. While many studies of children, youth, and media have for decades stressed the status of young people as competent and full social subjects, digital media increasingly insist that we acknowledge this viewpoint. Not only must we see youth as legitimate social and political actors, but we must also recognize them as potential innovators and drivers of new media change.

This does not mean that we are uncritical of youth practices or that we believe that digital media necessarily hold the key to empowerment. Rather, we argue against technological determinism, stressing the need for balanced scholarship that recognizes the importance of our current moment within the context of existing structures and unfolding histories. This means placing contemporary changes within a historical context as well as working to highlight the diversity in the landscape of media and media uptake. Neither youth nor digital media are monolithic categories; documenting how specific youth take up particular forms of media with diverse learning outcomes is critical to this series as a whole. Digital media take the form they do because they are created by existing social and cultural contexts, contexts that are diverse and stratified.

As with earlier shifts in media environments, this current turn toward digital media and networks has been accompanied by fear and panic as well as elevated hopes. This is particularly true of adult perception of children and youth who are at the forefront of experimentation with new media forms, and who mobilize digital media to push back at existing structures of power and authority. While some see "digital kids" as our best hope for the future, others worry that new media are part of a generational rift and a dangerous turn away from existing standards for knowledge, literacy, and civic engagement. Careful, socially engaged, and accessible scholarship is crucial to informing this public debate and related policy decisions. Our need to understand the relation between digital media and learning is urgent because of the scale and the speed of the changes that are afoot. The shape and uses of digital media are still very much in flux, and this book series seeks to be part of the definition of our sociotechnical future.

Mizuko Ito
Cathy Davidson
Henry Jenkins
Carol Lee
Michael Eisenberg
Joanne Weiss
Series Advisors

Introducing Identity

David Buckingham

Institute of Education, University of London, Centre for the Study of Children, Youth and Media

Identity is an ambiguous and slippery term. It has been used—and perhaps overused—in many different contexts and for many different purposes, particularly in recent years. As we shall see, there are some diverse assumptions about what identity is, and about its relevance to our understanding of young people's engagements with digital media.

The fundamental paradox of identity is inherent in the term itself. From the Latin root *idem*, meaning "the same," the term nevertheless implies both similarity and difference. On the one hand, identity is something unique to each of us that we assume is more or less consistent (and hence the same) over time. For instance, as I write, there is an intense debate in the U.K. about the government's proposed introduction of identity cards and their potential for addressing the problem of "identity theft." In these formulations, our identity is something we uniquely possess: it is what distinguishes us from other people. Yet on the other hand, identity also implies a relationship with a broader collective or social group of some kind. When we talk about national identity, cultural identity, or gender identity, for example, we imply that our identity is partly a matter of what we share with other people. Here, identity is about *identification* with others whom we assume are similar to us (if not exactly the same), at least in some significant ways.

Much of the debate around identity derives from the tensions between these two aspects. I may struggle to "be myself" or to "find my true self," and there are many would-be experts and authorities who claim to be able to help me to do this. Yet I also seek multiple identifications with others, on the basis of social, cultural, and biological characteristics, as well as shared values, personal histories, and interests. On one level, I am the product of my unique personal biography. Yet who I am (or who I think I am) varies according to who I am with, the social situations in which I find myself, and the motivations I may have at the time, although I am by no means entirely free to choose how I am defined.

An explicit concern with questions of identity is not a novel development, although it has undoubtedly taken on a new urgency in the contemporary world.[1] Identity is not merely a matter of playful experimentation or "personal growth": it is also about the life-or-death struggles for self-determination that are currently being waged in so many parts of the world. According to the social theorist Zygmunt Bauman, the new prominence that is accorded to identity is a reflection of the fact that it is becoming ever more problematic.[2] Globalization, the decline of the welfare state, increasing social mobility, greater flexibility in employment, insecurity in personal relationships—all these developments are contributing to a sense of fragmentation and uncertainty, in which the traditional resources for identity formation are no longer so straightforward or so easily available. Like many contemporary authors,

Bauman emphasizes the fluidity of identity, seeing it as almost infinitely negotiable, and in the process perhaps underestimates the continuing importance of routine and stability. Nevertheless, his general point is well taken: "identity" only becomes an issue when it is threatened or contested in some way and needs to be explicitly asserted.

Accounting for Identities

Within the human sciences, several disciplinary specialisms have laid claim to identity. The most obvious distinction here is between psychological and sociological approaches, but a whole range of subdisciplines and intellectual paradigms—developmental psychology, social theory, symbolic interactionism, cultural studies, and many others—have also sought to generate definitive accounts. In the first part of this chapter, I discuss five key approaches to thinking about identity and briefly identify some of their implications for understanding young people, digital media, and learning. These latter issues are then dealt with more explicitly in the second main part of the chapter.

Identity Formation: The Psychology of Adolescence

The first two approaches I discuss here are explicitly concerned with *youth* identities. The modern psychological account of youth can arguably be traced back to G. Stanley Hall's classic accounts of adolescence, published in the early years of the last century.[3] Hall is often credited with introducing the popular notion of adolescence as a period of "storm and stress," characterized by intergenerational conflicts, mood swings and an enthusiasm for risky behavior. From this perspective, the discussion of adolescence often leads inexorably to the discussion of drugs, delinquency, depression, and sexual deviance. Hall's approach is perhaps best termed "psycho-biological": his symptomatically titled book *Youth: Its Education, Regimen and Hygiene* (1906) includes extensive proposals for education and moral and religious training, incorporating practical advice on gymnastics and muscular development (not to mention quaint discussions of "sex dangers" and the virtues of cold baths).

Another classic psychological account of adolescence can be found in the work of Erik Erikson, most notably in his book *Identity: Youth and Crisis*, published in 1968.[4] Erikson's developmental theory extends Piaget's account of "ages and stages" into adulthood and old age. Each of his eight stages is characterized by a fundamental psychological conflict, whose successful resolution allows progression to the next stage. In the case of adolescence, the conflict is between identity and "role confusion." Resolving this conflict involves finding a more or less settled role in life, and it results in the formation of a "virtue" (a form of psychological strength)—in this case, loyalty or fidelity—that enables the young person to progress to early adulthood and to form the intimate attachments that are the key tasks of that stage. Unsuccessful resolution results in a "maladaptation," for instance in the form of fanaticism or a repudiation of adult responsibility.

Erikson therefore sees adolescence as a critical period of identity formation, in which individuals overcome uncertainty, become more self-aware of their strengths and weaknesses, and become more confident in their own unique qualities. In order to move on, adolescents must undergo a "crisis" in which they address key questions about their values and ideals, their future occupation or career, and their sexual identity. Through this process of self-reflection and self-definition, adolescents arrive at an integrated, coherent sense of their identity as something that persists over time. While this is partly a psychological process—and indeed a function of general cognitive development—it also occurs through interaction with peers and care givers. Identity is developed by the individual, but it has to be recognized and confirmed by others. Adolescence is thus also a period in which young people negotiate their separation from their family, and develop independent social competence (for example, through participation in "cliques" and larger "crowds" of peers, who exert different types of influence).

James Marcia builds on Erikson's account, focusing particularly on the notion of adolescence as a period of "identity crisis."[5] Through this period, the young person has to consider potential life choices and eventually make a commitment or psychological investment in particular decisions. Marcia identifies four "identity statuses," which represent different positions in this process. In the case of "foreclosure," the individual has effectively avoided the crisis by following others' expectations; in "diffusion," the person has given up on the attempt to make the necessary commitment; in "moratorium," the individual is still actively in the period of crisis, testing out various alternative commitments, while "achievement" only arrives when the person has been through the crisis and made clear choices about who he or she wants to become.

Of course, it is possible to debate the validity of such stage-based theories: is adolescence in fact a distinctive stage with a beginning and an end, or is human development more appropriately seen as a matter of gradual progression? Erikson and his followers claim that the stages they identify are universal, although it could be argued that "adolescence" as such does not exist in earlier historical periods, or in other cultures.[6] Others, like the psychologist Carol Gilligan, have argued that moral development takes a different path for males and females, which again implies that such generalized models may not take a sufficient account of social differences.[7] Furthermore, like most developmental theories, this approach is ultimately very normative. The healthy, mature individual is one who has attained a stable, integrated identity. Continuing "confusion" about one's identity is a mark of incomplete development, and may result in deviant or antisocial behavior. From this perspective, adolescence is seen primarily as a state of transition, a matter of "becoming" rather than "being."[8] Adolescents' key dilemmas are to do with what they will become, particularly in terms of their future occupation and their relationships: their current experiences are only significant insofar as they help them resolve their crisis and hence move on.

Despite the criticisms that can be made here, psychological accounts of adolescence do provide some useful concepts with which to interpret young people's relations with digital media. Erikson's notion of adolescence as a "psychosocial moratorium," a period of "time out" in which young people can experiment with different potential identities—and indeed engage with risks of various kinds—seems particularly appropriate in this respect. These kinds of approaches are exemplified (and indeed contested) by several of the contributors to this volume. For example, Susannah Stern's discussion of young people's online authorship of blogs and home pages suggests that this activity can provide important opportunities for self-reflection and self-realization, and for expressing some of the conflicts and crises that characterize this period. Some of the young people whom she discusses explicitly see adolescence as an "in-between stage," in which they are consciously seeking future directions in their lives. In a different vein, danah boyd's chapter also implies that social networking sites like MySpace provide opportunities for social interaction and affiliation that are crucial developmental tasks for this age group—opportunities that are all the more important now, as their access to "offline" public spaces has become increasingly restricted.

Youth Culture and the Sociology of Youth

Sociologists generally take a very different perspective on youth compared with the psychological accounts I have just outlined. Of course, there are some similarities between psychological studies of *development* and sociological analyses of *socialization*, despite the differences in terminology: both are essentially concerned with the ways in which young people are gradually prepared, or prepare themselves, to take up their allotted roles in adult life. A traditional, functionalist account of socialization would see this in equally normative terms: the young person is a passive recipient of adult influences, a "becoming" rather than a "being" in their own right.

Mainstream sociologists have also been particularly concerned with issues of youthful deviance and delinquency, in ways that often entail a pathological view of young people. Youth—particularly youth in marginalized or subordinated social groups—are frequently constructed as a "social problem" or "at risk." This then serves to legitimate various forms of treatment—the work of social, educational, and clinical agencies that seeks to discipline or rehabilitate troublesome youth, or to define and correct their apparent deficiencies. Nevertheless, sociologists generally understand these phenomena in terms of social factors such as poverty and inequality rather than as a matter of "raging hormones": their interest is not so much in internal personality conflicts, but more in the social uncertainties that young people face, for example as they make the transition from the parental home to the labor market.[9]

Furthermore, sociologists acknowledge that the nature of youth varies significantly according to the social context, and particularly in relation to factors such as social class, gender, and ethnicity. Indeed, social historians have argued that "youth" is a relatively modern invention, which has resulted from the extension of the period of transition that lasts from the end of compulsory schooling to the entry into waged labor; and this is clearly something that varies significantly between different social groups and between different cultural settings (in parts of the world where children leave school at the age of eleven, for example, "youth" is unlikely to be seen as a distinct category).[10] More recently, one could argue that youth is increasingly defined through the operations of the commercial market. The category of the "teenager," for example, was effectively brought into being in the 1950s through market research; and in contemporary marketing discourse, we can see the emergence of a whole series of newly invented categories such as "tweens," "middle youth," "kidults," and "adultescents"—categories that crucially blur the distinctions between children, youth and adults.[11] The invention and use of a category like "Generation X" (and its subsequent mutations) reflects both the importance and the complexity of age-based distinctions in contemporary consumer culture.[12] As this implies, "youth" is essentially a social and historical construct, rather than a universal state of being.

More radical youth research within Cultural Studies has contested the view of youthful expression as simply a function of adult attempts at socialization. There is a long tradition here of empirical research on youth culture, dating back to the early 1970s, and it is mostly concerned with the ways in which young people appropriate cultural commodities and use them for their own devices. Much of this work has focused on specific youth "subcultures"—groups such as hippies, skinheads, punks, goths, ravers, and others—who are seen to be resisting or opposing the imperatives of the parent culture, for example, through fashion, dance, music, and other cultural forms. Subcultures are seen here not just as a subordinate, but also as subversive: they arise from contradictions and tensions in the dominant social order and represent a threat to established social norms.[13]

Initially, much of this research focused on male, working class "street culture," although there is now a growing body of research on the youth cultures of girls and young women, and (to a lesser extent) on specific ethnic subcultures.[14] The emphasis here—as in some work on the anthropology of childhood and youth[15]—has been on attempting to understand youth cultures in their own terms, "from the bottom up," rather than judging them in terms of adult-oriented notions such as socialization. However, more recent research has pointed to the dangers of romanticizing youthful resistance and the tendency to overstate the political dimensions of youth culture. It has also challenged the rather simplistic opposition between "subversive" and "mainstream" culture, arguing that youth cultures can be just as hierarchical and exclusive as any other social groupings.[16] Some recent research has suggested that contemporary youth cultures are increasingly diverse and fragmented, and that they are best seen, not as a matter of self-contained "subcultures" but in a more fluid way, as "scenes" or "lifestyles" to which young people may be only temporarily attached.[17] Even so, there has been relatively little research on the more mundane, even conformist, cultures of young people who are not members of such "spectacular" or oppositional groupings (or indeed on affluent middle-class youth).

Despite its limitations, this kind of research focuses attention on the social and cultural dimensions of young people's identities, in ways which are particularly relevant to their interactions with digital media. On the one hand, we clearly need to acknowledge how commercial forces both create opportunities and set limits on young people's digital cultures; and we should also not forget that access to these media—and the ways in which they are used—is partly dependent upon differences to do with factors such as social class, gender, and ethnicity. Yet, on the other hand, we also need to consider how these media provide young people with symbolic resources for constructing or expressing their own identities, and, in some instances, for evading or directly resisting adult authority.

These points are taken up in different ways in several of the contributions that follow. Sandra Weber and Claudia Mitchell, for example, provide a series of case studies taken from very different cultural contexts that illustrate some of the diverse ways in which young people use digital media to reflect particular subcultural allegiances, or indeed to claim "spaces" that escape adult control. Likewise, Shelley Goldman, Meghan McDermott, and Angela Booker provide an example of how young people can use media production to address social issues that are of particular concern for them, and to make their voices heard by a wider audience. On the other hand, Susan Herring's chapter offers an important challenge to the assumptions that are often made about young people and their relations with technology—assumptions that frequently seem to veer between moral panics about the dangers of new media and an exaggerated romanticism about their liberating potential.

Social Identity: The Individual and the Group

Both the approaches outlined so far are directly concerned with *youth* identities, and the contrast between them amply illustrates some of the broader differences between psychological and sociological perspectives. Yet the discussion of identity obviously extends much more widely than this. The remaining three perspectives I discuss here are concerned with broader questions about the changing nature of identities, and the means of identify formation, in modern societies.

There is a large and diverse body of work within sociology, social psychology, and anthropology concerned with the relations between individual and group identities.[18] Researchers have studied how people categorize or label themselves and others, how they identify as members of particular groups; how a sense of group belonging or "community" is developed and maintained, and how groups discriminate against outsiders; how the boundaries between groups operate, and how groups relate to each other; and how institutions define and organize identities. These processes operate at both social and individual levels: individuals may make claims about their identity (for example, by asserting affiliation with other members of a group), but those claims need to be recognized by others. In seeking to define their identity, people attempt to assert their individuality, but also to join with others, and they work to sustain their sense of status or self-esteem in doing so. As a result, the formation of identity often involves a process of stereotyping or "cognitive simplification" that allows people to distinguish easily between self and other, and to define themselves and their group in positive ways.

Drawing on this approach, Richard Jenkins argues that social identity should be seen not so much as a fixed possession, but as a social process, in which the individual and the social are inextricably related.[19] Individual selfhood is a social phenomenon, but the social world is constituted through the actions of individuals. As such, identity is a fluid, contingent matter—it is something we accomplish practically through our ongoing interactions and negotiations with other people. In this respect, it might be more appropriate to talk about *identification* rather than *identity*.

One classic example of this approach is Erving Goffman's *The Presentation of Self in Everyday Life*, first published in the late 1950s.[20] Goffman provides what he calls a "dramaturgical" account of social interaction as a kind of theatrical performance. Individuals seek to create impressions on others that will enable them to achieve their goals ("impression management"), and they may join or collude with others to create collaborative performances in doing so. Goffman distinguishes here between "front-stage" and "back-stage" behavior. When "on stage," for example in a workplace or in a social gathering, individuals tend to conform to standardized definitions of the situation and of their individual role within it, playing out a kind of ritual. Back stage, they have the opportunity to be more honest: the impressions created while on stage may be directly contradicted, and the team of performers may disagree with each other.

Critics have argued that Goffman tends to overstate the importance of rules and to neglect the aspects of improvisation, or indeed sheer habit, that characterize everyday social interaction. More significantly, he suggests that back-stage behavior is somehow more authentic, or closer to the truth of the individual's real identity, which appears to imply that front-stage behavior is somehow less sincere or less honest. This could be seen to neglect the extent to which *all* social interaction is a kind of performance. Like some other researchers in this tradition, Goffman sometimes appears to make a problematic distinction between *personal* identity and *social* identity, as though collective identifications or performances were somehow separate from individual ones, which are necessarily more "truthful."[21]

Nevertheless, this approach has several implications for our understanding of young people's uses of digital media. It is most obviously appropriate for understanding online interactions, for example, in the case of instant messaging, chat or social networking, and for mobile communication, where questions of rules and etiquette are clearly crucial—not least because of the absence of many of the other cues (such as visual ones) we conventionally use to make identity claims in everyday life. The issue of performance is also very relevant to the ways in which young people construct identities, for example, via the use of avatars, e-mail signatures, IM nicknames, and (in a more elaborate way) in personal homepages and blogs. The question of whether online identities are more or less honest or truthful than offline ones has of course been a recurrent concern in studies of computer-mediated communication.[22]

These kinds of issues are explored in various ways in the subsequent chapters. For example, Gitte Stald's discussion of young people's uses of mobile phones points to several ways in which mobile technologies may be changing—or at least intensifying—the forms of social connectedness that characterize their interactions both with friends and family. The use of mobiles requires young people to develop new social and communicative skills and new social norms that enable them to regulate these relationships. Similarly, danah boyd's analysis of how friendships are conducted in MySpace draws attention to the complex ways in which hierarchies are formed, impressions are managed and social roles are played out; and while these processes have much in common with those that apply in traditional "offline" relationships, they have nevertheless generated significant anxiety for many adults.

Reclaiming Identities: Identity Politics

Questions of social power are implicit in social identity theory, but they come to the fore in what is often termed "identity politics." Clearly, different groups of individuals will lay claim to positive identities in quite different ways, and these claims may be recognized as more or less legitimate by those who hold power in society. As such, questions of identity are inevitably tied up with the issue of social status. The term "identity politics" refers primarily to activist social movements that have explicitly sought to challenge this process: they have struggled to resist oppressive accounts of their identities constructed by others who hold power over them, and claimed the right to self-determination. The most obvious aspects of this relate to "race," ethnicity, gender, sexuality, and disability; although the term "identity politics" is also often used in relation to forms of indigenous nationalism, religious groupings (and indeed forms of "fundamentalism"), and so on.

Identity politics thus entails a call for the recognition of aspects of identity that have previously been denied, marginalized, or stigmatized. Yet this call is not in the name of some generalized "humanity": it is a claim for identity not *in spite of* difference, but *because of* it. As this implies, identity politics is very much about transformation at the level of the group, rather than merely the individual: it is about identification and solidarity. Issues of representation—about who has the right to represent, or to speak, and for whom—are therefore also crucial here.[23]

Identity politics has been popularly criticized, both from the political right (as a kind of special pleading) and from the political left (as a diversion from the imperatives of the class struggle). But even in its own terms, identity politics has raised some significant problems that do not seem capable of easy resolutions. Perhaps the most fundamental issue here is that of essentialism, that is, the tendency to generalize about the members of a particular group and assimilate them to a singular identity. This approach runs the risk of fixing identity, for example in terms of people's biological characteristics or their historical origins, and ignoring their diversity. It neglects the fact that people have multiple dimensions to their identities, and may well resist having to select one that will override all the others.

Exponents of identity politics have argued that a kind of strategic essentialism may be necessary for particular purposes, and that different coalitions may be formed at different times. But such alliances can founder on the almost infinite factions and subdivisions that can emerge: does "race" override gender, for example, and who has the right to say that it does? Furthermore, different forms of power can operate within groups as well as between them: for example, women may unite to resist male oppression, but middle-class women will have access to other ways of exercising social power that are not available to their working-class counterparts. There is often a tension within such social movements between two contrasting aims—on the one hand, a claim for separatism (which can result in marginalization), and on the other, a move towards integration with the mainstream (which can result in the erasure of identity).

In some respects, therefore, the difficulties of identity politics follow from the fundamental paradox of identity with which we began. It could be argued that this kind of identity categorization is inevitably reductive; and yet all sorts of well-established social practices—and indeed laws—are based on such categories, for example, in the case of racial profiling, citizenship laws, immigration priorities, as well as the various "isms" of racism, sexism, homophobia, and so on. Of course, emphasizing aspects of identity that are shared inevitably means playing down aspects that differ. Yet claiming authenticity for a given identity is problematic when that identity is defined in opposition to another. To assert what is uniquely female (or feminine), for example, is to run the risk of reinforcing the binary opposition (male/female) that one is seeking to challenge. To assert "racial" authenticity with reference to unique historical origins or roots is to reassert the differences (and indeed the socially constructed category of "race") that one is seeking to undermine.[24] Yet to do the opposite—to celebrate gender fluidity or ethnic "hybridity"—is to run the risk of dissolving the very identities on which political claims can be made.

Queer theory offers a radical challenge to identity politics on precisely these grounds. It challenges established identity categories—including "gay" and "lesbian"—on the grounds that they inevitably lead to essentialism, to normative conceptions of identity, and to exclusion.[25] Judith Butler, for example, argues that attempts to articulate the interests of "women" as a specific, unified group merely reinforce binary views of gender and close down possibilities for other, more fluid or subversive, formations of gender and sexuality.[26] Interestingly, there are several similarities between Butler's notion of identity and Goffman's apparently more traditional one: she too argues that identity is performed, although (unlike Goffman) she does not seem to imply that there is a "back-stage," personal identity that is more authentic than the "masquerade" of everyday social life. Likewise—although queer theorists might well resist such comparisons—they have much in common with the social identity theories outlined above, not least in the idea of identity as a fluid, ongoing process, something that is permanently "under construction." From both perspectives, identity is something we *do*, rather than simply something we *are*.

Of course, there are some significant criticisms that can be made of such an approach. It can be seen to imply that identity is just a matter of free choice—that individuals can simply assume a particular identity at will. Furthermore, it emphasizes the potential for diversity and resistance to dominant identities, while neglecting the pressure to conform, and the comparative predictability of everyday behavior. Ultimately, it can be seen to result in a kind of relativism that undermines any attempt to speak of, or on behalf of, a particular identity—although that, of course, is precisely the point.

These debates around identity politics suggest some quite different ways of understanding young people's relationships with digital media. For example, on the one hand, it could be argued that the Internet provides significant opportunities for exploring facets of identity that might previously have been denied or stigmatized, or indeed simply for the sharing of information on such matters. Such arguments presume that media can be used as a means of expressing or even discovering aspects of one's "true self," for example, in relation to sexuality.[27] Yet on the other hand, these media can also be seen to provide powerful opportunities for identity play, for parody and subversion of the kind promoted by queer theory. Here, the emphasis would lie not on honesty and truth, but on the potential for performance and even for deception. Sherry Turkle's discussion of the fluidity of online identities—for example, in the form of "gender bending" in Internet communities—provides one well-known (and much debated) instance of this kind of approach.[28]

Several authors in this volume address the complexities of identity politics, particularly in relation to gender ("race" is the focus of a separate volume in this series). Rebekah Willett, for example, looks at how girls' online play with dressing up dolls raises questions about body image and sexual politics; and while the girls in her study are very self-consciously critical about these issues, they also differentiate themselves from invisible "others" whom they believe to be more at risk of negative media influences. Sandra Weber and Claudia Mitchell also address questions of gender and ethnicity, looking at how the markers of positive identities can be quite subtly coded in young people's online expressions; and they also explore some uses of digital technologies by socially excluded groups, who tend to be largely ignored by research in this field.

The Modern Subject: Identity in Social Theory

Finally, we need to address some of the ways in which identity has been defined and addressed within more general social theories. Two specific—and quite contrasting—perspectives will illustrate some of the tensions at stake here.

Anthony Giddens is probably the best-known exponent of a broader argument about the changing nature of identity in what he terms "late modern" societies.[29] Giddens argues that many of the beliefs and customary practices that used to define identities in traditional societies (such as those of organized religion) are now less and less influential. In this "post-traditional" society, people have to make a whole range of choices, not just about aspects such as appearance and lifestyle, but more broadly about their life destinations and relationships. They are offered a plethora of guidance on such matters by experts of various kinds and by the popular media (for example, in the form of lifestyle news, makeover shows, and self-help books), although ultimately the individuals are required to make these choices on their own behalf.

As a result, Giddens suggests, modern individuals have to be constantly "self-reflexive," making decisions about what they should do and who they should be. The self becomes a kind of "project" that individuals have to work on: they have to create biographical "narratives" that will explain themselves to themselves, and hence sustain a coherent and consistent identity. Like many of the other authors I have discussed, Giddens sees identity as fluid and malleable, rather than fixed. He recognizes that this new freedom places new burdens and responsibilities on people; particularly in a world of increasing risk and insecurity, the individual is placed under greater emotional stress. Yet in general, he regards this as a positive development and as part of a broader process of democratization; modern consumer culture has offered individuals multiple possibilities to construct and fashion their own identities, and they are now able to do this in increasingly creative and diverse ways.

There are several problems with Giddens's argument, but the most significant one has to do with his evidence. It is by no means clear that the processes he is describing are distinctive to the "late-modern" era, and, more significantly, that they actually apply to the majority of the population (rather than merely to academic social theorists). Some of the difficulties here become apparent when we contrast Giddens's approach with that of Michel Foucault and some of his followers. What Giddens appears to regard as a form of liberation (or at least self-actualization) is seen by Foucault as simply another means of exercising disciplinary power. Foucault argues that who we are—or who we perceive ourselves to be—is far from a matter of individual choice; on the contrary, it is the product of powerful and subtle forms of "governmentality" that are characteristic of modern liberal democracies.[30]

Foucault asserts that there has been a shift in the ways in which power is exercised in the modern world, which is apparent in a whole range of social domains. Rather than being held (and indeed displayed) by sovereign authorities, power is now diffused through social relationships; rather than being regulated by external agencies (the government or the church), individuals are now encouraged to regulate themselves and to ensure that their own behavior falls within acceptable norms. What Giddens describes as self-reflexivity is seen by Foucault in much more sinister terms, as a process of self-monitoring and self-surveillance. Giddens' "project of the self" is recast here as a matter of individuals policing themselves, and the forms of self-help and therapy that Giddens seems to regard in quite positive terms are redefined as modern forms of confession, in which individuals are constantly required to account for themselves and "speak the truth" about their identities.

Nikolas Rose extends Foucault's argument to the operations of what he calls the "psy complex"—the forms of academic, therapeutic and institutional expertise that make up modern psychology.[31] This "technology of the self," he argues, actively forms what it means to be human, and in the process, it seeks to regulate and control individual behavior in line with limited social norms. While appearing to act in the name of individual freedom, autonomy, and choice, such technologies ultimately give the power to experts to determine the ways in which identity can be defined.

As with Giddens's theories, there are questions that might be raised here about how this very generalized analysis actually plays out in individuals' everyday lives. Yet although there are some striking differences between these approaches, they do draw attention to some significant shifts in how identity is constructed and experienced in the contemporary world. In my view, this is important to bear in mind when we consider the specific nature of young people's interactions with digital media. As I shall argue below, one of the major problems with popular debates in this field is the tendency to regard technology as the driving force of social change. Social theory of the kind I have discussed here reminds us that technological change is often merely part of much broader social and historical developments. In particular, I would suggest that the *individualization* made possible by digital technology could be seen as an instance of much more general shifts in the ways in which identity is defined and lived out in modern societies, although (as this section has made clear) it is possible to interpret these developments in very different ways.

Here again, these questions are taken up by several of the contributors to this book. Gitte Stald's account of the role of mobile phones in generating a sense of (and indeed a requirement for) constant "presence," Susannah Stern's discussion of how teenagers construct and fashion particular forms of identity online, and danah boyd's analysis of how young people "write themselves into being" on social networking sites indicate just some of the ways in which these broader social theories might be used in analyzing specific aspects of young people's digital cultures. Rebekah Willett's chapter confronts some of these arguments more directly, drawing on Giddens and Rose to challenge the emphasis on "compulsory individuality" that she sees as a characteristic of contemporary "neo liberal" discourses. She argues that young people are being encouraged to construct identities in terms that are aligned with consumer culture: far from being free to "express themselves," the forms of that expression are in fact being regulated in ever more subtle ways. Finally, Kirsten Drotner's chapter suggests that the new forms of identity work that are required in complex, "late-modern" societies call on new forms of cultural competence that schools need to address much more directly than they currently do.

Digital Media, Young People, and Learning

Among the different views of identity outlined in the first part of this chapter, there is often a shared assumption that the ways in which identity is defined (and hence what *counts* as identity) are undergoing far-reaching changes in the contemporary world. This is certainly debatable, but it does imply that one place to look for evidence of change would be young people, and perhaps specifically young people's relation with new technologies. In the second part of this chapter, therefore, I intend to raise some broad points about how we understand digital technology, youth, and finally learning.

Technology: The Limits of Determinism

Technology is frequently held to be transforming social relationships, the economy, and vast areas of public and private life. Such arguments are routinely recycled in popular debates, in advertising and publicity materials, and indeed in academic contexts as well. As Carolyn Marvin (1988) has indicated, such discourses have a long history. She shows how the introduction of electricity and telecommunications in the late-nineteenth and early-twentieth centuries was both encouraged and challenged by discourses that attributed enormous power to technology. On the one hand, these technologies were promoted through forms of expert "boosterism," which glorified the opportunities they presented, yet on the other, there were frequent claims that technology might be threatening established social relationships. The telephone, for example, was celebrated for the way in which it could make business more efficient and facilitate more democratic forms of social life, yet it was also condemned for its disruption of intimate relationships and its unsettling of established social hierarchies.

Needless to say, there are striking similarities between these debates almost a century ago and those that currently surround the use of digital technology. Popular discussions of the Internet, for example, veer between celebration and paranoia; on the one hand, the technology is seen to create new forms of community and civic life and to offer immense resources for personal liberation and empowerment, while on the other, it is believed to pose dangers to privacy, to create new forms of inequality and commercial exploitation, as well as leaving the individual prey to addiction and pornography. On the one hand, the technology is seen to liberate the individual from constraint and from narrowly hierarchical ways of working, while on the other, it is regarded as a false substitute for the supposedly authentic values it is seen to be replacing.

Such discourses typically embody a form of *technological determinism*.[32] From this perspective, technology is seen to emerge from a neutral process of scientific research and development, rather than from the interplay of complex social, economic, and political forces. Technology is then seen to have effects—to bring about social and psychological changes—irrespective of the ways in which it is used, and of the social contexts and processes into which it enters. Like the printing press, television, and other new technologies that preceded it, the computer is seen as an autonomous force that is somehow independent of human society and acts upon it from outside. In the case of education, this often takes the form of what might be called "information determinism." Information is seen as a neutral good, which appears as if from nowhere. Learning often seems to be equated simply with access to information, and in providing this access, technology is seen to perform an essentially beneficial function.[33]

This "transcendent" view of technology and of information has been widely challenged. Kevin Robins and Frank Webster, for example, argue that it leads to a "desocialized" view of technology, which ignores its social history and sees it as somehow "influencing society yet beyond the influence of society."[34] Likewise, notions of the "information society" and the "knowledge economy," which are often used to justify the growing use of information technology in schools, involve some highly debatable assumptions about the changing nature of employment and about the skills that workers will need in order to function effectively in the new economic and technological order. More broadly, the claim that the "information society" represents a new mode of social organization, in which established forms of economic, political, and social activity are being fundamentally altered—and the assumption that this change is somehow an inevitable consequence of technology—has been widely challenged.[35]

However, such critics also point to the dangers of an opposite view—the notion that technology is somehow entirely shaped by existing social relations. Crudely, this approach sees technology as simply a matter of what people choose to make of it: it has no inherent qualities and is regarded as essentially value free. This ignores the fact that technologies have inherent potentialities or "affordances": it is much easier to use them for some purposes than for others. Relatively few of these affordances are inevitable: the history of technology is full of examples of unanticipated consequences and even subversive uses. Even so, the forms that technology takes are largely shaped by the social actors and social institutions that play a leading role in producing it, and in determining where, when, and how it will be used, and by whom.

In his influential discussion of television, Raymond Williams makes a powerful argument for a more dialectical approach, in which technology is both socially shaped and socially shaping.[36] In other words, its role and impact is partly determined by the uses to which it is put, but it also contains inherent constraints and possibilities which limit the ways in which it can be used, and which are in turn largely shaped by the social interests of those who control its production, circulation, and distribution. This approach thus begins to move beyond the notion of technology as a simple "cause" of social change (on the one hand) and the idea of technology as an easy "fix" for complex social problems (on the other).

Similar arguments can be made about media or modes of communication. For example, the so-called "medium theory" of Marshall McLuhan implies that specific media necessarily create or promote particular forms of consciousness, and hence particular forms of social organization.[37] Likewise, theories of "multimodal communication" appear to assume that changes in the dominant modes of communication—for example, from the predominantly verbal to the more visual style of the contemporary media—necessarily result in changes in social relationships.[38] These kinds of arguments have often been used to support far-reaching assertions about the liberating impact of new media. Yet here again, such theories tend to neglect the diverse ways in which these different media or modes of communication are used, and they ignore the complex and sometimes quite contradictory relationships between media change and social power.

Rethinking the Digital Generation

These kinds of ideas about the impact of technology tend to take on an even greater force when they are combined with ideas about childhood and youth. The debate about the impact of media and technology on children has always served as a focus for much broader hopes and fears about social change.[39] On the one hand, there is a powerful discourse about the ways in which digital technology is threatening or even destroying childhood.[40] Young people are seen to be at risk, not only from more obvious dangers such as pornography and online pedophiles, but also from a wide range of negative physical and psychological consequences that derive from their engagement with technology. Like television, digital media are seen to be responsible for a whole litany of social ills—addiction, antisocial behavior, obesity, educational underachievement, commercial exploitation, stunted imaginations . . . and the list goes on.

In recent years, however, the debate has come to be dominated by a very different argument. Unlike those who bemoan the media's destruction of childhood innocence, advocates of the new "digital generation" regard technology as a force of liberation for young people—a means for them to reach past the constraining influence of their elders, and to create new, autonomous forms of communication and community. Far from corrupting the young, technology is seen to be creating a generation that is more open, more democratic, more creative, and more innovative than their parents' generation.

For example, Marc Prensky makes a distinction between digital "natives" (who have grown up with this technology) and digital "immigrants" (adults who have come to it later in life) that has been widely influential in popular debate.[41] Prensky argues that digital natives have a very different style of learning: they crave interactivity, they value graphics before words; they want random access, and they operate at the "twitch speed" of video games and MTV. As a result, they are dissatisfied with old styles of instruction, based on exposition and step-by-step logic: they see digital immigrants as speaking in an entirely alien, outdated language. Prensky even suggests that digital natives have a very different brain structure from that of immigrants, as though technology had precipitated a form of physical evolution within a period of little more than a decade.

Likewise, Don Tapscott's *Growing Up Digital: The Rise of the Net Generation* is based on two sets of binary oppositions, between technologies (television versus the Internet) and between generations (the "baby boomers" versus the "net generation").[42] Tapscott's oppositions between these technologies are stark and absolute. Television is a passive medium, while the net is active; television "dumbs down" its users, while the net raises their intelligence; television broadcasts a singular view of the world, while the net is democratic and interactive; television isolates, while the net builds communities; and so on. Just as television is the antithesis of the net, so the "television generation" is the antithesis of the "net generation." Like the technology they now control, the values of the "television generation" are increasingly conservative, "hierarchical, inflexible and centralized." By contrast, the "N-Geners" are "hungry for expression, discovery, and their own self-development": they are savvy, self-reliant, analytical, articulate, creative, inquisitive, accepting of diversity, and socially conscious. These generational differences are seen to be *produced* by technology, rather than being a result of other social, historical, or cultural forces. Unlike their parents, who are portrayed as incompetent "technophobes," young people are seen to possess an intuitive, spontaneous relationship with digital technology. "For many kids," Tapscott argues, "using the new technology is as natural as breathing." Technology is the means of their empowerment, and it will ultimately lead to a "generational explosion."

From this perspective, technology is seen to have brought about fundamental changes in a whole range of areas. It has created new styles of communication and interaction, and new means for constructing community. It has produced new styles of playful learning, which go beyond the teacher-dominated, authoritarian approach of old style education. It is creating new competencies or forms of "literacy," which require and produce new intellectual powers, and even "more complex brain structures." It provides new ways of forming identity, and hence new forms of personhood; and by offering communication with different aspects of the self, it enables young people to relate to the world and to others in more powerful ways. Finally, these technologies are seen to be leading to the emergence of a new kind of politics, which is more distributed and democratic: the Internet, for example, is "a medium for social awakening," which is producing a generation that is more tolerant, more globally oriented, more inclined to exercise social and civic responsibility, and to respect the environment.

Wishful thinking of this kind undoubtedly has its pleasures, but it is important to address some of the fundamental limitations of these arguments. The technologically determinist stance adopted by these authors means that there are many issues and phenomena that they are bound to ignore. They tend to neglect the fundamental continuities and interdependencies between new media and "old" media (such as television)—continuities that exist at the level of form and content, as well as in terms of economics. A longer historical view clearly shows that old and new technologies often come to coexist: particularly in the area of media, the advent of a new technology may change the functions or uses of old technologies, but it rarely completely displaces them. On average, members of the "net generation" in fact spend more of their time watching television than they do on the Internet; and of course there are many members of the "television generation" who spend much of their working and leisure time online.

This relentlessly optimistic view inevitably ignores many of the down sides of these technologies—the undemocratic tendencies of many online "communities," the limited nature of much so-called digital learning and the grinding tedium of much technologically-driven work. It also tends to romanticize young people, offering a wholly positive view of their critical intelligence and social responsibility that is deliberately at odds with that of many social commentators. It is also bound to ignore the continuing "digital divide" between the technology rich and the technology poor, both within and between societies. Technology enthusiasts are inclined to believe that this is a temporary phenomenon, and that the technology poor will eventually catch up, although this is obviously to assume that the early adopters will stay where they are. The possibility that the market might not provide equally for all, or indeed that technology might be used to exploit young people economically, does not enter the picture.[43]

Finally, this account of the "digital generation" is also bound to ignore what one can only call the *banality* of much new media use. Recent studies suggest that most young people's everyday uses of the Internet are characterized not by spectacular forms of innovation and creativity, but by relatively mundane forms of communication and information retrieval.[44] The technologically empowered "cyberkids" of the popular imagination may indeed exist, but even if they do, they are in a minority and they are untypical of young people as a whole. For example, there is little evidence that most young people are using the Internet to develop global connections; in most cases, it appears to be used primarily as a means of reinforcing local networks among peers. Young people may be "empowered" as consumers, at least in the sense of being able to access a much wider range of goods and services much more easily. But as yet there is little sense in which they are being empowered as citizens; only a minority are using the technology to engage in civic participation, to communicate their views to a wider audience, or to get involved in political activity.[45] As Mark Warschauer points out, the potential for multimedia production—which requires the latest computers and software, and high bandwidth—is generally quite inaccessible to all but the wealthy middle-classes.[46] Research also suggests that young people may be much less fluent or technologically "literate" in their use of the Internet than is often assumed: observational studies suggest that young people often encounter considerable difficulties in using search engines, for example, although this is not to suggest that they are necessarily any *less* competent than adults in this respect.[47]

Aside from those who are denied access to this technology, there are also many who positively refuse or reject it, for a variety of reasons.[48] Only a relatively small proportion of young people are driven by a desire to purchase the latest technological gadgets or participate in the latest form of online culture, and rather than being regarded as "cool," they are still often dismissed by their peers as "geeks."[49] In general, one could argue that for most young people, technology per se is a relatively marginal concern. Very few are interested in technology in its own right, and most are simply concerned about what they can use it for.

Ultimately, like other forms of marketing rhetoric, the discourse of the "digital generation" is precisely an attempt to construct the object of which it purports to speak. It represents not a description of what children or young people actually are, but a set of imperatives about what they should be or what they need to become. To some extent, it does describe a minority of young people who are actively using this technology for social, educational and creative purposes, yet it seems very likely that most of these people are the "usual suspects," who are already privileged in other areas of their lives and whose use of technology is supported by their access to other forms of social and cultural capital.

Of course, none of this is to deny that different generations or age cohorts will have different kinds of experiences, and that these may result in "generation gaps." Generations can be defined—and come to define themselves—through their relationships to traumatic historical events, but also through their experiences of rapid social change (as, for example, in the case of the "Sixties generation.")[50] Nor is it to deny that contemporary developments in technology do indeed present new opportunities—and indeed new risks—for young people. Some differences between generations are a perennial function of age—the interests of the young and the old are bound to diverge in systematic and predictable ways—but others are a consequence of broader historical developments, which include technological change. Even so, the emergence of a so-called "digital generation" can only be adequately understood in the light of other changes—for example, in the political economy of youth culture, the social and cultural policies and practices that regulate and define young people's lives, and the realities of their everyday social environments. These latter changes themselves can also be overstated, and frequently are, but in any case, it makes little sense to consider them in isolation from each other.

These issues are taken up in various ways in later chapters. The authors are generally wary of easy assumptions about the impact of technology on young people, and of the dangers of romanticizing youth. They are also keen to locate contemporary uses of technology in relation to older forms of communication or of teenage social interaction. Susan Herring's chapter provides the most direct challenge to these kinds of assumptions, puncturing some of the easy rhetoric about the "digital generation," and locating adults' views of young people and technology in a broader historical context. At the same time, she is keen not to fall into the trap of merely suggesting that "we've seen it all before." Technology—in combination with a whole series of other social and economic changes—is transforming young people's experiences, albeit in ways that (as Herring suggests) may only become fully apparent several years further down the line.

The Place(s) of Learning Finally, what are the implications of these arguments for our thinking about learning? Learning is undoubtedly a central theme in popular debates about the impact of digital technology.[51] On the one hand, critics have often seen technology as incompatible with authentic learning. For example, the use of computers in schools has been condemned for undermining students' creativity and for emphasizing mechanical rote learning, and it has also been seen to promise instant gratification, at the expense of encouraging students to develop the patience that is required for the hard work of education.[52]

On the other hand, advocates of technology have extolled its value for encouraging creative, student-centered learning, for increasing motivation and achievement, and for promoting demanding new styles of thinking.[53] Don Tapscott and Marc Prensky, for example, wax lyrical about the interactive, playful styles of learning that are promoted by the Internet and by computer games. Prensky's "digital natives" and Tapscott's "net generation" are seen as more inquisitive, self-directed learners: they are more sceptical and analytical, more inclined toward critical thinking, and more likely to challenge and question established authorities than previous generations. Above all, learning via these new digital media is seen as guaranteed "fun," as the boundaries between learning and play have effectively disappeared.[54]

Academic analyses of learning in relation to digital media have drawn on a wide range of perspectives. It is sometimes forgotten that one of the key advocates of behaviorist theories of learning, B. F. Skinner, was also an enthusiast for what he termed "teaching machines"—machines that have some striking similarities with contemporary computers.[55] Behaviorism is certainly alive and well in the design of contemporary "drill and skill" software, although most enthusiasts for computers in education tend to espouse a form of "constructivism" that emphasizes active, student-centered learning rather than instruction.[56] More recent approaches have drawn on social theories of learning, such as the "situated learning" approach. From this perspective, learning is seen to be embedded in social interactions (or "communities of practice"), and it can take the form of a kind of apprenticeship, as newcomers observe and gradually come to participate in particular social practices by modeling and working alongside "old timers." This theory also suggests that learning entails the development (or "projection") of a social identity; in learning, we take on, or aspire to take on, a new role as a member of the community of practice in which we are seeking to participate. Such theories have an obvious relevance to the study of online social networks, for example in the case of gaming and fan communities.[57]

One key emphasis in these debates is on the importance of the "informal learning" that characterizes young people's everyday interactions with technology outside school. Seymour Papert, for example, extols the value of what he calls "home-style" learning, seeing it as self-directed, spontaneous, and motivated in ways that "school-style" learning is not,[58] while Marc Prensky and Don Tapscott also look outside the school for alternatives to what they regard as the old-fashioned, instructional style of Baby Boomer teachers. Similar arguments have increasingly been made by academic researchers, who have looked to young people's leisure uses of digital technology—for example, in the form of computer games—as a means of challenging the narrow and inflexible uses of information and communications technology (ICTs) in schools.[59]

To be sure, young people's everyday uses of computer games or the Internet involve a whole range of informal learning processes, in which there is often a highly democratic relationship between "teachers" and "learners." Young people learn to use these media largely through trial and error. Exploration, experimentation, play, and collaboration with others—both in face-to-face and virtual forms—are essential elements of the process. Playing certain types of computer games, for example, can involve an extensive series of cognitive activities: remembering, hypothesis testing, predicting, and strategic planning. While game players are often deeply immersed in the virtual world of the game, dialogue and exchange with others is crucial. And game playing is also a "multiliterate" activity: it often involves interpreting complex three-dimensional visual environments, reading both on screen and off screen texts (such as games' magazines, and websites), and processing auditory information. In the world of computer games, success ultimately derives from the disciplined and committed acquisition of skills and knowledge.[60]

Likewise, online chat and instant messaging require very specific skills in language and interpersonal communication.[61] Young people have to learn to "read" subtle nuances, often on the basis of minimal cues. They have to learn the rules and etiquette of online communication, and to shift quickly between genres or language registers. Provided youths are sensible about divulging personal information, online chat provides young people with a safe arena for rehearsing and exploring aspects of identity and personal relationships that may not be available elsewhere. Again, much of this learning is carried out without explicit teaching: it involves active exploration, "learning by doing," apprenticeship rather than direct instruction. Above all, it is profoundly social: it is a matter of collaboration and interaction with others, and of participation in a community of users.

In learning with and through these media, young people are also learning how to learn. They are developing particular orientations toward information, particular methods of acquiring new knowledge and skills, and a sense of their own identities as learners. They are likely to experience a strong sense of their own autonomy, and of their right to make their own choices and to follow their own paths—however illusory this may ultimately be. In these domains, they are learning primarily by means of discovery, experimentation, and play, rather than by following external instructions and directions.

Even so, there are some important limitations to all this. Media content is, of course, not necessarily neutral or reliable: it represents the world in particular ways and not others, and it does so in ways that tend to serve the interests of its producers. Activities such as chat and game play are heavily bound by systems of rules, even if the rules are not always explicitly taught and even if they can sometimes be broken or bent. The structure or "architecture" of software itself (for example, of links on the Internet) imposes very significant constraints on the ways in which it can be used. And the social worlds that users enter into as they participate in these activities are by no means necessarily egalitarian or harmonious. For all these reasons, we need to be wary of simply *celebrating* young people's "informal" experiences of media and technology, and there are good reasons to be cautious about the idea of simply extending those experiences into the more "formal" context of the school.

This raises the important question, not so much of *how young people learn* with technology, but of *what they need to know* about it. The need for "digital literacy" is fast becoming a growing concern among educators and policy-makers in many countries. To date, however, most discussions of digital literacy have been confined to a fairly functional approach; the emphasis is on mastering basic skills in using technology, with some limited attention to evaluating the reliability or credibility of online sources (an issue addressed in detail in another of the volumes in this series). These are undoubtedly important issues, but digital literacy clearly needs to be seen much more broadly. Literacy is more than a matter of functional skills, or of knowing how to access information; we need to be able to evaluate information if we are to turn it into meaningful knowledge. Critical literacy is not just about making distinctions between "reliable" and "unreliable" sources: it is also about understanding who produces media, how and why they do so, how these media represent the world, and how they create meanings and pleasures.[62]

In this respect, I would argue that digital literacy should be seen as part of the broader field of media literacy. There is a long history of media literacy education in many countries, and there is a well-established conceptual framework and a repertoire of classroom strategies that are recognized and shared by teachers around the world.[63] Clearly, new media such as games and the Internet require new methods of investigation, and new classroom strategies, and schools need to think hard about how they should respond to the more participatory forms of media culture that are now emerging (for example in the form of blogging, social networking, fan cultures, video production, game making, and so on).[64] Nevertheless, media educators' long-standing concerns with questions about representation, about the characteristics of media "languages," and about the ownership and production of media continue to be highly relevant here, as does the emphasis on connecting these more critical concerns with the practical production of media (enabling students to create websites or digital videos, for example).

The issue of learning is addressed indirectly by several of the contributors here, but it is taken up most explicitly in the two final chapters. Kirsten Drotner's key concern is with the implications of young people's emerging digital cultures for the institution of the school. How should teachers and schools build on the forms of creativity and learning that young people are experiencing in their everyday uses of digital media? Rather than making the school redundant, Drotner argues that it has a new role to play, both in addressing inequalities in access to technology and in providing new forms of literacy. Meanwhile, Shelley Goldman, Meghan McDermott and Angela Booker focus on the possibilities and the challenges of "informal" learning in out-of-school contexts. While technology does provide important new possibilities for self-expression and communication, they clearly show that technology in itself does not make the difference. On the contrary, we need to think hard about the "social technologies"—the other forms of social interaction—and the types of pedagogy that surround the technology, and which crucially determine how it will be used. (These authors' concern with the role of digital media in young people's civic participation is taken up in another volume in this series.)

Conclusion

Simply keeping pace with the range of young people's engagements with digital media is an increasingly daunting task. Inevitably, there will be many gaps in our account here. Some of them are more than amply filled by other books in this series, such as the volumes on games, on ethnicity, and on civic engagement. Other gaps relate to the types of young people who are addressed here. To date, research on young people and digital media has tended to focus on the "early adopters," who, as I have suggested, are also likely to be privileged in other areas of their lives. Some of the chapters here—such as those by Sandra Weber and Claudia Mitchell, and by Shelley Goldman, Meghan McDermott, and Angela Booker—do focus explicitly on disadvantaged young people, although this is an issue that needs to be addressed more effectively in future research.

Even so, our hope for this book is that the theme of identity will provide a useful lens through which to view particular aspects of young people's relations with digital media more clearly. Identity is a very broad and ambiguous concept, yet it focuses attention on critical questions about personal development and social relationships—questions that are crucial for our understanding of young people's growth into adulthood and the nature of their social and cultural experiences. Focusing on this theme gives us a particular "take" on the relationship between the individual and the group. It raises questions about social power and inequality, and it enables us to connect the study of technology with broader questions about modernity and social change.

Perhaps most importantly, a focus on identity requires us to pay close attention to the diverse ways in which media and technologies are used in everyday life, and their consequences both for individuals and for social groups. It entails viewing young people as significant social actors in their own right, as "beings," and not simply as "becomings" who should be judged in terms of their projected futures. In our view, the needs of young people are not best served either by the superficial celebration or the exaggerated moral panics that often characterize this field. Understanding the role of digital media in the formation of youthful identities requires an approach that is clear sighted, unsentimental, and constructively critical. We trust that this collection will be read, and its contents debated, in an equally rigorous manner.

Notes

1. Richard Jenkins points to the long history of debates about identity in *Social Identity* (2nd Edition, London: Routledge, 2004).

2. Zygmunt Bauman, *Identity* (Cambridge, UK: Polity, 2004).

3. G. Stanley Hall, *Adolescence* (New York: Appleton, 1904) and *Youth: Its Education, Regimen and Hygiene* (New York: Appleton, 1906).

4. Erik Erikson, *Identity: Youth and Crisis* (New York: Norton, 1968).

5. James Marcia, Identity in Adolescence, in *Handbook of Adolescent Psychology,* ed. Joseph Adelson (New York: Wiley, 1980), 159–187.

6. For histories of "youth," see John Gillis, *Youth and History* (London: Academic Press, 1974); Michael Mitterauer, *A History of Youth* (Oxford, UK: Blackwell, 1992).

7. Carol Gilligan, *In A Different Voice* (Cambridge, MA: Harvard University Press, 1982).

8. This distinction between "being" and "becoming" is a key theme in the sociology of childhood: for a thoughtful discussion, see Nick Lee, *Childhood and Society* (Buckingham, UK: Open University Press, 2001).

9. Christine Griffin gives a useful overview of sociological perspectives in *Representations of Youth* (Cambridge, UK: Polity, 1993). For a good sociological overview, see Andy Furlong and Fred Cartmel, *Young People and Social Change* (Buckingham, UK: Open University Press, 1997).

10. For historical studies, see note 6 above. Cross-cultural accounts may be found, for example, in Sharon Stephens, ed., *Children and the Politics of Culture* (Princeton, NJ: Princeton University Press, 1995) and Vered Amit-Talai and Helena Wulff, eds., *Youth Cultures: A Cross-Cultural Perspective* (London: Routledge, 1995). Some of the complexity of this definition is apparent in the very diverse ways in which national legal systems and international agencies like the UN and the European Commission define the age boundaries of "youth."

11. Bill Osgerby gives a useful overview of these issues in *Youth Media* (London: Routledge, 2005).

12. See John Ulrich and Andrea Harris, eds., *Genxegesis: Essays on Alternative Youth (Sub)Culture* (Madison: University of Wisconsin Press, 2003).

13. Key examples of this early work would include Stuart Hall and Tony Jefferson, eds., *Resistance Through Rituals: Youth Subcultures in Post-War Britain* (London: Hutchinson, 1975); Angela McRobbie, *Feminism and Youth Culture: From "Jackie" to "Just Seventeen"* (London: Macmillan, 1991); and Paul Willis, *Learning to Labour* (Farnborough, UK: Saxon House, 1977). Ken Gelder and Sarah Thornton provide a useful, broad-ranging compilation in their *Subcultures Reader* (2nd Edition, London: Routledge, 2005).

14. Examples of more recent research can be found in Tracy Skelton and Gill Valentine, eds., *Cool Places: Geographies of Youth Culture* (London: Routledge, 1998) and Andy Bennett and Keith Kahn-Harris, eds., *After Subculture* (London: Palgrave Macmillan, 2004).

15. See, for example, Barrie Thorne, *Gender Play: Girls and Boys in School* (Buckingham, UK: Open University Press, 1993) or JoEllen FisherKeller, *Growing Up With Television* (Philadelphia: Temple University Press, 2002).

16. See particularly Sarah Thornton, *Club Cultures: Music, Media and Subcultural Capital* (Cambridge, UK: Polity, 1995).

17. Andy Bennett, *Popular Music and Youth Culture* (Basingstoke, Hants, UK: Palgrave Macmillan, 2000) and Steven Miles, *Youth Lifestyles in a Changing World* (Buckingham, UK: Open University Press, 2000).

18. Key examples of this work would include Henri Tajfel, *Human Groups and Social Categories* (Cambridge, UK: Cambridge University Press, 1981); Michael Hogg and Dominic Abrams, *Social Identifications* (London: Routledge, 1988); and Anthony Cohen, *Self Consciousness: An Alternative Anthropology of Identity* (London: Routledge, 1994).

19. Richard Jenkins, *Social Identity* (2004).

20. Erving Goffman, *The Presentation of Self in Everyday Life* (New York: Anchor Books, 1959).

21. A summary of some critiques of Goffman, and a response, may be found in Simon Williams, Appraising Goffman, *British Journal of Sociology,* 37, no. 3 (1986): 348–369, and the special issue of *Sociological Perspectives* 39, no. 3 (1996).

22. See, for example, Andrew Wood and Matthew Smith, *Online Communication: Linking Technology, Identity, and Culture* (Mahwah, NJ: Erlbaum, 2001).

23. See the insightful discussion by Cressida Hayes in the *Stanford Encyclopaedia of Philosophy.* http://plato.stanford.edu/entries/identity-politics/ (accessed May 29, 2007).

24. See Stuart Hall, The Question of Cultural Identity, in *Modernity and its Futures*, eds. Stuart Hall, David Held, and Anthony McGrew (Cambridge, UK: Polity, 1992).

25. See Annamarie Jagose, *Queer Theory: An Introduction* (New York: New York University Press, 1996).

26. Judith Butler, *Gender Trouble* (London: Routledge, 1990).

27. See, for example, some of the papers collected in *Digital Generations: Children, Young People and New Media,* eds. David Buckingham and Rebekah Willett (Mahwah, NJ: Erlbaum, 2006).

28. Sherry Turkle, *Life on the Screen* (New York: Simon and Schuster, 1995).

29. The key text here is *Modernity and Self-Identity* (Cambridge, UK: Polity, 1991) by Anthony Giddens. Other authors who appear to me to be making related arguments include Ulrich Beck and Zygmunt Bauman.

30. The most accessible way in here is via Michel Foucault, *The History of Sexuality: Volume 1* (Harmondsworth, UK: Penguin, 1979).

31. Nikolas Rose, *Governing the Soul* (2nd Edition, London: Free Association, 1999).

32. See Kevin Robins and Frank Webster, *Times of the Technoculture* (London: Routledge, 1999) and Frank Webster, *Theories of the Information Society* (London: Routledge, 1995).

33. These ideas are debated at length in David Buckingham's (forthcoming) *Beyond Technology: Children's Learning in the Age of Digital Culture* (Cambridge, UK: Polity, 2007).

34. Op. cit.: 74.

35. See, for example, Nicholas Garnham, Information Society as Theory or Ideology, *Information, Communication and Society,* 3, no. 2 (2000): 139–152; Christopher May, *The Information Society* (Cambridge, UK: Polity, 2002); and Frank Webster, op. cit.

36. Raymond Williams, *Television: Technology and Cultural Form* (Glasgow: Fontana, 1974).

37. Marshall McLuhan, *Understanding Media: The Extension of Man* (New York: New American Library, 1964).

38. See, for example, Gunther Kress, *Literacy in the New Media Age* (London: Routledge, 2003).

39. See David Buckingham, *After the Death of Childhood: Growing Up in the Age of Electronic Media* (Cambridge, UK: Polity, 2000).

40. A useful compendium of such arguments may be found in the Alliance for Childhood report: See Colleen Cordes and Edward Miller, *Fool's Gold: A Critical Look at Computers in Childhood.* http://www.allianceforchildhood.net (accessed May 29, 2007), op. cit.; Alison Armstrong and Charles Casement, *The Child and the Machine: How Computers Put our Children's Education at Risk* (Beltsville, MD: Robins Lane Press, 2000); and Jane Healy, *Failure to Connect: How Computers Affect Our Children's Minds—For Better and Worse* (New York: Simon and Schuster, 1998).

41. Marc Prensky, *Don't Bother Me, Mom—I'm Learning!* (St. Paul, MN: Paragon House, 2006).

42. Don Tapscott, *Growing Up Digital: The Rise of the Net Generation* (New York: McGraw-Hill, 1998).

43. See Ellen Seiter, *The Internet Playground: Children's Access, Entertainment, and Mis-Education* (New York: Peter Lang, 2005).

44. See, for example, Keri Facer, John Furlong, Ruth Furlong, and Ros Sutherland, *Screenplay: Children and Computing in the Home* (London: Routledge, 2003); Sarah Holloway and Gill Valentine, *Cyberkids: Children in the Information Age* (London: Routledge, 2003); and Sonia Livingstone and Magdalena Bober, *U.K. Children Go Online: Surveying the Experiences of Young People and their Parents* (London: London School of Economics and Political Science, 2004).

45. See Sonia Livingstone, Magdalena Bober, and Ellen Helsperm, Active Participation or Just More Information? Young People's Take-Up of Opportunities to Act and Interact on the Internet, *Information, Communication and Society,* 8, no. 3 (2005): 287–314.

46. Mark Warschauer, *Technology and Social Inclusion: Rethinking the Digital Divide* (Cambridge, MA: MIT Press, 2003).

47. Susan Cranmer, Families' Uses of the Internet, Unpublished PhD thesis, Institute of Education, University of London, 2006; Sonia Livingstone and Magdalena Bober, op. cit.; Janet Ward Schofield and Ann Lock Davidson, *Bringing the Internet to School: Lessons from an Urban District* (San Francisco: Jossey-Bass, 2002).

48. Keri Facer and Ruth Furlong, Beyond the Myth of the "Cyberkid": Young People at the Margins of the Information Revolution, *Journal of Youth Studies,* 4, no. 4 (2001): 451–469; Keith Roe and Agnetha Broos, Marginality in the Information Age: The Socio-Demographics of Computer Disquietude, *Communications,* 30, no. 1 (2005): 91–96; and Neil Selwyn, What's in the Box? Exploring Learners Rejection of Educational Computing, *Educational Research and Evaluation,* 4, no. 3 (1998): 193–212.

49. Sarah Holloway and Gill Valentine, op. cit.

50. See June Edmunds and Bryan Turner, *Generations, Culture and Society* (Buckingham, UK: Open University Press, 2002).

51. For fuller discussion, see David Buckingham (2007), particularly Chapters 3 and 6.

52. See Colleen Cordes and Edward Miller, op. cit.; Alison Armstrong and Charles Casement (2000) and Jane Healy (1998).

53. For example, Seymour Papert, *The Children's Machine: Rethinking School in the Age of the Computer* (New York: Basic Books, 1993); Milton Chen and Sara Armstrong, eds., *Edutopia: Success Stories for Learning in the Digital Age* (San Francisco: Jossey-Bass, 2002).

54. A more academic treatment of this argument is provided by James Gee, *What Video Games Have To Teach Us About Learning and Literacy* (Basingstoke, Hants: Palgrave Macmillan, 2003); and see the critique in David Buckingham (forthcoming), Chapter 6.

55. Burrhus Frederick Skinner, The Science of Learning and the Art of Teaching, *Harvard Educational Review,* 24, no. 2 (1954): 86–97.

56. The most influential advocate of this approach in relation to ICTs is undoubtedly Seymour Papert, *Mindstorms: Children, Computers and Powerful Ideas* (New York: Basic Books, 1980).

57. See James Gee, *Situated Learning and Literacy: A Critique of Traditional Schooling* (London: Routledge, 2004).

58. Seymour Papert, *The Connected Family* (Atlanta, GA: Longstreet, 1996).

59. For example, Bridget Somekh, Taking the Sociological Imagination to School: An Analysis of the (Lack of) Impact of Information and Communication Technologies on Education Systems, *Technology, Pedagogy and Education,* 13, no. 2 (2004): 163–179 or Jerry Wellington, Exploring the Secret Garden: The Growing Importance of ICT in the Home, *British Journal of Educational Technology,* 32, no. 2 (2001): 233–244.

60. For a multidimensional account of game play, see Diane Carr, David Buckingham, Andrew Burn, and Gareth Schott, *Computer Games: Text, Narrative and Play* (Cambridge, UK: Polity, 2006).

61. See Julia Davies, Hello Newbie! **Big Welcome Hugs** Hope U Like It Here as Much As I Do! An Exploration of Teenagers' On-Line Learning, in *Digital Generations: Children, Young People and New Media*, eds. David Buckingham and Rebekah Willett (Mahwah, NJ: Erlbaum, 2006); and Vebjørg Tingstad, *Children's Chat on the Net: A Study of Social Encounters in Two Norwegian Chat Rooms* (Unpublished PhD thesis, NTNU Trondheim, 2003).

62. For further discussion, David Buckingham, *Beyond Technology: Learning in the Age of Digital Culture* (Cambridge: Polity, 2007).

63. See David Buckingham, *Media Education: Literacy, Learning and Contemporary Culture* (Cambridge, UK: Polity, 2003).

64. See David Buckingham and Sara Bragg, eds., *Media Education Goes Digital,* Special issue of *Learning, Media and Technology,* 32, no. 2 (2007).

PART I: OVERVIEWS

Imaging, Keyboarding, and Posting Identities: Young People and New Media Technologies

Sandra Weber

Concordia University, Montreal, Department of Education

Claudia Mitchell

McGill University, Montreal, Faculty of Education

Introducing Youth, Technologies, and Identities-in-Action

New Technologies and Young People

Among the many cartoons we clip out of the newspaper for our growing collection, one of our favorites shows a baby popping out of the womb with a cell phone in one hand, a computer mouse in the other, and an iPod plugged into his or her ears (a view of the genitalia is obscured by the arms of whoever is holding the baby). Minutes old, the baby already seems to be communicating the birth experience to a group of as yet unborn cohorts, text messaging in some sort of "baby code" incomprehensible to adults, while presumably also listening to self-selected MP3 files (downloaded perhaps via the umbilical cord?!). It all seems so very . . . "unbaby-like." The boundaries between teens and babies are blurred[1] and adults seem out of the loop altogether. Cartoons such as this are becoming commonplace, almost a cliché, but are still capable of eliciting a smile or a grimace from adults who are wondering about the impact of new technologies on society in general, and on children and youth in particular. Offering a humorous commentary on contemporary societies, the cartoon poses some very interesting questions about how new technologies are forcing us to reexamine identities, bodies, interaction, intergenerational dialogue, and the nature of childhood. It also evokes the influence of popular culture and the increasing role of technology in even the most "natural" aspects of life such as birth.

There are popular assumptions underlying the cartoon that need to be challenged. It is important, for example, to remember that not all children are "born into new technologies" to the same extent. Even in North America there are still homes without computers or Internet access; not every adolescent has a cell phone, an MP3 player, and a Game Cube or Play Station (although it certainly is beginning to seem that way). As research by Seiter[2] and many surveys confirm, there is an economic digital divide that is overlooked and possibly growing. And even amongst the economic elite, it would be naïve to assume that all life is digital. Sports, arts, books, camping, bicycles, hobbies, offline games, and hanging out with friends offline are still a part of childhood for many.

The cartoon also ignores the growing cohort of adults whose engagement mirrors those of the cartoon techno-tot. Whether it is in the quest to remain young and "with it," the desire to keep in touch or keep up with their children and grandchildren, or the necessity of adapting to the changing requirements of the job market, adults are catching up with youth in terms of hardware adoption and use, something that is explored in Susan Herring's chapter in this volume. Some are even co-opting or integrating aspects of youth culture such as the lingo and conventions of text messaging into their own. Cross-generational dialogue and evolving adult role models challenge the cartoon's assumptions that digital technologies are only for the young. Perhaps the adults witnessing the cartoon birth understand more digital language than the baby realizes. Nonetheless, most of the scholars who write about new technologies and their impact on children are writing about an experience they themselves never had as a child. Text messaging and online gaming, for example, were not available to young people twenty years ago. There is thus a very real danger of misunderstanding what growing up in a digital age is really like from young people's perspectives. It would be a mistake to assume that adults' learning and engagement with new technologies mirror childhood processes.

And so, returning to our image of the techno-newborn, we ask: Who is this new baby and who will she become? How will she view herself in relation to her peers as she approaches adulthood? How will she use technologies to express and learn about herself? To explore these questions, we will examine a series of four case studies that highlight the roles that digital media can assume in the construction of youth identities. Before presenting the cases, however, we will first set the scene by raising some of the assumptions, problems, and questions that are central to investigations of young people and new technologies.

Adolescence and Identity Processes As we have seen in the introduction to this volume, adolescence has often been viewed as a key period in identify formation, and indeed as a period of "identity crisis," in which fundamental dilemmas have to be resolved. Instead of referring to an arbitrary age range, adolescence can perhaps more usefully be viewed as a series of questions that youth ask of themselves, the world, and each other, and that others ask of them. "Just who am I?," "What will I do when I leave school?," "Where do I fit in?," "Who do I love?" There is also an assumed plasticity to adolescence (although that assumption may be mistaken). Poised on the cusp of adulthood, adolescents are believed to be at a key stage of identity formation, a time of visible and invisible "becoming" when the biological changes of puberty, emergent sexuality, transitions to more adult roles, and the formation of significant peer relationships all intersect. It is, for most young people, a time of transitions—to new schools, new jobs, new bodies, new relationships, and new responsibilities. In Western discourse, adolescence is often portrayed as a heightened, and perhaps emotional, experiencing of life, a questioning or yearning for . . . some unknown future, the need to situate oneself, to find out who our friends are, to take one's place in society, the ambivalent wish to belong and not belong, to be the same yet stand out. This search may not be unique to adolescence nor typical of all young people, but, in the popular culture of youth at least, it seems to be "writ large."

One could legitimately argue that not all of these assumptions apply to all youth or that they apply to a much broader range of people, but if indeed identity processes during adolescence apply to other ages and phases, then the case for studying this period becomes even more compelling. New technologies are a good place to start these investigations. For many young people, especially in industrialized parts of the world, digital media are significant modalities through which they are seeking, consciously or unconsciously, the answers to identity questions, looking for what Buckingham and Sefton-Green describe as "the me that is me."[3]

Digital Production and "Identities-in-Action" Like youth identities, new technologies keep changing, converging, morphing—seemingly always in flux, and like youth identities, young people's own digital productions facilitate a blending of media, genres, experimentations, modifications, and reiterations, which Mizuko "Mimi" Ito describes as a "media-mix."[4] Digital productions tell stories of sorts (often nonlinear and multivoiced) and leave a digital trail, fingerprint, or photograph of "where I was then," "where we are now," "who I would like to be," and so on. In other words, young people's interactive uses of new technologies can serve as a model for identity processes. We propose labeling such cultural production activities *identities-in-action* as a reminder that, like digital cultural production, identity processes are multifaceted and in flux, incorporating old and new images.

Following the leads of scholars such as Henry Jenkins,[5] we use the term "production" not only to refer to the creation of digital products, but also to the interactive consumption that is embedded in production, that is, the ways in which youth often take up or consume popular images, and combine, critique, adapt, or incorporate them in their own media productions. Lister proposes that we abandon former distinctions between producers and consumers, collapsing them into one word, "prosumers."[6] As the cases we will present illustrate, the processes of producing, consuming, and being consumed or shaped by digital media are intertwined and often simultaneous. This makes them perfect entry points for investigating learning and identity, for it is at least partially through these processes of interacting with technologies (including hardware, software, and design) that identities are constructed, deconstructed, shaped, tested, and experienced.

Youth digital productions are mostly viewed or consumed by youth audiences, and these often include the very people who are the producers in the first place. Young people revisit their own web productions, not only to see how they might update them, but also to see what has happened to them in terms of "hits" or response messages and so on. They are their own audience. There is a reflexivity to this process, a conscious looking, not only at their production (themselves), but at how others are looking at their productions.

Producing Identities: Four Cases

From data collected in Britain, Canada, and South Africa, we have selected cases that involve a range of technologies and contexts, from adult-mediated activities in schools and community centers to spontaneous media production done in private at home. Moreover, since gender, race, ethnicity, social group, culture, and local context all play important roles in identity processes, we used these factors as well to vary our selection. Although it may seem counterintuitive, focusing on experiences that differ actually helps make what is common to all the cases stand out.

Three of the four cases we present below are taken from a body of funded research that we and our international team have conducted under the umbrella of two major projects over the last six years.[7] One project investigates young people's everyday experiences of new technologies. The other focuses on the use of digital photography and video to enable young people to express their views around issues of violence, gender, and sexuality. A fourth case is based on the viewing and transcription of a video from a community-based youth project led by British researcher and activist Liz Orton.[8]

Case 1. Personal Websites and Friendship: Situating Personal and Social Selves

To illustrate the complexities and nuances of identities-in-action through multimedia production, we will begin with a very detailed case drawn from a series of studies of girls' everyday uses of digital technology conducted by the *Digital Girls* research team in Canada.

During the project, we interviewed several girls from different economic, ethnic, and cultural backgrounds. The focus of the open-ended interviews was on their use of new technologies, and in particular their activities around personal websites. By following their friends' posts and links to their websites, we were able to trace and examine friendship groups, some of which included boys.

A bubbly and outgoing eleven-year-old girl raised in a religious North American Catholic family of Italian heritage, Isabella (not her real name) has created three major reiterations of her MySpace home page in the last year. For her large circle of friends and cousins (which includes boys), sharing websites, signing each other's guestbooks, and leaving comments in the chatboxes is de rigueur. The same holds true for her older sister, Maria, and her peers who are two grades ahead, marching into adolescence (there are no boys in this older group). In fact it was watching the older girls create webpages that got Isabella going. And go she did; her site is one of the most elaborate amongst the two groups of youths we followed. We were able to interview the two sisters and view multiple iterations not only of their sites, but also those of their circles of friends too. We focus more on Isabella's site than on others because her site offers the greatest variety of postings and because she was able to articulate clearly her views of website construction and identity. Since she is the youngest of the group, her case affords us a glimpse of the roots, the beginnings of the kinds of things we see in the older teen sites, a point of comparison to see how views and practices change in adolescence. Moreover, it quickly became apparent that so much of what Isabella knows, in terms of technical skills and conventions of display, she has learned from her older sister.

Updated almost daily as soon as she comes home from school, Isabella's site includes many features of a gossipy journal or blog combined with instant messaging and elements of scrapbooking. Despite the fact that it is sitting right out in plain sight in public cyberspace, the site is geared specifically toward her friends and, in many ways, acts as a personal diary with pictures; it is a form of what could be called public privacy. On the site's home page, Isabella clearly indicates both her intended audience (her circle of friends) and her desire to include them, to welcome them, to create a sense of "we-ness" to her site:

> If there's anything you would want me to change like pictures of you or something like a page or wtv don't be shy to tell me! I really don't care.... so tell me your corrections on msn [she gives her MSN address below this message].

In looking across the websites of the two friendship circles of young people (aged eleven to thirteen), a common general template or structure is readily apparent. They have developed a group genre and set of codes that incorporate some features that can be found on popular websites and magazines directed at tweens and teens with other aspects, such as daily postings, that are more often found on popular blogs. The organization and content of their sites are also dependent on what the templates, website tools, and site host permit or facilitate.

Almost all of the sites we examined feature:

- a home page that links to all the other pages;
- a "best friends" section (listing members of one's circle and often providing links to their sites);
- a personal page revealing a range of information and opinions (favorite music, "my cute dog," sports, a blog-like posting of snippets of daily experience, love notes to friends, jokes, gossip, candid photos, posed photos, and more);

- a guest book or message board where visitors (assumed to be one's best friends) can sign in and leave messages;
- an instant messaging chat box;
- a "goodbye—come again" page;
- elements of fandom, participation in popular culture, sharing likes and dislikes—popular movies, sport, music idols, and so forth;
- declaration of their friendship group, their heritage group, and in some instances, their family; in other words, certain elements selected to show where they fit in, where they belong;
- inclusion of friends' site addresses;
- a bulletin board for friends to leave messages;
- coded "private" messages for certain friends, sometimes inserted within the main text of the site;
- personal photos (often downloaded from cell phones) and artwork;
- use of the prevailing norms for "cool" language;
- photographs (posed and/or candid shots of oneself, pets, and others, downloaded or scanned photos, often of idols);
- images—sometimes original drawings, but more often clip art taken from other sites, popular images, and commercial logos.

Isabella's site is colorful and cheerful, full of creative combinations of pop-culture images, author-produced layout and script, private coded messages to friends, personal information, photographs of friends and family, jokes, cartoon images, lists of favorites, and more. Sexily posed photos of Isabella herself (à la Hillary Duff or Paris Hilton, two popular teen icons) are juxtaposed with images taken from younger children's cartoons. Combining elements that range from childlike naivete to adult pseudosophistication, the content is poignant, whimsical, funny, occasionally profane, and perhaps to some adult eyes a bit disconcerting. Both the images and the written text evoke a sort of savvy innocence, a playfulness that does not seem to be sexual but that is very affectionate. The written text is a casual and interesting mixture of unconventional and very "in" spellings (e.g., buhh byee, tataa, crazzzy, woww) filled with extra letters for ordinary words, coded abbreviations for swear words (e.g., it was so fkn funni), and typical IM codes (e.g., lol, omg, u r nuts).

The "Best Friends" page is extensive and features an ark full of cartoon animals derived from popular culture (for example, *Hello Kitty*). Clicking a name on the list of her best friends leads to a photo of that person displayed above a message Isabella has written both proclaiming her love for that friend and recalling some shared event ("remember when") or "secret." These messages are written in a creative blend of coolspeak and text message language. For each page devoted to a friend, Isabella changes fonts, wallpaper, and styles, finding ways to improve upon or circumvent the space provider's templates, showing off her growing skill with HTML, experimenting, but also personalizing the page to suit her image of each friend (some of whom are boys). How might they view themselves as posted through her eyes, we wonder.

Most of the friends who visit Isabella's site and who are featured on her best friends' page have sites of their own as well. The look, arrangement of photos, personal information, and preferences vary; so do opinions for and against Hillary Duff and Paris Hilton! Some talk about their pets, others are more interested in adventures they've had, but in many respects, the sites are similar. One interesting commonality across the sites of those in the circle who have an Italian background is the inclusion on their fan pages of a conscious nod to their heritage though the posting of photos of one or more of the "Hottie Gottis" from the recently cancelled reality TV show *Growing Up Gotti*, a series that featured the three teenaged grandsons of John Gotti. This posting of images reflecting linguistic and national heritage roots does not emerge in conversation with the sisters as central to their identity, but it is important to them. For circle members of Italian heritage, posting such images appears to be a "this is what you are required to do to keep your standing in the community" gesture, as the crosses some of them wear on a chain around their necks are a taken-for-granted symbol that does not necessarily signpost deep religious belief as much as simply proclaim "I am a member in good standing of a particular social group"—or as Isabella puts it, "ya gotta show respect." (There is further discussion of how friendships and identities are constructed in MySpace in danah boyd's chapter in this volume.)

The sites of the three boys in Isabella's circle resemble the girls' sites in many ways. They use similar templates, feature fan pages (more sports icons here), personal information (for example, likes and dislikes, hobbies), candid photographs, similar text message style writing, and more. Their sites seem less elaborate, however, and their popular images veer more toward cars, sports images, and pictures of athletes, stereotypic markers of masculinity. The colors tend to be stronger (fewer pastels, more red and black) and the affectionate outpouring of love for friends a bit more restrained (but only a bit—we were surprised at the frank affection and support for friends expressed on these sites). Like the girls, some token expression of identifying with Italian heritage seems mandatory for the boys, especially during the World Cup months when Italian flags went up on two of the sites. Following the lead of their female friends, the boys also posted pictures from the TV show *Growing Up Gotti*, although unlike the girls, they don't refer to the male Gotti teens as "hot." Without interviewing the boys, it is hard to know the extent to which they might identify with the Gottis in more direct ways than the girls do, or the extent to which these and other fan posts see them as "objects of desire."

Meanwhile, the older girls' sites bear many similarities to those of the younger girls (although they would probably deny this rather vehemently) in terms of structures and genre. However, the content is different—there are fewer nostalgic icons of childhood, more sarcasm, more obvious references to sexuality, and more critique of adults (especially teachers). They draw on a wider color palette, using more austere colors and a lot more black. White text on dark background is, for the moment, considered "cool." There is also more attempt at animation and more links to sites that are beyond one's circle of friends (although, as for the younger girls, a friends page is central to most of their sites). It's as if they have a greater awareness or appreciation of the world wide web beyond their own site, and are more curious about other people's ways of constructing sites. Through experimentation, peer tutoring, and seeking out information, they are actively learning site construction skills and acquiring wider knowledge of genres and esthetic possibilities. Their construction or posting of self seems more deliberate and reflexive.

These web postings demonstrate or even constitute a form of embodiment. The posting of photographs extends their bodies into cyber space; their sites bear their "fingerprints," the traces of their activities, the imprint of their inventive spellings and font choices, the visual evidence that they exist, a signpost to who they think they are or who they want you to think they are or who they would like to become. As they choose and post a plethora of photographs that include candid photographs of groups of friends, impromptu "clowning around" snaps as well as posed, stylized, and sometimes altered photos, they are presenting themselves, performing their bodies, and trying on "looks." The choice of photographs of their idols can also be viewed as an extension or projection of their bodies, a desiring or coveting of another's appearance. They want their own images and their sites to have a certain look, but the desired look changes as new trends emerge or as someone gets a creative inspiration. There is a tentative experimentation evident in the frequency with which they change certain images, and a growing commitment or certainty about other images that they keep across multiple iterations.

The performance[9], sexualization, and gendering of their bodies was quite prominent. Some of the girls were very intent on posing and dressing their bodies to look "sexy." But what they mean by sexy and what older teens or adults label sexy might be very different, as suggested by the following excerpt from an interview:

Interviewer: What do you mean by "sexy?"
Tween (female): You know . . . cute . . . pretty!

While most of their language suggests a normative emphasis on heterosexuality (the older girls, especially, all talk as if they are mainly into "hot guys"), it is interesting to note that the girls lavish affection and love on female idols (crushes perhaps) which far outnumber the male images they post, and that the boys posted images of male as well as female idols. Same-sex as well as cross-sex (one could also argue sexless) affection is very much the norm for both the older and the younger groups and perhaps reflects strong identification or aspirations to be like those objects of affection. In appropriating images of others for posting, are they trying to incorporate aspects of their identities into their own?

The presentation or expression of self on these sites also contains many contrasting, ambivalent, or even contradictory elements of "self." For example, one trend that runs through most of the girls' sites is the nostalgic inclusion of cuddly animals and images that are associated with younger children, right alongside the sexy poses and images more typical of teen magazines. When questioned, none of them felt that there was any problem with using "childish" cartoons or clichés mixed with sexual images. These images modified and contextualized each other: for example, in the younger group, the word "sexy" can just mean "cute" in one posting and "sexy" in the more conventional adult sense in another.

In summary, this case study illustrates some of the ways in which personal website production provides young people with diverse means of constructing and fashioning their identities through images and words. Their sites contain a variety of pictures, expressions, and references relating to the popular culture of media, new and old. This improvised and almost natural combining of analog and digital components (e.g., scanning analog photos or using old fashioned scrapbooks as website templates) illustrates that young people's evolving media productions reflect what Jenkins calls a "convergence culture,"[10] where the boundaries between old and new media are blurred, and elements of each are blended and adapted to meet emerging needs. The resulting visual and textual collages often contain contrasting elements, all imbued with both personal and social meanings. Highly original artwork sits right alongside popular images and drawings poached from other websites. Many of their postings constitute a declaration of belonging to or identifying with a peer group, a family group, an ethnic or linguistic or heritage group, a stream of popular culture, a particular time, space, and place. These young people teach each other, borrow images or ideas from each other, and in a sense co-construct identities. But it is also important to emphasize that their posted identities are neither predictable nor homogeneous. As the sometimes subtle, sometimes blatant differences and variations across websites attest, even if they all eat from the same popular buffet, they are not all alike.

Case 2. Why I Love My Cell Phone: Seeing Voice

When she was a fifteen-year-old, Walia, an African refugee living in East London, took part in a digital storytelling (photovoice) project called *Moving Lives*.[11] The goal of the project is to help young refugees make the transition to life in the U.K. by building their confidence in their own voices and empowering them to speak out using digital media. Given *carte blanche* as to the subject matter they choose, young people learn to use digital cameras, PowerPoint, and the Internet to "represent themselves as they want to be seen and heard: as individuals with hopes, histories, ideas, and dreams." Some of the resulting photo stories have been posted on the project's website.

Walia seems to have had no trouble choosing her topic and title: Get my *phone back or die trying*, a recounting of actual events and a creative expression of her passionate feelings about her cell phone. Through a sequence of photographs (some of her, some of the objects she mentions, and others obviously posed using parts of other people's bodies) accompanied by her own voice and words, she tells a story about having her cell phone stolen and how she managed to get it back. When Walia found out from a friend of hers that a school bully (whom she represents as holding a knife) had stolen it, she worked up the courage to approach him to ask if she could buy it back. As the photo essay progresses, we realize she has arranged a sting operation with the vice principal of the school. She gets to keep her money, the bully gets caught and reprimanded, and Walia gets her phone back. Confronting and getting the better of a male bully can be quite a risk, and one might wonder about the wisdom of her plot. But she tells us: "I love my phone. I love it enough to risk my life for it." It's always on, she says, and she keeps it beside her bed at night. She sometimes talks all night, busting her budget and spending her month's money in a few days.

In the course of telling her digital story, Walia weaves in a love poem to her phone, using similes illustrated with photographs to convey what this technology means to her. "My phone," she says, "is like a dog—because it's so cute and loyal. My phone is like New York. It's always busy." And later on in the story, "My phone is like a chicken supreme pizza with stuffed crust—it's the tastiest thing there is.... My phone is like boots (photo of knee high black suede sexy boots) to go out clubbing and have fun.... My phone is like earrings, I never leave home without it."

This case is interesting for many reasons. For one, it illustrates the use of one digital medium (photography/PowerPoint) to evoke and illustrate the personal significance of another medium, the cell phone. As the Danish youth Gitte Staid describes in her chapter, Walia has incorporated this technology extensively into her daily life. One particular cell phone (hers) seems to act as an extension of self, almost as part of her body. She has invested this object with significant personal meanings. Getting it back seems very important; she doesn't mention even considering buying another one. She seems to be literally saying that she would die without it, or at least, be less of who she is. At the very least, we can conclude that an important dimension of her identity is that "I am a person who has and uses her own cell phone." For Walia, the cell phone seems to act symbolically as a mediator or link between social and personal identities, connecting her to others, even when she is not using it. Perhaps it acts as a stand-in for the people she can "touch" via her phone. She imbues it with so much meaning, perhaps bestowing on it the affection she feels for the people with whom she chats all evening.

The identity Walia constructs in her online photovoice posting is of a young woman who is sociable, strong, and perhaps stylish (judging from the boots and the earrings). In talking about her friends, her phone, her clubbing, she evokes other people, her desire to be connected and available to her friends. In publicly using a poetic voice and carefully posed photographs to describe her feelings toward her phone, she comes out as an artist. In confronting and besting a bully, she expresses her values and affirms an identity that firmly states what she is NOT. She is not a victim. Nor are the girls in the next case which also involves photography and PowerPoint, albeit in a very different context.

Case 3. In My Room: Power Point Projections

. . . the bedroom is an important place for most adolescents, a personal space in which they can experiment with possible selves. (Brown et al.)[12]

What do girls' digital images of their bedrooms reveal about identity and self-image, and how do girls' public rerepresentations of their bedrooms using PowerPoint technology add another dimension to the presentation of self? Here we look at visual data collected as part of a study that involves a group of 50 eleven- and twelve-year-old girls from Pietermaritzburg in South Africa. All of them are English first-language speakers from middle-class backgrounds who participate in a "digital bedroom" project as part of a second-language class where they are learning Isizulu.[13] At their teacher's suggestion, the girls used digital cameras to take still pictures of their bedrooms. Then, using a selection of these images, they each created a PowerPoint presentation which they showed in class. They use Isizulu in the print text that accompanies the photos, as well as in the actual oral presentation to the rest of the class. Their teacher was eager to do this project because she hoped that this use of a personal frame of reference would motivate the girls and enhance their language learning. The rationale for creating visual images and including these images as part of a PowerPoint presentation reflects a recognition of the visual world of the girls, and indeed might even be read as an extension of the photo-sharing practices that are increasingly associated with cell phones.

Most of the girls took pictures of their bedrooms in their own homes, although a few boarders who live in a hostel took pictures of their "home away from home." The images produced by the girls represent a fascinating array of "girl stuff" ranging from photos of favorite objects—floppy stuffed animals, dolls—to photos-of-photos of a horse or a pet dog. Surprisingly, given the influence of popular culture, there was very little overlap in terms of the actual favorite objects selected.[14] Their chosen objects include the various forms of technology in the bedroom (televisions, computers, iPods, DVD players, and so on) as we see in Figure 1, a photo that combines a cell phone and a CD player with candy sours. They also took pictures of "girl spaces": images of special places for hiding things (a drawer or a special box), and images of favorite hiding places where they go when they want to be alone (under a bed, in a wardrobe).

Beyond the single photographs are the actual PowerPoint productions where each girl has rerepresented her bedroom creatively and artistically. Like Walia's photo story noted above, it is the personal narrative that is important. Each girl could use up to four or five images in a PowerPoint presentation. In the presentations the girls make full use of the various features of PowerPoint, including color schemes and backdrops, text layout, particular animation features (bounce, ellipsis, etc.), and slide design and layout.

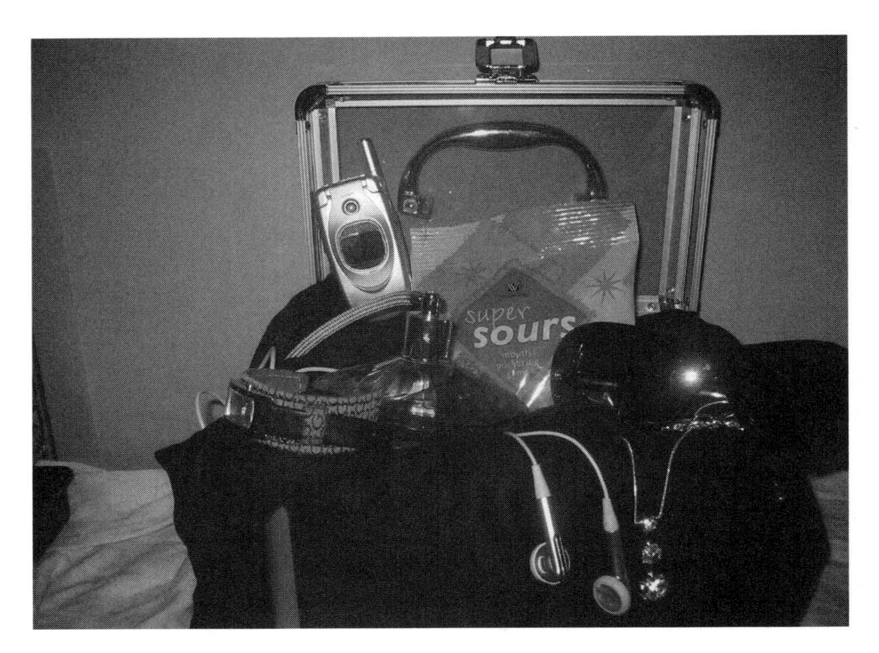

Figure 1
Slide of technologies in a girl's bedroom.

As one small example of their editing work, the image in Figure 2 is taken from a PowerPoint presentation, which brings life to the stuffed animals through such features as boomerangs and title arcs. They personalize their images in other ways too. One girl, for example, adds in a small image of a stylized dog to accompany each of her images; the dog in a sense becomes the commentator. The girls respond enthusiastically to doing the project on their own, as well as to looking carefully at each other's work. As their Isizulu teacher observes: "Up to now I have always taught the theme "My Bedroom," in an old-fashioned way during Isizulu lessons in the Grade 7 class. The girls would use pictures from magazines and posters to improve their vocabulary and to carry out their oral work. I am of the opinion that the girls were in some ways detached from the task." In other words, allowing girls to express their identities more authentically and freely based on their home life outside of school turned out to be an effective school-initiated teaching strategy, one that empowers and respects students.

The images and projections of the bedrooms complement and extend the work of McRobbie and Garber, who coined the term "bedroom culture" in 1976 to describe the cultural space of girls and young women.[15] They wanted to address the invisibility of girls in studies of youth subcultures. In their work they found that while the girls' bedrooms were not public spaces as such, they were nonetheless social spaces—places where girls talked on the phone to friends, covered the wall with pin-up posters, had pajama parties, and interacted socially in terms of reading novels, writing in diaries, and so on. These private yet social spaces, they argue, contrast with the public street spaces dominated by boys and young men. More recently, Julian Sefton-Green and David Buckingham have explored the idea of the "digital bedroom" to account for the location of children's cyber play.[16] They observe

Figure 2
Slide of a girl's teddy bear from her bedroom.

that whether it be gaming, surfing the Web, or home page construction, much of this is done on a home computer, often located in the bedroom. However, as we explore elsewhere in an analysis of websites produced for and by girls,[17] the term "digital bedroom" is also an apt descriptor of girls' websites, which themselves often resemble bedrooms (featuring digital "pin-ups," décor, blogs and messaging, and so on)—something we noted before in the description of the websites created by Isabella.

When Adrienne Salinger embarked upon her project, *In My Room: Teenagers in Their Bedrooms,* with young people (boys and girls) a few years ago, she commented on the constructed nature of the photographs of the bedrooms. In that project, Salinger and a photographer visited young people in their bedrooms. Although her participants were instructed not to clean up, it became clear as the project evolved that what young people say about their own rooms, and how they talk about them, is indeed an extension (or projection) of themselves. Certain objects have particular currency. As Salinger writes, "Our bedrooms tell stories about us. They become the repository for our memories and the expression of our desires and self-image" (1995, np)[18]. Demonstrating their "tween" status, the girls in the digital bedroom project took photographs of "big girl" clothing accessories such as belts and handbags mixed in with their images of various types of dolls (from Barbies to porcelain dolls and meilie-meil African dolls). In this respect, their digital play resembles the cyber-paper doll play described by Rebekah Willett in the next chapter.

These digitized images of bedrooms, while located within an adult-organized project, offer us a glimpse into the world of girls that links the construction of identity, space, and digital technology. Like Isabella's website construction described in our first case, and the video-making process that will follow in the next one, the use of the digital camera along with

PowerPoint offers the girls an opportunity to project themselves in particular and personal ways. The girls worked in a relatively autonomous manner, with very few restrictions on what they could photograph. And unlike the use of point-and-shoot cameras, where the photographer is forced to wait for the photographs to be developed and where even access to the pictures may be constrained by adult supervision, using digital cameras to represent their bedrooms meant that the girls could edit their images on the spot. Although the girls worked individually, what they have chosen to photograph and project in a public space also represents a social act, not just in relation to what they initially chose to photograph but also in relation to what they chose to project to their peers and teacher. In this respect, their work is not that different from the photo-sharing associated with their cell phone use or within the social networking sites, described in danah boyd's and Susannah Stern's chapters later in this volume. The girls' choices of images raise fascinating questions about their personal–public identities. What meaning, for example, does the addition of the little commentator dog have? How does a certain font or text layout personalize the projection? It is through the use and the reading of these seemingly mundane details that identities emerge.

Case 4. Our Collective Selves: Participatory Video

This last case looks at youth identities-in-action in relation to the idea of collective selves. How do young people create a collective identity through video production? We explore this question through the following excerpt taken from a participatory digital video-making project involving young people in a rural district of KwaZulu-Natal, South Africa.[19] The video-making workshops are part of a community-based "every voice counts" project, addressing HIV and AIDS in a context where more than 25 percent of young people between the ages of fifteen and twenty-four are HIV positive.[20] An ongoing issue in these communities relates to engaging youth in addressing what has come to be known as the "sick of AIDS" phenomenon, an expression that is intended both literally, given the grim statistics noted above, and figuratively, in the sense that there has been an overdose of "fighting AIDS" messages.[21]

Set against this backdrop, groups of young people between the ages of fourteen and sixteen at two secondary schools (along with teachers, community health care workers, and parents) participated in one-day video-making workshops. The work with digital cameras is linked to other participatory approaches such as photo-voice and drama that have also been used at the two schools. The overall purpose of the workshops is to look at ways that the participants can explore concerns that are meaningful to them. Digital video offers a unique "take" on their engagement with the issues.

This section focuses primarily on an all-boy group that produced a video called *Rape*. Most of the youth groups elected to focus in one way or another on gender violence, a critical issue throughout South Africa, and given that young women are four to five times more likely to be HIV positive than young men of the same age, not separate from the high rates of HIV infection amongst girls and young women. The story line of *Rape* is organized around the multiple rapes of one girl (G) by her boyfriend (S). The actual narrative is broken up into eight short scenes, four of which directly depict staged rapes. As we see in the scene below, the encounters between the boy and his girlfriend start off in a loving way, but quickly move to forced sex. We offer an English translation of the scene that was originally produced in Isizulu:

2nd RAPE SCENE
S: *Where do you live now my baby? Give me a hug. No way, lets sit down.*
G: *Take a break and have some fresh air.*

S: [Grabs her.]
G: *Just wait a bit. Wait! Stop!*
S: *What is the matter with you?*
G: *I don't like to do it. I don't like it.*
S: *What don't you like?*
G: *To do it. I don't like to.*
S: *What?*
G: *Eh . . . eh . . . I don't like to do it . . . Eh . . . eh . . . You know what, I'll cry out loud.*
S: *Come on now baby* (Rape takes place). *But who are you going to cry out to? Come on baby.*

G. reports her boyfriend to the police. He is imprisoned, and as we see below in the last scene of the video, he appears to show some remorse for what he has done, although not because of the impact of his actions on his girlfriend so much as what has happened to him in prison, where he himself is subjected to sexual violence.

8th Scene
S: Ei! I am now regretful. I raped my sweetheart. When I get out of here she will not even want to see me. Ei, I raped a person really. I am in prison now. Its tough . . . even to eat. It is me that is getting raped now. They mount me. Ei, now I regret what I did.
I don't know what to say. I don't know what to do. I am in prison now. I raped a female person. I raped her and beat her and am in prison now. I don't know what to do now. The men in here mount me and beat me. Just look now, when I get out of here the babes in the location will leave me. I won't get another cherry because I am known to be a rapist now.
But you, my brothers out there, I'm telling you, restrain yourselves, be strong, don't rape females because you will be sentenced and grow old inside (prison).

At one level, the video production can simply be read as a very disturbing and graphic representation of aggressive masculinity, one which reinforces negative stereotypes about boys and young men.[22] Indeed, in many ways the scenario depicted here is no different from the kinds of testimonies that are described in face-to-face interviews with young people in various South African locations where boys report that it is "okay to hit your girlfriend" and where it is "okay to expect sex," and where girls talk about the inevitability of forced sex and unprotected sex.[23] In one of the all-girl video groups, for example, the first point that they brought up during a brainstorming session was "we worry about getting pregnant before we finish school."

However, at another level, the boys' video invites us to consider what difference it makes that this is a "production" (and not just an interview), and to ask how working with new technologies such as digital video (and not, for example, just performance or still photographs) contributes to a deeper understanding of identity construction. The availability of relatively inexpensive equipment (cell phones, webcams, digital cameras with a video function, and inexpensive camcorders) clearly has made this kind of work more feasible even in a rural school in South Africa—even where, as in this case, the only electricity is in the principal's office. One of the groups, for example, managed to import a soundtrack from a cell phone into the video. This was particularly interesting, given that no one in any of the groups had ever used a video camera before.

One might also ask what difference the collective process makes—particularly in evoking and exploring questions of gender identity. *Rape* was clearly a group effort. Indeed, as we review the footage that was shot during the production process, we can see groups "in action" negotiating particular scenes, as well as working out who would be behind the camera and who would be in front of the camera. In participatory video, there is the possibility of creating a strong sense of a collective response, one that includes both producers and viewers, directors, actors, technicians, and so on. While it is possible that individual responses may sometimes be overshadowed in this collectivity, we would argue that in the case of gender violence, which is social in nature and multilayered in meaning, the collective response is vital. The group chooses the themes, decides on the images, "constructs" the stage, and so forth. In the case of video (as opposed to live performance), there is a whole array of techniques that expand the possibilities for constructedness—from shot angles to dialogue to theme music. Participants can stop the process, view, and review the work, and indeed, can even easily "see themselves" in action. Each frame is considered and reconsidered. Nothing is accidental. And although we employed a "no editing required" approach, so that each scene was shot as a final cut, participants did have the opportunity to reshoot the scene from the beginning if they wished. Several groups rehearsed the entire episode first, offering yet another way of playing not only with the various components of the video, but also and especially with gendered identities. In *Rape,* the boys work to construct the girlfriend as weak and passive, and themselves as cool and powerful. S appears after each of the rape scenes with his shirt half hanging out, and later in the prison scene appears in one of the "cool" woolen beanies that boys wear outside of school (but which are not part of the mandatory school uniform).

As we have illustrated throughout this chapter, digital media allow for a trying on of various identities. In the process of making the video, the boys seemed to be consciously (and insistently) trying on identities that reproduce the masculine role images that they see around them in school, village, and the media, while at the same time they are also testing out new identities, not the least of which is a type of "prison hero" as we saw earlier in S's final soliloquy.[24] The plea is to feel sorry for him and not to wonder what happened to his girlfriend.

It is also interesting to note that in order for them to project what they feel is a satisfactory macho or male identity, the boys are adamant that they need to "borrow" a girl from one of the other video-making groups so that they could enact the rapes on screen. Although the facilitator tries to convince the group that they could "suggest" rape by using off-camera voices (another group production which also deals with gender violence uses "behind closed door" screaming, not unlike the school rape scene in the film *North Country)* or through the use of an item of clothing as a trace, the boys convince one of the girls to join their group for the purposes of filming the rape. This leads us to ask what role does the "other"—in this case, girls and young women—play in constructing gender identity?

We might also read this process of negotiating and "trying on" identities as an explicit form of reflexivity during the video making, whereby the boys were not only testing out particular scenarios of rape and remorse, but also experimenting with particular technical features such as camera angles and set arrangements. For example, while several of the scenes involve the rapist, S, along with his mates or his girlfriend, the final scene of regret and anguish works so well because of his soliloquy. At a later point in the process when the group screens the video again for the purposes of thinking through the ways in which such a video might be used in the community, their comments reveal the possibility for what Gary Barker[25] and others might describe as an example of an alternative masculinity, one that does not require that boys and young men take on a more normative or hegemonic masculinity that relies solely on dominance and power over girls and young women. They comment, for example, that a critical element of addressing gender violence is to revisit the statement "when no means no," a point that relates to the fact that G, in the video, repeatedly says some version of "no." What is clearly important here is the idea of setting up a space where it is possible for participants to look back at their production, to reflect on the multiple meanings it might have to different audiences, *including themselves*, and to allow for revision.

Reading Identities Across the Cases

Several of the specific media forms and technologies we have introduced here are considered in much more detail in subsequent chapters in this book, particularly in Part 2. Through our "sampling" of these different youth production practices, we have sought to provide an initial indication of some of the broader issues that cut across these seemingly diverse media forms. A careful reading across the examples reveals certain shared features of digital production that can be useful to understanding both youth as cultural producers and youth *identities-in-action*.

Constructedness

One of the most salient characteristics of identity processes to emerge across the cases is the "constructedness" of the various media productions. Borrowing from the phenomenon of construction toys, we are referring here to the manner of playful yet more or less deliberate creative "assembling" involved—whether it be of the virtual components of websites or the constructing and deconstructing of gender as part of on- and offline role play. As with construction block play, in media productions like those described earlier, you usually start out using the materials at hand, respecting or finding ways to get around their limitations, working with others or alone. Suggested blueprints or models may be included with both toys and media design, but individual and collective uses and interpretations of them may differ; negotiation, subversion, and adaptation are commonplace. Once you have acquired some skills and have explored possibilities, you may find yourself improvising and seeking out additional materials to incorporate into your construction. What you end up with may have unintended potential uses or effects on others. The creative construction that is involved in digital production permits the manipulation of gendered, raced, and sexualized identities, both online and offline.[26] Moreover, in looking across the cases, it strikes us that, like the products of construction toys, the identities emerging through multimedia production retain traces of the original materials, faint outlines of the building blocks as it were. As in a collage, you can see remnants of other images that contribute to identity—bits of media material, fragments from personal life, original poems, family photos, social symbols, shared memories, cut-and-paste resources of media tools, and site hosts—that in combination add up to a unique image—an identity work-in-progress that, like block construction, can be toppled, changed, or rearranged.

Collectivity and Social Construction

The notion of collectivity follows from these socially constructed and co-constructed images and identities described above. As we saw in the case of Isabella and Maria, for example, digital technology enables them to present their identities in various guises to a select audience and to examine them in the reflected light of the comments and reactions of their friends (and in Isabella's case, her older sister). The sites could be regarded as montages of group and individual identities, improvisations that draw on and blend a variety of genres and sources that provide the raw material for construction. They are created not only as expressions and explorations of individual identities, but also very much as a way of including others in their own personal "identity work" and of extending and linking themselves to significant others. Through this process, they become part of a collaborative, participatory culture.[27] Identity constructions on these sites evoke the wider collectives of peer group and family, and facilitate a dialectical relationship between personal and social identities, one that shifts and flows, reacting to new information, situations, and contexts.

Exploring the collective process in group video making (as in our final case) may help to deepen our understanding of social construction more broadly. The fact that each of the videos is produced by the group (from group brainstorming to group decision making about the scripting, planning, and filming) reflects both the idea of constructedness noted above and the idea of negotiation. The technology of the camera and the "no editing required" constraint means that groups must collectively arrive at decisions about *who* (will play the rapist, do the filming, play the police), *what* (the number of scenes, dividing them up, and so on) and *how* (choosing locations, deciding on props and sound, etc.). In the case of *Rape* (as well as most of the other videos that were produced about gender violence), the group itself participates in performing gender. At one point, for example, when one of the groups is still brainstorming the various "in-my-life" critical issues, there is a discussion about gangsterism and the "look" of a local gang member, wherein various group members physically stand a certain way, pull up their collars, put their hands in their pockets, and so on. In line with Judith Butler's ideas about gender identity[28] discussed in the introduction to this volume, the technology of video making and the group effort accentuates the dimension of performance. The fact that most groups rehearsed their scenes before they actually filmed them meant that group members were able to offer suggestions, and in some cases even role play what the person who was being filmed should be doing. And while this could be true for any type of performance, it is the capturing on film that adds to the identity-in-action process and the possibilities for social action.[29] This collective and social aspect of construction is also evident in the two case studies of youth activism described by Shelly Goldman, Meaghan McDermott, and Angela Booker later on in this volume.

Convergence

Reading digital production both within and across the cases offers a unique glimpse into the intersection and blending of old and new media more generally. As Henry Jenkins writes:

> Media convergence refers to a situation in which multiple media systems coexist and where media content flows fluidly across them. Convergence is understood here as an ongoing process or series of intersections between different media systems, not a fixed relationship (282).[30]

In the video production of *Rape*, for example, young people "perform" identities using traditional forms of role play, although one might look at some of the parallels to role play on the Internet.[31] Through their use of digital cameras to capture these performances, they are able to work with an instant replay, whereby they can see if they have caught the scene exactly as they want it, and, as noted earlier, one of the group members imports a sound track from a cell phone into the video. As a different example, the long established media practice of the photo essay is central to the PowerPoint narrative of "I love my cell phone" where Walia has visually portrayed the various scenes of her story. Capturing these performed events digitally and rerepresenting them through a PowerPoint presentation that focuses on a cell phone results in a compelling document that uses one medium to comment on the significance of another. In the case of "In my room," the girls work with the conventions of display and the techniques of photovoice, each of which could have been presented without digital technology. Using PowerPoint as a type of storytelling, however, enables them to play around with and explore how they (and their private bedrooms) can be represented in a more public setting. And finally, returning to the first case, even in the most seemingly "new" technologies of website construction, we see blends of older ones—journal writing, photo albums, slide projectors, scrapbooking, and more. This ongoing convergence mirrors or reflects identities-in-action, which similarly incorporate and merge old and new elements of experience.

Reflexivity and Negotiation

One of the key ways in which media production contributes to the construction of identities is through the facilitation of *reflexivity*. By this we mean to suggest three things: Firstly, their own media production (both through its processes and its outcomes) forces young people to look at themselves, sometimes through new eyes, providing feedback for further modification of their self-representations. Secondly, the source materials and modes of young people's media production are often evident or transparent; the choices and processes that they use reveal and identify them in ways that they themselves might not even realize. Thirdly, through built-in response mechanisms or simply through audience response, media production invites other people's feedback and readings, sparking a dialectic that is inherent to mediating and reshaping how we see ourselves and how we think others see us. Even so, as Buckingham indicates in his discussion of Giddens's and Foucault's theories of identity in the preceding chapter, the question of *whose* eyes we see ourselves through and whose language we use to express ourselves is not so easily answered. A reflexive regard is not necessarily as critical as one might think; it too is shaped by culture and experience. Because we are not always aware that seeing is something we are taught to do and that language is something into which we are socialized, our ability to read and represent ourselves can lose its critical edge. It is, therefore, the ability of media production to occasionally provoke this awareness that makes it so useful to identity construction.

The expression and construction of identities through digital media production usually relies heavily on the visual, and it is this visual component that can jolt us into a more critical reflexivity. Visual anthropologists such as Sarah Pink[32] and Jay Ruby[33] assert that there is an element of reflexivity inherent in working with images. Much of what we have described in this chapter—the photo sharing, the constructed images, and so on—is visual and closely linked to the identities that young people are reflecting upon and exploring.[34] When we look across the cases, we see evidence of this in different ways. As one example, through the visual structure and content of their websites, Isabella and her friends were constantly negotiating their standings and identities within general pop culture, their heritage community, and their circle of friends, closely examining and giving each other feedback on their posts, subtly suggesting through example what can and cannot be posted, what is "cool," and so forth. Posting the image of a flag or a particular pop idol is an identification that strengthens a sense of belonging. In visiting and adapting their own and each other's sites, these young people were in a sense gazing at themselves, critiquing and consuming their own images.

Embodiment

There is a tendency, when discussing identity in the context of new technologies, to forget that identities are always and inescapably embodied.[35] Although we may forget our bodies when cruising in cyberspace, all our actions are taken through them. Indeed, if there is anything that gives a sense of permanence and stability to the flux of identity processes, it is the body, which even as it changes in appearance, remains at the heart of identity. While theorists may ignore the role of actual bodies in both individual and collective identities (they seem to prefer theoretical ones), young people most certainly understand that identity is always embodied. For example, by posting photos of themselves which they have taken, often deliberately posed (e.g., à la Hillary Duff) as we saw in the first case, young people are examining, modifying, dressing, adorning, and putting their bodies out there. During adolescence, they sometimes treat or read appearance as the very substance of identity, something alluded to in more detail in the following chapter by Willett.

Embodiment is also evident in a more subtle way in our third case study, of girls' photos of their bedrooms. The digital images that they chose for their PowerPoint presentations evoke their everyday embodied world of sleeping, eating, playing, collecting, caring for pets, and so on. Moreover, objects such as those found in their bedrooms can be markers or even the material of identity production. Clothes, for example, display and shape embodied identities, something that explains to a certain extent the obsession some gamers have with dressing and reconstructing their avatars. A garment, accessory, or piece of jewelry, like Walia's boots and earrings (and, one could argue, her cell phone) in case 2, can extend, represent, and reconstruct the body. In the *Rape* video, we see the various characters "trying on" identities: rapist, gangster, repentant prisoner. Items of clothing and body gestures become markers of these identities: the shirt half hanging out, the "cool" walk of the gangster, and the beanie of the prisoner.

At times, bodies are front and center, the very focus of media production. In the horrifying rape scene, S is filmed overpowering G. with a simulated attack on her body which could be interpreted in one way as an attack on her "person," on who she is. However, as a reminder that the *Rape* video was simulated or "made up," it is important to observe that someone has put down two sheets of flip chart paper so that G. does not have to lie on the dirty cement floor of the classroom during the shoot, a protection of the very body that is being violated, but also a further reminder that media productions, like identities, are always embodied.

Learning

Learning is another theme that we see running across the cases. The differences in educational structures and settings, for example, can have an impact on both the skills and content of young people's media productions. In the first case, where girls construct websites on their own without direct adult supervision, the learning is informal and self-motivated, embedded in their daily lives outside school, and occurring at their own pace and in their own space. As the need arises during the website production or posting process, Isabella turns to her sister to learn such things as where to find templates and how to modify them, a good example of sibling-as-mentor. She also turns to her peers for ideas, feedback, and guidance. There is an experimentation and authenticity to her learning as well as pleasure and satisfaction in what she achieves. Far from being a solitary process, learning in this kind of situation involves interacting with friends whose responses fuel and shape media production.

The learning processes that occur in the more formal school and community center settings of the last three cases differ in some ways from the first case, especially in terms of the power and freedom afforded to young people. For example, unlike the first case, the type of production (PowerPoint, photovoice essay, video) is predetermined by adults (teacher or community worker or animator). Moreover, the skills needed to do the media production are modeled and taught before production begins during hands-on workshops, and then coached as necessary during production. Although the young people can freely choose specific content and write their own stories in all of the cases, there are varying degrees of adult control over the general topic from case to case. It is perhaps not too surprising to realize that it is the production project (photographing bedrooms) initiated by a teacher as schoolwork that has the most restrictive general parameters (it is taken up, nonetheless, very enthusiastically by her students).

Access to technology also emerges as a critical feature of learning. In the first case, for example, the girls and their friends clearly had access to various digital media in their homes and communities. In the third case, the girls who created their own PowerPoint presentations had access to digital cameras outside of school, making it possible for them to experiment on their own. In the fourth case, however, none of the participants (teachers and other adults as well as the students) had access to any digital media outside the workshop. A point worth making here, therefore, relates to the important role of other community members and community resources in expanding the possibilities for young people to experiment with media.

In all the cases, the young people we observed learn *through* media production which often exemplifies constructivist notions of learning, a self-motivated learning through play, through trial and error, and through actively engaging with the world. Not only do they acquire technical skills, they also learn to create and critique, developing their own sense of esthetics and learning goals. Their emerging media literacy enables them to further articulate and experiment with multiple identities as they refine their productions. And while the idea of cultural production and media literacy has often been taken up elsewhere,[36] it remains critical to understanding learning in the context of digital media and youth identities.

Conclusion: Identity Production as Bricolage

Many contemporary theories of identity—such as those reviewed in the introduction to this book—conceive of identity as a process, rather than a fixed possession or label. From this perspective, identity is not something that can ever be achieved once and for all: it is fluid and open to negotiation, but also subject to many constraints. Similarly, the structural features or characteristics of digital production we have described in this chapter also reflect a broader view of identity as an ongoing process, one that is always under construction but that also has a permanence or longevity, an existence tied to embodiment. To encapsulate our conceptualization of identity, we draw in this section on the concept of *bricolage*, a French term often used to refer to a construction or creation (for example, of a work of art or a craft project) that is improvised, using whatever materials are at hand. Like "identity," the word bricolage can be used to refer to a process as well as a product. It relates, in some ways, to the metaphor of block building we used earlier.

Turkle[37] speaks of identities in the digital age as fragmented, shifting, partial. In contrast, our notion of identity as personal and social bricolage[38] places those fragments within a single work-in-progress, an evolving active construction that constantly sheds bits and adds bits, changing through dialectical interactions with the digital and nondigital world, involving physical, psychological, social, and cultural agents. Identities, whether individual or collective, are not unitary wholes cut out of a single cloth—they are constructed in action, using whatever cultural and life material is at hand. Like bricolage, identity construction involves improvising, experimenting, and blending genres, patching together contrasting or even contradictory elements, creating and modifying meanings to suit the context and in response to the requirements, affordances, and meanings of the situation. For many young people, digital media (whichever ones are "at hand") provide tools and display possibilities that are well suited to bricolage.

Several years ago, Julian Sefton-Green and David Buckingham took us into the digital bedroom to survey young people's esthetic and cultural production practices. While they were somewhat despairing of what they described as a form of "lego creativity" which falls short of a more autonomous use of new media, they nonetheless highlight the significance of young people's cultural production and the fact that they do "muck around" in ways that are uniquely their own.[39] "Mucking around" is part of what bricolage entails, an experimentation that gradually leads, with or without help, to production skills as well as knowledge of available materials and how to manipulate them, both to create new meanings and reproduce old ones.

Our conception of bricolage as both shaping and being shaped by "what is at hand" reflects a dialectical model of identity, similar to Bakhtin's, wherein identities are simultaneously both personal and social.[40] We construct and deconstruct and reconstruct ourselves in dialectical relationship with the world (which includes the material cultural world and other people), and we construct others in relation to ourselves and our situation. Identities are negotiated and tested in the context of circles of relationships and the wider community, and fed back into the ongoing bricolage. Social and individual identities co-constitute each other.

Clicking, posting, and text messaging their way through a shifting digital landscape, young people are bending and blending genres, incorporating old ideas, activities, and images into new bricolages, changing the face, if not the substance, of social interaction and altering how they see themselves and each other. Whether it be the frequent postings on websites, the improvisations in the filming of a story, the incorporation of objects at hand in a PowerPoint, the cases we have described in this chapter give us a way to view and interrogate the ongoing production of youth identities.[41] As technologies become more deeply integrated into ever widening areas of our lives, their roles as mediators of identities and learning are likely to be taken for granted, perhaps becoming almost invisible. That's why it is so important to examine and reflect on them now.

Notes

1. For an interesting discussion of this blurring, see David Buckingham, *After the Death of Childhood: Growing up in the Age of Electronic Media* (Cambridge, UK: Polity, 2000); for earlier although more alarmist views, see Neil Postman, *The Disappearance of Childhood* (New York: Vintage Books, 1994).

2. For an informative discussion of Internet access and the economic divide in the United States, see Ellen Seiter, *The Internet Playground: Children's Access, Entertainment, and Mis-Education* (New York: Peter Lang, 2005); for one in Britain, see Sonia Livingstone, and Magdalena Bober, *U.K. Children Go Online: Surveying the Experiences of Young People and Their Parents* (London: London School of Economics and Political Science, 2004).

3. David Buckingham and Julian Sefton-Green, *Cultural Studies Goes To School* (London: Taylor and Francis, 1994).

4. Mizuko Ito (in press), Mobilizing the Imagination in Everyday Play: The Case of Japanese Media Mixes, in *International Handbook of Children, Media, and Culture,* eds. Sonia Livingstone and Kirsten Drotner (London: Sage).

5. Henry Jenkins, *Convergence Culture: Where Old and New Media Collide* (New York and London: New York University Press, 2006), 290.

6. Martin Lister et al., *New Media: A Critical Introduction* (Routledge: London and New York, 2003).

7. We gratefully acknowledge the financial support of the Social Sciences and Research Council of Canada for *Digital Girls: Girls' Everyday Experiences of Technology: From Play to Policy.*

8. *Moving Lives* is a digital photovoice storytelling project for young refugees run by Liz Orton and based in Trinity Community Centre in England. For more information, see http://www.photovoice.org/html/projectgallery/photovoiceproj/movinglives/ (accessed October 29, 2006).

9. Performance as we use it here not only refers to the roles that Erving Goffman claims we are *always* assuming, whether onstage or backstage, but more along the lines of embodiment as proposed by Judith Butler, *Gender Trouble: Feminism and the Subversion of Identity* (New York: Routledge, 1990), and then wonderfully critiqued and extended by Elizabeth Grosz, *Volatile Bodies: Toward a Corporeal Feminism* (Bloomington: Indiana University Press, 1994).

10. Jenkins, 2006.

11. Liz Orton, ibid (note 8).

12. See Jane Brown, Carol Reese Dykers, Jeanne Rogge Steele, and Ann Barton White, Teenage Room Culture: Where Media and Identities Intersect, *Communication Research* 21, no. 6 (1994): 813–827.

13. We wish to acknowledge the work of Maureen St. John Ward and her students at Wykeham Collegiate.

14. Even if the girls had photographed similar objects, it is the personal meanings, as Christian Boltanski points out in his Favourite Objects project, that is the point. See Claudia Mitchell and Jacqueline Reid-Walsh, Virtual Spaces: Children on the Cyber Frontier, in *Researching Children's Popular Culture: Cultural Spaces of Childhood* (London and New York: Routledge Taylor Francis, 2002).

15. See Angela McRobbie and Jane Garber, Girls and Subcultures: An Exploration, in *Resistance Through Rituals: Youth Subcultures in Post-War Britain*, eds. Stuart Hall and Tony Jefferson (London: Hutchinson, 1976), 209–222.

16. See Julian Sefton-Green, Digital Visions: Children's Creative Uses of Digital Technologies, in *Digital Diversions: Youth Culture in the Age of Multimedia*, ed. Julian Sefton-Green and David Buckingham (London: Routledge, 1998), 62–83.

17. See also Mitchell and Reid-Walsh (2002).

18. See Adrienne Salinger, *In My Room: Teenagers in Their Bedrooms* (San Francisco: Chronicle Books, 1995).

19. Here we would like to acknowledge the participation of the Learning Together research team at the Centre for Visual Methodologies for Social Change, University of KwaZulu-Natal. The Learning Together team is headed up by Naydene de Lange.

20. Centre for the AIDS Programme of Research in South Africa (CAPRISA). http://www.caprisa.org/Projects/women_and_aids.html# (accessed August 18, 2006).

21. See Claudia Mitchell and Ann Smith, Sick of AIDS: Literacy and the Meaning of Life for South Africa Youth, *Culture, Health and Sexuality* 5, no. 6 (2003): 513–522.

22. In their work with youth in South Africa, Catherine Campbell and Catherine McPhail, *Letting Them Die* (Cape Town: Double Storey, 2003), found that the notion of the male sex drive as uncontrollable was assumed. Here they are also confirming the work of Janet Holland, Caroline Ramazanoglu, Sue

Sharpe, and Rachel Thomson, Feminist Methodology and Young People's Sexuality, in *Culture, Society and Sexuality: A Reader,* eds. Richard Parker and Peter Aggleton (London and Philadelphia: UCL Press, 1999), 457–472. They note that male sexuality is often portrayed as "a train that cannot be derailed once engaged."

23. Reshma Sathiparsad, *Perceptions of Rural Zulu Male Youth on Sexual Violence,* University of KwaZulu-Natal, 2006 explores the links between hegemonic masculinity in Zulu culture and sexual violence in her unpublished doctoral dissertation.

24. At the time of the video-making workshop, Jacob Zuma, the deputy prime minister of South Africa, was embroiled in a court case where he was being accused of having raped a young woman who was visiting the family home. Much media attention through radio, television, and newspaper was given over to a public interrogation of Zulu male culture.

25. Gary Barker et al., Engaging Young Men in Violence Prevention: Reflections from Latin America and India, in *Combating Gender Violence in and Around Schools,* eds. Claudia Mitchell and Fiona Leach (Trent, UK: Trentham Books, 2006).

26. Jacqueline Reid-Walsh takes up this idea of construction further in a conference paper, "Virtual Spaces as Critical Spaces: Girls' Consumption and Production of Popular Culture Web Sites as Instances of Critical Digital Literacy," presented at the Researching New Literacies: Consolidating Knowledge and Defining New Directions conference, October 16 and 17, 2006, Memorial University of Newfoundland, St. John's, NL. She also discusses construction and multimedia in "Harlequin Meets *The SIMS*: A History of Interactive Narrative Media for Children and Youth from Early Flap Books to Contemporary Multi Media," in eds. Sonia Livingstone and Kirsten Drotner (in press), *International Handbook of Children, Media, and Culture* (London: Sage).

27. Jenkins, 2006.

28. Butler, 1990.

29. Michael Schratz and Rob Walker, *Research as Social Change* (New York: Routledge, 1995) argue that a critical feature of various interventions like the video making workshops which lend themselves to social change is that they are in fact social in nature in the first place. They involve the group and cannot be managed "individually and in isolation." As they go on to write: "It (Motivation) requires a collaborative effort and a reassessment of the nature of self in relation to social context, not a submerging of the individual within the collective, but a recognition that the person only exists in the light of significant others."

30. Jenkins, 2006.

31. Here we are thinking of the role play involving online interactive societies such as *World of Warcraft* and *Second Life.*

32. See Sarah Pink, *Visual Ethnography* (Thousand Oaks, CA: Sage, 2001).

33. See Jay Ruby, *Picturing Culture: Explorations of Film and Anthropology* (Chicago and London: University of Chicago Press, 2000).

34. In their work, *Finding Our Voices: Gendered and Sexual Identities and HIV/AIDS in Education* (Nairobi: UNICEF ESARO, 2003), Rob Pattman and Fatuma Chege argue that "identities such as male, female, black and white, only exist in relation to each other . . . " and that individuals are always "producing and negotiating—whether consciously or not" these identities.

35. For a very interesting account of embodied identity, see Grosz (1994).

36. For example, in Buckingham and Sefton-Green (1994).

37. Sherry Turkle, *Life on the Screen* (New York: Simon and Schuster, 1995) was one of the first to examine identity in relation to new technologies.

38. Although Joe Kincheloe's passage is intended as a description of research processes [Joe Kincheloe, *Qualitative Inquiry* (Sage, 2001), 679–692] the elaboration of bricolage (following Yvonne Lincoln's extension of Levi-Strauss's famous term) very well describes or fits our notion of identity processes.

39. This observation is reminiscent of the earlier work of David Buckingham and Julian Sefton-Green in their study of young people constructing identity posters. See David Buckingham and Julian Sefton-Green, *Cultural Studies Goes to School* (London: Falmer Press, 1994). (Quote is from page 73.)

40. Mikhail Bakhtin, *The Dialogic Imagination: Four Essays,* eds. Carol Emerson and Michael Holquist (Austin: University of Texas Press, 1981).

41. For further cases and discussion, see Sandra Weber and Shanly Dixon, eds., *Growing Up Online: Children and Technologies* (New York: Palgrave, 2007).

Consumer Citizens Online: Structure, Agency, and Gender in Online Participation

Rebekah Willett

Institute of Education, University of London, Centre for the Study of Children, Youth and Media

An interesting shift occurs within educational settings when the formality of learning environments is relaxed and students are given "free time" on the Internet. Educational websites disappear, music comes on, and different people in the room become experts. The screens, the sounds, the way students interact with technology, and the interactions between them change as they immerse themselves in games, social networks and commercial sites of their own choosing. Students update their profiles on websites, changing their photos as well as their lists of favorite films, television shows, and music. They play games, search for cheats, and find out what other gamers are saying about particular games and gaming systems. They look for clothes, shopping around for the best deals and identifying outfits through which they can express an individual style.

One of the popular free-time activities I have observed in these situations is to play with online paperdolls on "dollmaker" sites. Particularly, though not exclusively, used by girls I observed aged eight to twelve, paperdoll sites contain clothes, hair, makeup, and accessories to drag and drop onto curvaceous cartoon-like figures. Wanting to look more closely at this shift between formal and free time, I ran a workshop in a school in London in which girls aged eleven to twelve designed their own dollmaker sites. One of the designs from the project is shown in Figure 1. The clothes, hair, earrings, and purse in this design are all stylized to match current trends. The outfit, with the display of midriff and peeking thigh, suggests a sexualized girl's body. However, the body itself (colored lurid turquoise) was completely ignored by the girls, treated like a mannequin, and left unchanged from the template provided.

On the surface, we could argue that the design reflects the influence of the fashion and beauty industries on girls. Given a space to design a body and clothing, this eleven-year-old produced an image that positions girls as sexual, as needing to be skinny, and as constant consumers of fashion and accessories. However, on the basis of the interviews and conversations I conducted with the girls, I was not willing to describe them as passive dupes of the beauty industries. Similarly, I was unwilling to see their other interactions during "free time" on the Internet as a matter of engagement in senseless violence, as video gaming is sometimes described, or as immersion in music which is manufactured and mind-numbingly dull, as some popular music is sometimes seen. Clearly, engagement on the Internet, even within the context of commercial culture, is not a passive activity. So how can we analyze online activities in ways which account for the power and influence of commercial industries, while at the same time recognizing how young people actively engage with the commodities these industries offer?

Figure 1
Dollmaker design.

This chapter examines identity within the context of online consumer cultures. The consumerism I am discussing may not take the form of overt advertising or marketing, as, for example, on a website such as Barbie.com. Instead, the chapter focuses on cultures which exist in more blurred areas of the kind described above, in which young people can be seen to be contributing to online media, through written text, images, and music. It is in this blurred area that I am seeking to explore the relationships between the *structures* of consumerism (and wider societal discourses) and the *agency* (the capacity to think and act freely) of the young consumer/producer. My focus, then, is on the tension which underlies many debates about young people's online activities, between seeing young people as acted upon by societal forces and seeing them as independent actors in their own right.

Popular debates about young people's online activities often focus on elements that are seen as harmful or problematic, as in the arguments about violence in games, or sexual images on social networking sites, for example. Yet these assertions have been criticized by some as being overly deterministic, as positioning young people as passive and ignoring the complexity of children's and young people's consumption of media. Instead, it is suggested that media, particularly new digital media, offer young people the chance to be powerful and to express their creativity as media producers. In this view, young people are doing important identity work—finding like-minded peers, exploring issues around gender, race, and sexuality; and defining themselves as experts within particular communities. However, there is a risk here of celebrating young people's interactions with media without taking a critical look at some of the inherent structures which are at play in young people's lives. More importantly, it can lead us to overlook particular values that young people are buying into through their engagements with digital media.

The aim of this chapter is to look past the structure–agency dichotomy implied in the arguments above, and to see how, as Anthony Giddens describes, human agency and social structure act through each other.[1] In drawing on work by Giddens and others, the chapter discusses identity in the context of broader debates about late modernity, specifically considering how the agency offered to young people is structured by neoliberal discourses, for example, those of "individualization" and "responsibilization." It is through these discourses, I shall argue, that the modern "consumer citizen" is defined.

The chapter starts with a discussion of research on young people as consumers, tracing historical constructions as well as current debates about marketing to children online. The second section examines theories of identity, as described above, specifically looking at how these theories discuss consumerism, and then relating these ideas to an analysis of consumer activities online. The third section focuses specifically on research into girls' online activities, which provides an introduction to the final section—an analysis of girls' paperdoll activities online. The conclusion points to some of the implications of these ideas for research in the context of learning environments.

Young People as Consumers

Children and young people are increasingly at the center of critical debates about consumer culture. Numerous popular publications claim that childhood is being commodified as a result of manipulative and deceitful marketing strategies.[2] In this view, children are victims of powerful commercial industries, and childhood, once a natural and free space, is seen as being destroyed by the influence of consumer culture. Debates here are combined with arguments about media effects: media are seen single-handedly to promote various "ill effects," such as increases in violence, sexual activity, obesity, stereotyped beliefs, and behavioral disorders, to name but a few.[3] On the other hand, there are those who argue that children and young people are wise and authoritative consumers who carefully select and use consumer items to meet their desires and needs. Children are seen here to be discriminating and active consumers, as is evidenced by the fact that so many new children's products fail to generate a profit.

These debates, which are polarized in popular critical literature on consumer culture, provide a useful springboard for discussing the relationship between consumerism and identity. Whilst there can be no doubt that marketing is a key factor in children's lives, we also need to recognize times when it is not effective. Even so, children do not choose products and express themselves freely and independently. We need to be careful not to over-celebrate the agency of individuals. Structures, in this case from consumer cultures, frame individual choice and action: external factors shape, form, and constrain people's choices, although they are far from being all-powerful.

The focus on young people's consumer habits is not new. Since the "youth quake" of the 1950s, brought about partly by the baby boom and an increase in youth employment, markets in countries with developed economies have attempted to tap into the spending power of young people. This is reflected in the emergence in the 1950s of youth-oriented media, such as music, magazines, movies, and fashion. This trend continued through the 1960s and 1970s, with particular media such as music segmenting into specialist markets. Even with the "baby bust" of the 1980s (when the proportion of the population under age eighteen dropped) and the recessions running through the early 1980s and early 1990s, youth on the whole remained a lucrative market segment. However, the media industries in the 1980s and 1990s felt the impact of greater economic competition and deregulation of markets. Industries responded by increasing their efficiency through outsourcing and subcontracting, but also moving away from mass-market products. With greater flexibility, industries were able to develop new marketing techniques that could capitalize on niche markets. This set the trend for "cool marketing" and the commercial exploitation of "youthful" styles and values.[4]

As outlined by Buckingham in the introduction to this volume, sociological research has argued that the category "youth" is a social and historical construct; yet at the same time, there has been research which examines how young people actively construct youth identities. Within studies of "youth subcultures," analyses have focused on how material objects are used as markers of identity, defining specific social groups and distinguishing them on the grounds of class, race, and gender as well as age.[5] Products from popular media are seen here as shared "symbolic resources," providing easily accessible markers of interest and identity amongst young people. As society becomes increasingly fragmented by age, so too does the growth in products available to specific age groups. For example, Cook describes how the children's clothing industry worked to define particular subcategories of the children's market, through developing the "toddler" and "teen girl" categories of clothing.[6] However, this is not to say that markets single-handedly *create* different categories of childhood. As Cook argues, "they provide, rather, indispensable and unavoidable means by which class specific, historically situated childhoods are made material and tangible."[7]

Ideas about the relationship between consumer items and identity apply equally well to online cultures. For example, social-networking sites which combine blogs, profiles, and photo- and video-sharing can be viewed as cultural resources which are used by young people as a way of performing and perhaps playing with their identity. These sites often contain references to consumer culture—for example, personal web pages often feature the author's favorite music that plays when a user accesses the page. Furthermore, commercial websites offer children and young people specific identities connected with the consumer culture. Websites targeted at tween girls, for example, reflect a particular market discourse that attempts to capitalize on the emergence of the category "tween."[8] Referring to the dual nature of the audience and marketing culture, Quart describes how consumer culture not only brands teens as subjects, but also positions teens as branded objects.[9] However, young people are not simply passive victims of this process; on the contrary, consumer culture increasingly positions them as active participants within it.

In 2006, U.S. teenagers had an estimated spending power of $153 billion.[10] It is not surprising that marketers are keen to capitalize on the new ways in which young people are using media to mark their identities. However, the process of researching and then capturing a market is not simple or straightforward. As "cool hunters" will testify, as soon as something is identified by marketers as "cool" within youth culture, the "opinion leaders" within the peer group are forced to move on.[11] On the web, the popularity of sites follows these "cool" trends, where Habbohotel was once a preferred site of young people, MySpace is currently the market leader, no doubt to be replaced over time as new ways of interacting online become available and popular.

It is also important to recognize that young people do not necessarily consume an item "straight off the shelf." For example, McRobbie discusses how with girls, personal style becomes a focus for display, particularly as they grow older and interact independently in more public spaces (away from shopping trips with mum, for example).[12] Furthermore, using the example of how girls use second-hand clothing, McRobbie argues that girls resist, rework, and recreate consumer trends. Several researchers in this field use Levi-Strauss's notion of "bricolage,"[13] also employed in the chapter by Weber and Mitchell in this volume to describe how young people draw on a variety of sources and then piece together, recontextualize, and transform cultural items to create a new self-image or identity. Home pages, for example, are analyzed by Chandler and Roberts-Young in terms of "bricolage," referring to the processes involved in creating a page made up of references and images from various sources which have been appropriated and recontextualized.[14] In including, omitting, adapting, and arranging these references, the "bricoleur" is also constructing and performing an identity. Viewing consumption in these terms, we can see young people as active agents, appropriating consumer culture for their own uses.

Yet these markings of identity are not freely chosen. If we are to believe any of the numerous critiques of consumer culture, children (and their parents) are subject to increasingly devious marketing strategies that are serving to exploit children and work against their best interests.[15] This is ever more relevant when discussing online marketing. Online advertising is a booming market: Jupiter Research has forecast that the online advertising market will reach $18.8 billion by 2010.[16] Increasingly, immersive advertising in the form of e-cards, ring tones, wallpaper, contests, clubs, games, and quizzes is being used in everything from computer games to children's edutainment websites.[17] Compared with television, online advertising is seen by marketers as more effective in terms of cost, impact, and measurability. The interactive nature of many forms of online advertising assures marketers that children are engaging with a promotion, or at least more so than TV audiences who may not even be in the room when an ad is shown. According to Montgomery, advertisers are seeing the Internet as the best place to develop brand loyalty and regard online ads as an important part of "cradle to grave marketing."[18] As Montgomery points out, with 98 percent of children's websites permitting advertising and two-thirds depending on ads for revenue, website owners are relying on new advertising techniques to keep afloat. Interestingly, the rise of more immersive and less visible forms of advertising is also a result of legislation in the United States which dictates that websites are not allowed to sell directly to children.[19]

According to Montgomery, advertising has been "turned on its head" by the web, where once brands sponsored a website and now sites are brands unto themselves. The sale of YouTube to Google in October 2006 for $1.65 billion demonstrates this point; although Google already had a videosharing site, it did not have the audience that YouTube offered, and so YouTube was seen as a valuable brand identity that could be purchased. Neopets, a website which involves nurturing a pet and preparing it for contests, was an early adopter of immersive advertising.[20] Interactions on the site take place in a branded world (e.g., users can "eat" at McDonalds), and it is easiest to acquire points for the survival of one's pet through consuming interactive advertising. Seiter describes how viewing ads, completing surveys, and doing advertised price comparisons through Neopets give users far more "Neopoints" than training one's pet or winning contests.[21] Importantly, Seiter found that children had no awareness of the economics of the site, seeing it not as a commercial venture but as a lone individual's fun invention. According to Seiter, "the high level of involvement helped to dull [children's] awareness of the commercialism" (p. 100).

Discussions of consumer culture often play into a wider argument about the blurring of boundaries between public and private spaces. These issues are more prevalent as households with access to the Internet increase and, therefore, private domestic space increasingly becomes an extension of public space. Thus, in her work on UK children's online activities, Livingstone refers to debates about the commercialization of public space, and the blurring of the boundary between consumers and citizens.[22] She outlines a change in young people's media use, toward greater individualization. These issues have serious consequences for media regulators, as can be seen in countries such as Sweden and Greece, where radio and TV advertising to children is banned or restricted. With an increase in private and individual media consumption, there is a need to look closely at how spaces of consumption are structured. For example, we might want to question the portrayal of the Internet as a completely open democratic space in which children navigate freely. Although the concept of "walled gardens" sometimes refers to safe spaces on the internet for children to "play," Livingstone describes how enclosed commercial sites constrain Internet use, by making it difficult to leave a site and not including links to outside sites. Montgomery also highlights the fact that commercial search engines, particularly those used by children and young people such as Yahooligans! and Disney's Internet Guide, most frequently lead users to commercial sites.[23] These arguments highlight the need not only to examine young people's active engagement online but also to understand the structures through which that engagement is taking place. Furthermore, these studies highlight the importance of Internet literacy in navigating the Internet, detecting commercial strategies, and recognizing consumer rights, for example.

To summarize this section, children and young people are increasingly being targeted by marketers, and they are interacting in ever-more sophisticated commodified spaces online. Although surrounded by these market structures, young people can be seen as "bricoleurs," appropriating and reshaping consumer culture as they define and perform their identities, and in some instances rejecting or simply ignoring marketing techniques and discourses. This is not to say that marketing structures are the only ones which need to be accounted for in an analysis of young people's media consumption: obviously there are important structural factors such as class, race, and gender which play key roles in consumer practices. However, my focus here is primarily on market structures and consumer practices, and their implications for identity formation. The next section looks more specifically at identity in relation to consumer culture, examining how social theories discuss the "self" as a consumer, and relating those theories to online consumerism.

Consumerism and the Reflexive Self

As I have argued, modern consumers are faced with a plethora of objects and information through which identities can be defined and performed. Yet, as Appadurai suggests, consumer choice is also shaped and constructed through merchandising. Consumers may feel that they exercise power and agency, but as Appadurai argues: "These images of agency are increasingly distortions of a world of merchandising so subtle that the consumer is consistently helped to believe that he or she is an actor, where in fact he or she is at best a chooser."[24] Drawing on these ideas, Kenway and Bullen argue that marketing creates possible lifestyle choices which position consumers in terms of desire and belonging, as well as separation and distinction.[25] In other words, consumption can mark social status—defining oneself (or who one wishes to be) as well as defining those whom one is not (or wishes not to be).

One area for discussion raised by these ideas is consumers' awareness of their role in consumer culture. Are consumers consciously choosing products to mark their identities? Are there structures which make consumers think they are choosing freely, when actually the choices are limited? As Buckingham has described in the introduction to this volume, social theorists such as Foucault imply that individuality itself is socially constructed, and emphasize the structures which impact on people's choices. In line with Foucault's theory, consumerism can be seen as a "technology of the self"—a mechanism through which people present and "police" their identities in society. From this perspective, people are seen to regulate their behavior, expression, and view of themselves in accordance with the surrounding texts and practices—for example, advertising and make-over features which suggest how clothes, cosmetics and various body treatments can transform the self through altering one's physical appearance. This view is complemented by Giddens's idea of the reflexive self—the idea that we are continuously working and reflecting on our identity—and the idea that we choose, develop and project a "lifestyle."[26] As Buckingham suggests, Giddens takes a less deterministic view than Foucault, stressing the agency of individuals and the flexibility of resources that people use to develop their lifestyles.

These factors are particularly apparent when looking at young people's interactions online. Young people have numerous ways of projecting lifestyle choices online—through the sites they choose to visit, their written messages and responses, their own home pages and interactions on social networking sites. Much of this public work is reflexive, that is, people are rethinking and recontextualizing their ideas, as is apparent in the changes young people make to their websites (updating music and photographs, for example). Furthermore, as discussed earlier, we can see how this online "identity work" involves drawing on specific consumer cultures, for example, identifying oneself in terms of music choice or videogame preference and mastery. As Giddens writes, "Modernity opens up the project of the self, but under conditions strongly influenced by the standardizing effects of commodity capitalism."[27]

Rose draws on Giddens's ideas, arguing that modern neoliberal discourses offer new ways of understanding the self. Modern societies are governed, not by the overt exercise of power, but by inculcating subtle "norms of autonomy and self-realization," which appear to emphasize freedom, choice, and individuality.[28] Rose describes how citizenship is no longer about a relationship with government, but is about acts of "free but responsibilized choice."[29] In this new neoliberal discourse, it is up to the individual to self-monitor, make good choices and work toward self-improvement, or as Giddens writes, "we are, not what we are, but what we make of ourselves."[30] These ideas also explain our relationships with consumer cultures, in what Griffin labels the "compulsory purchase narrative."[31] Although as consumers we are positioned as having the freedom to make choices, consumption is framed by a positive requirement to better ourselves through our purchases: it is difficult to choose not to consume at all.[32]

These ideas are part of a wider trend in modern liberal societies over the past fifty years or so, according to Giddens.[33] In modern societies, consumer cultures offer diverse models of lifestyle and of the self; consumers believe they enjoy choice, autonomy, and self-realization; and part of being a "consumer citizen" is reflecting on the available choices and questioning the models that are presented to us and what is being sold to us. In some sense, consumers are seen to regulate industry by demanding innovation and quality.[34] However, industries also regulate consumers by offering particular lifestyles: as individual and responsible consumers, we have an obligation to choose a particular style, based on the available commodities. Thus, industries both reflect the world (through consumer citizens' choices) and also shape the world through offering a limited range of choices. According to Giddens, the range of choices may be larger than those that were traditionally on offer, and we do not adapt one lifestyle; rather we construct a life story, or what Beck calls a "choice biography," by reflecting on choices and navigating through them.[35]

Consumer citizens are individuals; they consume as a way of marking their identity and form their identities in relation to what is on offer, but they also resist and create new consumer cultures. We can see many examples online of young people's resistance to mainstream consumer culture, from culture jamming products, such as mashups and ezines, to civic activism, to the growing interest in alternative lifestyles. However, Heath and Potter warn us not to be unduly celebratory about these seemingly resistant and countercultural movements.[36] Instead of seeing modern society as enforcing conformity, these authors argue that capitalist society enforces individuality. Therefore, mainstream culture becomes about maintaining a distinct cultural identity, through manifesting an appearance of rebellion for example. Markets capitalize on this desire to be distinct: the proliferation of music genres in young people's online activities, for example, can be seen to reflect their attempts to conform to the need to present oneself as an individual. Although this argument might be accused of disqualifying young people's culture and agency, it does challenge the simplistic view of the so-called alternative culture as wholly resistant to the mainstream.

As discussed in the previous section, consumer cultures act both as the backdrop and the tool to many children and young people's online activities—through the sites they visit, their top search terms, the games they play, the music they download, not to mention the bricolage of consumer cultural items they display on their own web-authored spaces. Through these activities, one could argue that children and young people are carving out and reflecting on their distinct identities, marking who they are, who they would like to be, and also who they are not. Through civic participation sites, blogs, and other authored spaces, children and young people increasingly have a voice in cyberspace; however, we must ask who is listening and how that voice is being constructed. As Duncan and Leander describe in relation to their analysis of the website, gURL.com, "While the Web provides a space for writing activities that presents new opportunities for the construction of identity and the realization of agency, it also provides immediate and direct access to ideological influences that position online writers as consumers, as objects of consumption."[37]

From this perspective, we could argue that online cultures contain complex and contradictory possibilities, but that young people's agency is nevertheless framed within commodified spaces. Young people's voices online can also be seen as highly constrained and constructed through particular discourses. For example, in line with Rose's ideas about neoliberal discourses of individualism, we could argue that online spaces are framed by a kind of compulsory individuality, where the "freedom" to express oneself becomes a requirement, which then allows identities to be managed and regulated. On the other hand, we might want to question the determinism implied in such arguments and the way they tend to dismiss young people's culture. Furthermore, in analyzing young people's activities online, we need to consider other societal discourses which are impacting on the choices they make and the way these choices are discussed. The final section of this chapter, which discusses the dollmaker research introduced earlier, will provide an example of how this analysis might work specifically in relation to gender.

Summing up this section, we have seen that the relationship between structure and agency is taken into account in theories about consumerism and identity in quite different ways. Appadurai and Kenway and Bullen suggest that choice serves as a way of defining identity, although choice is structured by commercial mechanisms such as marketing. Foucault's theory of the "technology of the self" suggests that culture, and here we could include consumer culture, "polices" and structures our presentation of our selves. Likewise, Rose's work highlights the way choices are structured by neoliberal discourses of individualism and responsibility. On the other hand, Giddens's theory of the reflexive self accords less power to the structures of consumerism and places more emphasis on individual agency. In this theory, structures offer lifestyle choices that are then acted upon by consumers through a process of self-reflection. These theories therefore provide quite different ways of understanding the relationship between structure and agency—between the power of the individual to reflect on and make choices, and the power of the structures through which those choices are made.

The next section looks at how these ideas can be applied to analyzing online identities, specifically in relation to girls. There are several reasons for choosing to look at girls' interactions in this context. There has been a substantial body of work on "cyberfeminism" and identity, looking at the Internet as a feminized space as well as a space for women and girls to pursue feminist politics. Less work, however, has been done on the commodification of these spaces or how they are structured by the neoliberal discourses discussed above.[38] In relation to girls and young women, a body of work exists around consumer practices, but again there has been less attention to online practices. However, the work that has been done highlights the importance of analyzing gender in relation to consumer culture, as markets become increasingly gendered, and girls in particular operate in an arena in which the consumption and production of the self are crucial aspects of becoming a woman.[39] This next section looks at research into girls' performance, definition, and in some cases exploration of identity as they engage in various online activities.

Girls Online

One of the ways identity has been traditionally defined and constructed is through gender. A view of identity in which gender is seen as a matter of performance rather than a fixed state of being allows us to view consumer activities as part of the process of constructing one's gender identity.[40] Kacen describes how in consumer cultures, gender has been a particularly polarized field, with male producers and female consumers.[41] However, postmodernity has brought into question this polarized view of identity. Giving examples of how advertising has disrupted traditional representations of gender, Kacen argues that the future may offer "a utopian vision of a gendered paradise that is radically different from the existing social order."[42] She argues that online cultures offer particular challenges to a view of the world as "masculine" or "feminine," given the relative ease with which one can assume a range of masculine and feminine characteristics (though one would want to argue that assuming a different gender online is not straightforward or easy). Although many may not share Kacen's utopian vision, a significant body of literature focuses on the agency of girls as they explore their identity through online interactions.

Following on from landmark studies of women's media consumption, recent research on girls has included analyses of their consumption of magazines, computer games, and television, as well as their production of countercultural products such as zines.[43] Over the past decade, studies of girls' online production activities (ezines, webpages, blogs, discussion groups) have also been proliferating, with "gURLs" emerging as a term to describe connected young feminists.[44] Researchers have reported on a wide range of girls' online activities, from punk feminist sites drawing on the Riot Grrrl tradition to everyday extensions of school conversations through blogs and instant messaging.[45]

Although there has been less research on the commodification of girls' online culture, Shade's work has highlighted the need to consider this area. Shade focuses on "the tensions between . . . corporate strategies (the *feminization* of the Internet) and the use of the Internet by women for activism (*feminist* uses of the Internet)."[46] She discusses the site gURL.com, which started as a liberal feminist community presenting "a frank and feisty attitude toward dating, sex, and beauty" and was eventually bought up by the major media conglomerate, Hearst Publishing. Currently owned by iVillage, a subsidiary of NBC, the site maintains some of the original types of content: resources and advice on a large range of health and body issues, various "shout outs" which encourage gURLs to express opinions; outlets for poetry, stories, and photos; and specific discussions about media, emotions, dating, spirituality, and politics. However, the site is also highly commodified, containing various marketing strategies including a shopping mall and surveys as well as numerous banner advertisements on each page. The advice in the fashion and beauty section is largely based on mainstream representations of female body improvement, a far cry from the original gURL content such as "The Boob Files," a collection of first-person essays on breasts.

The commodification of gURL.com is one example of how the Internet is being seen and used by marketers as a profitable space for capturing the female market. As marketers continue to pour money into purchasing branded websites as well as immersive forms of advertising, spaces such as gURL.com are becoming "feminized" in line with market perceptions and demands. As Shade describes, the process of feminization involves "the creation of popular content where women's consumption is privileged and encouraged, rather than production or critical analysis."[47]

Looking at girls' online identity work, many researchers have attempted to show how the quality of the virtual experience, the kind of interactivity, and development of community complement and extend the existing forms of social interaction. Turkle argues that online communities can offer a safe virtual space for people to try out and experiment with multiple identities, and through these interactions "make meaning of the self and the world."[48] Harris also describes the safety of the Internet, its public yet private status, as an important "border space" for girls' creative political and cultural activities. This border space allows for the meeting of like minds without the surveillance they might receive in traditional public spaces. Harris writes, "The border space within which this process works is significant in transforming young women's spheres into productive places of activity instead of passive consumption, and in providing some room for overregulated young women to be in the world without leaving their homes."[49] Stern's work in this volume, focusing on girls' home pages, also examines the possibilities of the Internet for girls' self-expression. In previous work, Stern argues that the Internet offers a wide audience, giving girls the chance to connect with others who are sharing their concerns; it allows girls to express themselves in a carefully controlled way, using text as well as image, sound, and links; and it offers an anonymous environment for girls to explore ideas which otherwise would be difficult or impossible to express.[50] Stern concludes, "In light of these possibilities, personal WWW home pages may do more than just provide girls with another place to speak; they may actually facilitate girls' self-disclosure."[51] In these arguments, the Internet is seen to be providing a new kind of space for girls, one which potentially impacts on their social, cultural, and emotional development.

One of the activities in these online border spaces is feminist activism, which is present in loose groupings of cybergurls, cybergirls, cybergrrrls, geekgirls, and so on. Shade lists several ezine sites which resemble earlier printed zines and guerrilla graphics produced by "second-wave" feminists in the 1960s and 1970s, addressing such topics as cultural imperialism, capitalism, gender roles, and consumer cultures.[52] Shade argues that these new cybergurls, possibly the elusive third-wave feminists, are using popular culture in new self-reflexive ways, critiquing through parody, for example. Harris also discusses DIY ethics that are being advocated online, as girls are encouraged to resist lifestyles that are marketed to them and instead reappropriate and produce their own forms of culture and community.[53] Other examples of online activism abound, and as Harris outlines, given the ever-increasing commodification of girlhood, "other ways need to be found for reflective, political young women to conceive of girls as something other than consumer citizens."[54] There are many other online communities for girls which have been subjects of research, including wiccan, punk rock, and queer youth communities.[55] This research suggests that online environments are not just providing new kinds of spaces to support and extend girls' development, they are also providing particular cultures and communities which act as alternatives to the mainstream.

The studies outlined above show the powerful opportunities offered to girls online. However, such studies could be accused of overemphasizing individual agency and making too much of unrepresentative examples. In many of the accounts, the Internet seems to be offering girls an open space in which they can express themselves freely. Girls seem here to have an enormous power to resist particular ideologies, to construct new identities, and to form communities. There is little account of the structures, which operate on many different levels in these girls' lives.

There is concern amongst some feminists that this apparent celebration of girls' choice and agency leads to a neglect of structures, which continue to create inequitable power relations. Some complain of the "undoing of feminism" by a new generation of young women who, having grown up in a "postfeminist" society, no longer see a need for feminism.[56] According to some feminists, new forms of femininity include a "hyperculture of commercial sexuality," as well as a related silence and complicity with continuing forms of male oppression. These concerns also apply to girls' online activities, which frequently entail the presentation of themselves as highly sexualized and sexually active. Instead of seeing these girls as benefiting from the sexual revolution, which is allowing them to celebrate their sexual selves, we might want to ask whether these girls have simply dismissed feminism and the need to critique dominant cultures. In this respect, McRobbie argues that an overemphasis on agency in theories of modernity has led to a neglect of "the adverse consequences of new individualism."[57]

More broadly, various researchers have voiced concern over the way neoliberal ideas are acting to constrain women.[58] Within neoliberal discourses, girls' success in their personal life as well as their professional or educational career is seen to be due to personal choice and effort. This places girls who are "at-risk" as responsible for their position due to poor choices that they have made. Harris challenges "the idea that good choices, effort, and ambition alone are responsible for success that has come to separate the can-dos from the at-risks."[59] Griffin also reminds us that we need to consider gender in relation to inequalities based on ethnicity and socioeconomic status, particularly when considering consumer cultures.[60]

In this context, it is becoming increasingly important to examine how girls and young women are understanding and employing these new ideas about identity, particularly in relation to digital cultures, which are seen to offer new modes of consumption as well as new forms of empowerment. The final section of this chapter contains an analysis of girls' discussions of their online activities, with particular reference to their use of neoliberal ideas about individualism and responsibility. The conclusion goes on to consider the role of learning and education in the context of these discussions.

Girls' Online Dress-Up

To put some of these ideas into a specific context, this section focuses on the study referred to in the introduction of this chapter, in which twenty-six girls aged twelve to thirteen took part in workshops at a specialist ICT centre connected to a school in inner-city London. The girls recruited for the workshop were representative of the population of the school, which is ethnically diverse (about 75 percent of the pupils on roll are from minority ethnic groups, the largest being African Caribbean followed by Bangladeshi). The students came from a range of socioeconomic backgrounds, although the majority were from families with limited economic resources. The girls explored and discussed fashion as presented online, and produced their own interactive fashion design webpages, making decisions about body shapes, types of clothing, and audience. As described in the introduction, the focus for this study stems from a very popular online activity—dressing up online fashion figures (known as dollmaker or paperdoll sites). These simple drag and drop activities are readily available online and were used by a large majority of the girls studied across three research sites. The curvaceous online dolls include hundreds of clothing items (including sexually provocative ones), as well as options for hair, eyes, and skin color.

The main focus of my analysis here is on the meanings the girls are making from their interactions with online fashion, rather than how they are interacting online. As the study was conducted in a school setting, I also consider the role of learning and education in relation to girls' online identity work. My analysis uses poststructuralist theory to explore how particular societal texts and practices, construct (and restrict) possible identities. Drawing on Foucault's theories, poststructuralists use the term "discourse" to refer to conglomerations of practices which contain both ways of thinking and particular sets of power relationships.[61] Discourses are seen to produce "subject positions": for example, discourses of academic knowledge, authority, and childhood produce the positions of "teacher" and "pupil." Yet the theory also suggests that people are able to negotiate (to some degree), which subject positions to occupy (for example, within dominant discourses about gender, a girl can to some extent choose a "tomboy" or a "hyper-feminine" position or various positions in between). Furthermore, people shift their positions over time, and at any given moment people will hold multiple, sometimes contradictory positions. Hall describes how identity is not "who we are" but a process of becoming a never ending construction. In his words, "Identities are thus points of temporary attachment to the subject positions which discursive practices construct for us."[62]

The analysis here looks at girls' construction of identity in relation to three themes: body image, the pleasures of doll play, and self-confidence. In the first theme, the girls position themselves as resistant to media discourses, although in doing so they demonstrate how expressions of agency are framed by other discourses on individualism and choice, as discussed earlier in this chapter. In the second theme, the girls' statements about playing with dolls and fashion reveal both the pleasures of such play as well as the meanings girls are making within particular consumer structures. Finally, girls' statements about confidence and self-esteem in connection with dress are analysed in terms of discourses around individualism and autonomy.

Body Image and the Reflexive Self The workshops were relatively formal in structure, and involved a series of activities which the girls carried out either in small groups or individually. One of the activities involved designing and making a sales pitch for a fashion website. The girls discussed potential audiences for their site, and issues surrounding body shape emerged as part of those discussions. Most of the groups were careful to include clothes "for bigger people" as well as for "slim people." In conversations with the girls, they raised the topic of media effects, and we discussed how playing with fashion Web pages and dolls or reading magazines might affect how they feel about themselves. The issue of body dissatisfaction emerged in discussions of these questions, and the girls referred to adults and older teens as being anxious about their bodies, more so than themselves. This "third-person effect" (the belief that others are more affected by media than oneself) is well documented in media research.[63] The girls here indicated that it was other people who were affected by

Wolf's "beauty myth"—somehow the girls did not see themselves as being subject to these ideologies in the same way as older teens.[64] They could identify and resist "the tyranny of slenderness," while others could not:[65]

VALERIE: Most teenagers, when they go on a diet, they starve themselves.

DALIA: When they grow up, yeah, they could, like, worry about themselves, and they could do exercise or have a diet.

NEYLAN: They might start thinking, 'Ah, maybe I should diet.' And they might do it too much. Or eat less fat and sugar.

MACKENZIE: They'll want plastic surgery so they can be perfect 'cause they think they're not as pretty.

The girls here are showing an awareness of body dissatisfaction and a recognition that girls (or teenagers) compare themselves to an ideal image. On the one hand, the statements above appear politicized—the girls are resisting media influences, being self-reflexive and analyzing the "technologies of the self," which are produced, for example, through television shows which focus on body dissatisfaction (e.g., *Ten Years Younger, Extreme Makeover, Nip/Tuck*). On the other hand, as in the discussion of gender and citizenship earlier in the chapter, we can see these statements as instances of how girls themselves engage in the "project of the self," scrutinizing their interior lives, and importantly blaming individuals for their failure to maintain a healthy body.

The girls also draw on particular educational discourses, positioning themselves as healthy individuals, in control of their self-image and specifically their eating. These discourses reflect the girls' position here as students in an interview in a school setting, although the girls are also positioning themselves in relation to their friends in the group. By adopting an "us-them" stance (it is teenagers and older women, not us, who are affected), the girls are positioning themselves as a cohesive group, not only as younger but also as less susceptible to "the tyranny of slenderness." This reflects what Thorne calls "border work," in which children construct particular groups as "other," especially along gender lines.[66] Furthermore, as a conversation amongst friends, the girls' statements can be seen as part of their collective construction of identity: as in the research by Kehily and Nayak, talk amongst girl friends provides a space in which normative forms of femininity are established and maintained.[67] By discussing problems of self-image and eating disorders amongst older girls and women, the girls form a group consensus about what constitutes their own healthy identity, in opposition to the unhealthy identities of others. Using the ideas from Giddens referred to earlier in this chapter, this discussion demonstrates how girls are navigating through complex structures which demand self-reflexivity, as we see here, and also individual effort.

The girls' statements here suggest a degree of agency which is important to recognize—they are making judgments about societal discourses and seeing themselves as active and independent. They claim to have the power to resist the "tyranny of slenderness" which they detect in the unhealthy practices of older teens, positioning themselves as somehow less susceptible to such powerful structures. However, agency is implicitly defined here as a matter of individual responsibility and choice. It is individuals who "think they are not as pretty," it is the responsibility of the individual to "eat less fat and sugar," it is the choice of the individual to "starve themselves" or have plastic surgery. Therefore, we can see the girls' comments here as a demonstration of how "agency" is structured by neoliberal discourses of individualism and responsibility. More importantly, these structures work to conceal other societal structures, such as the role of social class, which exclude some people and privilege others. There are many factors which determine how much fat and sugar one eats, including personal history, school meals, the cost and availability of particular types of food, and knowledge of food preparation; and individual choice may have less to do with what one eats than is implied in "free choice" rhetoric.

Playing with the Truth—Dollmaker Pleasures In an attempt to engage the girls in a discussion about some of these ideas around media and body dissatisfaction, they were asked more directly if they felt that playing with fashion Web pages or fashion dolls or reading teen magazines affected how they felt about themselves. The girls had a variety of responses to this question, all centring on factors which affect the way media are read.

They argued that they did not compare themselves to images on dollmaker sites ("they're cartoons," explained Dalia) or to plastic dolls such as Barbie which are clearly not real. The girls were suggesting that *modality*—that is, the truth claims made by a text—affects how a text is read. As Dalia described, "like if you look at Bratz, they've got a really small body and like some big heads on it." The girls seemed perplexed that adults would consider to play with disproportionate plastic breasts as affecting them: one girl exclaimed, "my boobs are normal!" The girls' reflection on dolls' modality supports Driscoll's ideas about the "multiplicity of Barbie": "[Barbie] is woman/not-woman and human/not-human, a game that can seem to denaturalize gender despite the anxieties of interested parties."[68] The girls did not think adults would consider to play with fashion dolls or dollmaker websites as risky and instead would see it as they do, "only a game"—although one group did consider the possibility of becoming overly concerned with clothes, putting a financial strain on their families.

In the case of dollmaker sites and doll play, the girls indicated that the weak modality of the resources with which they were playing minimized the effects on, for example, body image. However, one group of girls indicated that body dissatisfaction might occur when looking at teen magazines:

VALERIE: It's mostly when you start seeing idols or celebrities in particular that you want to turn yourself like that.

GRACE: Ya, you wanna be like them.

. . .

VALERIE: Unless they see an actual body, they won't try and make themselves like them.

Resources with strong modality, therefore, are seen to have a greater effect than those with weak modality. We can also see the girls' statements as further evidence of the shift away from a perceived need for an imposed code of conduct, media regulation in this case, and toward an approach whereby individuals are responsible for making choices and shaping their lives.[69] As self-reflexive individuals, the girls claim that they are able to analyze when media might have an effect on them, as demonstrated in their statements here. In neoliberal terms, one could conclude that these girls are demonstrating their ability to take responsibility and make ethical choices. However, we may also want to look at how, as Rose describes, "Consumption requires each individual to choose from among a variety of products in response to a repertoire of wants that may be shaped and legitimated by advertising and promotion but must be experienced and justified as personal desires."[70]

This raises questions about how girls talk about the pleasures they gain from their consumption of fashion dolls. It is clear from the girls' interactions with dollmaker sites that part of the appeal is a pleasure in playing with fashion in a social context: they construct outfits together, they show each other their finished combinations, they try on outrageous clothes and "have a laugh." Dalia describes the pleasure in this play: "Like, you can make them weird or make them really nice like they're going to a party." This play is partly about fantasizing about their future bodies. Numeyra said, "I just like the hairstyles, and I just go, 'Oh, I wish I had long hair,' or something." When asked if dressing up on dollmaker sites would make the girls want to wear that sort of outfit, Jade said, "No, you would just think 'Oh, what would I look like if I wore that?'" Likewise, Davies and Thomas describe how girls experiment with online identities and avatars, fantasizing and performing different femininities.[71] As Thomas concludes, "they 'play' with the image and the text they use to present themselves in very particular ways to explore their fantasies of desire."[72] Similarly, Walkerdine looks at girls' fantasies as spaces in which girls play with and insert themselves into various discursive practices, and therefore fantasies "become discursive and material in the social world."[73]

Similarly, it could be argued that dollmaker images are offering spaces for play and fantasy. However, it is also important to consider Rose's suggestion that the pleasure is shaped by forms of advertising and promotion. Numeyra's desire to have long hair is not necessarily about the inherent properties of long hair, but about the social meanings associated with long hair, which are reflected and produced in advertisements, for example. Similarly, statements by the girls about modality provide a cautionary note to a celebratory stance in which "play" with images is seen as unproblematic. Images which center around "real" people perhaps are read more seriously than comic style graphic images. Here again, we may want to argue that girls are not affected by media images in a simplistic way, but we also need to avoid falling into the trap of saying they are not affected at all.

Dressing for Success—Self-Esteem, Confidence, and Dress In all of the interviews, the girls raised the topic of confidence and self-esteem. Feeling comfortable with your dress, which was mentioned by many of the girls, was predominantly seen as a matter of individual choice and confidence, as Giovanna indicates: "Because if you just copy someone else and don't feel comfortable, you're not really yourself." When the girls in the current study were asked what was in their wardrobes at home and what clothes they would like to buy in the shops, several specifically mentioned being "embarrassed" by seeing thongs at the front of a shop, feeling that "wearing skirts that are too short... looks stupid," or indicating that provocative styles "are not for me." The girls would not feel comfortable in thongs and short skirts, due in part to the discursive practices which position them as needing to express individuality as well as innocence, but also due to the scrutiny and surveillance which comes with self-reflexivity. Therefore, although dressing comfortably implies a kind of free choice, we can see how that choice is limited as the girls scrutinize their dress in order to portray an image which is "appropriate" for their age, fits in with their peer culture, yet also expresses individuality.

Ashley and Giovanna connect confidence with eating disorders and dress, and individuality with the ability to resist peer pressure:

GIOVANNA: Well, for me, to me I look at it... if you have good self-esteem then you shouldn't be worried. But then if you—

ASHLEY: —If you don't, if you're not really happy with yourself, then you'll be one of those people who will force themselves to lose weight.

GIOVANNA: But then again, um, that thing brings the person out of you. Because what you wear tells a lot about you, that you feel comfortable about yourself or if you, um, just want to fit in in a group, or . . . yeah.

These statements echo findings from Currie's study in which girls described how little influence magazine fashion had on their choice of what to wear, and instead how they strived for a look which was both an expression of individuality as well as a sign of their belonging to dominant peer cultures.[74] An interesting element in Ashley and Giovanna's discussion above is the contradiction between expressing one's individuality and maintaining one's belonging in a group. According to Giovanna, if you feel confident, then you are able to resist "just want[ing] to fit in in a group." All the groups of girls said that developing an individual style was important, and they also saw it as a benefit of creating fashion designs and playing on dollmaker websites. Part of the fun of playing with dollmaker is "to create your own image" and "to express what kind of clothes you like." The girls are drawing on a particular discourse in which the development of personal style is encouraged, for example, by teen magazines suggesting personalizing wardrobes by searching in second-hand clothing shops.[75] Although these girls use individuality as an argument to display their independence (from parents, crowds, or manipulative media), when asked where they would buy clothes if they were given £100, every girl named the same sports shop. The girls seemed comfortable with these apparent contradictions—on the one hand having an individual style, and on the other hand wearing very similar clothes from the same store. They argued that individual style can be expressed through sports clothes, for example, and different trainers (sport shoes) in particular are indicative of the "tribe" to which one belongs.[76] This is reminiscent of analyses of youth subcultures discussed earlier in this chapter, which show how material objects are used by young people as markers of identity. And, as Widdicombe and Wooffitt describe, there is a broader tension here around authenticity, between expressions of individuality and expressions of belonging to a particular subculture.[77]

The discourses of autonomy and individualism are important to recognize here, particularly in the way they conflict with the need to be part of a group and the ways in which choices are controlled. The girls in the current study are reflecting "girl power" discourses—the power to buy what they like and express their identity through consumerism. As discussed earlier in this chapter, consumerism is part of the way citizenship is enacted in late modernity.[78] According to Harris, citizenship is also defined through self-discipline, high self-esteem, and confidence—all characteristics which the girls in this study are drawing on in their production of the self-reflexive subject. This emphasis on individual strategies and personal responsibility is part of the "technologies of the self" which are enacted in different ways in these girls' lives. For example, educational discourse frames bullying as connected to confidence—pupils are told that bullies pick on people's insecurities, and that acting confident will dissuade bullies. Being confident and comfortable with oneself is also a message in drug education—pupils are told that they need to be confident to follow what they think is right, to be themselves, and thereby to resist peer pressure to consume alcohol, tobacco, or other drugs. Again, we need to consider how the construction of active citizens as self-disciplined, motivated, confident, and above all responsible for their own welfare may ignore social factors, placing particular groups of people in the category of "can-do" and others in the "at-risk" category.[79] Furthermore, we should look at how discourses of choice, which offer a space for pleasurable consumption, also contain ideas about girls who can navigate choices successfully, as responsible citizen consumers, and those who are seen to lack the discipline to make good choices.

Conclusion

I have argued in this chapter that young people's online identities must be viewed not only in terms of active engagement, but also in relation to the structures which frame those activities. I have chosen to focus on consumer cultures online, in light of research which suggests that online environments are becoming increasingly commodified and children and young people are becoming targets of ever-more sophisticated marketing. By focusing on girls' online activities, we see the tensions within the research, with many examples of how online communities provide important spaces for girls' development, expression, and access to alternative cultures, yet also evidence that these spaces are not "free" and "open" environments.

There are several conclusions to be drawn from this chapter that point to further areas for research. First, the online dress-up study demonstrates the important and powerful educational opportunities online cultures can offer to teachers and students. The activities in which girls were producing and consuming online dolls offered a space to make sense of curvaceous online figures and to consider and discuss wider identity issues such as body image. Drawing on these cultures enables educators to engage with and help students consider the complexity of meanings, how those meanings are constructed, and specific issues such as consumer rights, which are part of the development of media literacy. Importantly, these educational discussions can happen in the context of texts and activities that are valuable to students, in which they have a positive identity as experts, and in a context in which various cultures, personalities, and values can be expressed. The questions we might want to ask here are about how to recognize online cultures in educational contexts without colonizing them; how to maintain a balance between producing, consuming, and analyzing media; and how to recognize the complexity of the issues rather than giving online media a generic simplistic treatment.

Within research itself, the discussions here raise a number of key questions, some of which are also relevant for young people to be engaged with. How is the responsible, motivated, confident young Internet user being constructed within academic discourse, government policies, and popular rhetoric? To what extent do the debates on such issues construct and divide young people into can-do or at-risk Internet users? When analyzing young people's online communication, to what extent do we see this as a matter of their freely expressing and exploring identity issues, and how far do we take account of the ways in which their responses are regulated? Finally, are ideologies of "consumer citizenship" being recognized, resisted, or reinforced by young people online? These questions arise when considering children and young people as both producers and consumers—producers of meaning with the agency to resist, redefine, and recontextualize; and consumers being positioned by cultural products and discourses. Analyzing these dual positions and how they work through each other is essential if we are to understand how young people are making meanings and identities through their online interactions.

Notes

1. Anthony Giddens, *Modernity and Self-Identity: Self and Society in the Late Modern Age* (Cambridge, UK: Polity Press, 1991).

2. For a discussion of the popular debates around marketing to children, see David Buckingham, Selling Childhood? Children and Consumer Culture. *Journal of Children and Media*, 1, no. 1 (2007): 15–24.

3. Martin Barker and Julian Petley, *Ill Effects: The Media/Violence Debate* (London: Routledge, 1997).

4. For a more developed version of historical trends in youth media culture, see Bill Osgerby, *Youth Media* (London: Routledge, 2004).

5. See for example, Dick Hebdige, *Subculture: The Meaning of Style* (London: Methuen, 1979); Celia Lury, *Consumer Culture* (Cambridge, UK: Polity Press, 1996).

6. Daniel Cook, *The Commodification of Childhood: The Children's Clothing Industry and the Rise of the Chid Consumer* (Durham, NC: Duke University Press, 2004).

7. Cook, 2004, p. 144.

8. Rebekah Willett, Constructing the Digital Tween: Market Forces, Adult Concerns and Girls' Interests, in *Seven Going on Seventeen: Tween Culture in Girlhood Studies*, eds. Claudia Mitchell and Jacqueline Reid-Walsh (Oxford, UK: Peter Lang, 2005), 278–293.

9. Alison Quart, *Branded: The Buying and Selling of Teenagers* (London: Arrow Books, 2003).

10. Mintel International Group, *Spending Power of the Teen Consumer, US* (London: Mintel International Group Ltd., September 2006).

11. Douglas Rushkoff, *Open Source Democracy: How Online Communication Is Changing Offline Politics* (London: Demos, 2003).

12. Angela McRobbie, *Feminism and Youth Culture: From 'Jackie' to 'Just Seventeen'* (Basingstoke: Palgrave McMillan, 1991).

13. Claude Lévi-Strauss, *The Savage Mind* (London: Weidenfeld and Nicolson, 1974).

14. Daniel Chandler and Dilwyn Roberts-Young, *The Construction of Identity in the Personal Homepages of Adolescents*. 1998. http://www.aber.ac.uk/media/Documents/short/strasbourg.html (accessed November 16, 2006).

15. See, for example, Juliet Schor, *Born to Buy: The Commercialized Child and the New Consumer Culture* (New York: Scribner, 2004); Susan Linn, *Consuming Kids: The Hostile Takeover of Childhood* (New York: New Press, 2004).

16. Cited in danah boyd, *Friendster Lost Steam. Is MySpace Just a Fad*? Apophenia Blog 21. March 2006. http://www.danah.org/papers/FriendsterMySpaceEssay.html (accessed November 16, 2006).

17. Sara Grimes and Leslie Regan Shade, Neopian Economics of Play: Chidren's Cyberpets and Online Communities as Immersive Advertising in NeoPets.com. *International Journal of Media and Cultural Politics* 1, no. 2 (2000): 181–198; Grace Chung and Sara Grimes, Cool Hunting the Kids' Digital Playground: Datamining and the Privacy Debates in Children's Online Entertainment Sites. *Canadian Journal of Communication* 30, no. 4 (2005): 527–548.

18. Katherine Montgomery, Children's Media Culture in the New Millennium: Mapping the Digital Landscape. *Children and Computer Technology* 10, no. 2 (2000): 145–167.

19. The Children's Online Privacy Protection Act of 1998 (COPPA), established by the US Federal Trade Commission; and the US regulatory board, Children's Advertising Review Unit (CARU) place strict limits on advertisements to children online.

20. Grimes and Shade, 2000.

21. Ellen Seiter, The Internet Playground, in *Toys, Games, and Media*, ed. Jeffrey Goldstein, David Buckingham and Giles Brougere (Mahwah, NJ: Lawrence Erlbaum Associates, 2004), 93–108.

22. Sonia Livingstone, Children Online—Consumers or Citizens? *Cultures of Consumption Working Paper Series*. 2004. http://www.consume.bbk.ac.uk/publications.html (accessed November 17, 2006).

23. Montgomery, 2000.

24. Appadurai, 1996, p. 42.

25. Jane Kenway and Elizabeth Bullen, *Consuming Children: Education-Entertainment-Advertising* (Buckingham: Open University Press, 2001).

26. Giddens, 1991.

27. Giddens, 1991, p. 196.

28. Nikolas Rose, *Governing the Soul: The Shaping of the Private Self*. 2nd edition (Free Associations Books, 1999).

29. Rose, 1999, p. xxiii.

30. Giddens, 1991, p. 75.

31. Christine Griffin, Good Girls, Bad Girls: Anglocentrism and Diversity in the Constitution of Contemporary Girlhood, in *All about the Girl: Culture, Power and Identity*, ed. Anita Harris (London: Routledge, 2004), 29–44.

32. Russell and Tyler outline how these ideas are particularly relevant for teenagers, because of the move away from the security of childhood toward a less certain adulthood, combined with the compulsory nature of individuality and connected consumerism. See Rachel Russell and Melissa Tyler, Branding and Bricolage: Gender, Consumption and Transition, *Childhood* 12, no. 2 (2005): 221–237.

33. Giddens, 1991.

34. Rose, 1991.

35. Ulrich Beck, *Risk Society: Towards a New Modernity* (London: Sage, 1992).

36. Joseph Heath and Andrew Potter, *The Rebel Sell: How the Counterculture Became Consumer Culture* (Chichester: Capstone, 2005).

37. Barbara Duncan and Kevin Leander, Girls Just Wanna Have Fun: Literacy, Consumerism, and Paradoxes of Position on gURL.com. 2000. *Reading Online* 4, no. 5 (November 17, 2006). http://www.readingonline.org/electronic/elec_index.asp?HREF=/electronic/duncan/index.html (accessed May 29, 2007).

38. There is an increasing number of studies focusing on the commodification of internet spaces, including Shade's work on sites for women; see Leslie Regan Shade, *Gender and Community in the Social Construction of the Internet* (New York: Peter Lang, 2002), as well as studies of games (Chung and Grimes, 2005) and specific sites such as Neopets (Grimes and Shade, 2000).

39. Anne Cronin, *Advertising and Consumer Citizenship: Gender, Images, and Rights* (London: Routledge, 2000); Quart, 2003; Russell and Tyler, 2005; Elizabeth Chin, *Purchasing Power: Black Kids and American Consumer Culture* (London: University of Minnesota Press, 2001).

40. Judith Butler, *Gender Trouble: Feminism and the Subversion of Identity* (London: Routledge, 1990).

41. Jacqueline Kacen, Girrrl Power and Boyyy Nature: The Past, Present, and Paradisal Future of Consumer Gender Identity, *Marketing Intelligence and Planning* 19, no. 6/7 (2000): 345–355.

42. Kacen, 2000, p. 345.

43. Dawn Currie, *Girl Talk: Adolescent Magazines and their Readers* (Toronto: University of Toronto Press, 1999); Mary Celeste Kearney, *Girls Make Media* (London: Routledge, 2006); Valerie Walkerdine, Remember Not to Die: Young Girls and Video Games, *Papers: Explorations into Children's Literature* 14, no. 2 (2004): 28–37; Catherine Beavis and Claire Charles, Challenging Notions of Gendered Game Play: Teenagers Playing *The Sims*. *Discourse: Studies in the Cultural Politics of Education* 26, no. 3 (2005): 355–367; Gerry Bloustien, *Girl Making: A Cross-Cultural Ethnography on the Processes of Growing Up Female* (Oxford: Berghahn Books, 2003).

44. The term gURL originated on gURL.com, a website founded in 1996 as a reaction to commercialized teen culture.

45. Denise Sevick Bortree, Presentation of Self on the Web: An Ethnographic Study of Teenage Girls' Weblogs. *Education, Communication and Information* 5, no. 1 (2005): 25–39; Clare Dowdall, Dissonance Between the Digitally Created Words of School and Home. *Literacy* 45, no. 3 (2006): 153–163; Anita Harris, *Future Girl: Young Women in the Twenty-First Century* (London: Routledge, 2004); Shade, 2002.

46. Shade, 2002, p. 107 (original emphasis).

47. Shade, 2002, p. 9.

48. Sherry Turkle, *Life on Screen: Identity in the Age of the Internet* (New York: Simon and Schuster, 1995), 180.

49. Harris, 2004, p. 162.

50. Susannah Stern, Virtually Speaking: Girls' Self-Disclosure on the WWW, *Women's Studies in Communication* 25, no. 2 (2002): 223–253.

51. Stern, 2002, p. 229.

52. Shade, 2002.

53. Harris, 2004.

54. Harris, 2004, p. 173.

55. Julia Davies, Hello newbie! **big welcome hugs** hope u like it here as much as i do! An exploration of teenagers' informal online learning, in *Digital Generations: Children, Young People and New Media*, eds. David Buckingham and Rebekah Willett (Mahwah, NJ: Lawrence Erlbaum, 2006), 211–228; Susan Driver, Virtually Queer Youth Communities of Girls and Birls: Dialogical Spaces of Identity Work and Desiring Exchanges, in *Digital Generations: Children, Young People and New Media*, eds. David Buckingham and Rebekah Willett (Mahwah, NJ: Lawrence Erlbaum, 2006), 229–245; Barbara Guzzetti, Cybergirls: Negotiating Social Identities on Cybersites. *E-Learning* 3, no. 2 (2006): 158–169.

56. Griffin, 2004; Angela McRobbie, Notes on Postfeminism and Popular Culture: Bridget Jones and the New Gender Regime, in *All About the Girl: Culture, Power and Identity*, ed. Anita Harris (London: Routledge, 2004), 3–14.

57. McRobbie, 2004, p. 11.

58. McRobbie, 2004; Walkerdine, 2004; Harris, 2004.

59. Harris, 2004, p. 16.

60. Christine Griffin, Troubled Teens: Managing Disorders of Transition and Consumption, *Feminist Review* 55 (Spring 1997): 4–21.

61. Michel Foucault, *Discipline and Punish: The Birth of the Prison* (New York: Vintage, 1977).

62. Stuart Hall, Who Needs 'Identity'? In *Questions of Cultural Identity*, eds. Stuart Hall and Paul du Guy (London: Sage, 1996), 6.

63. Richard M. Perloff, Third-Person Effect Research, 1983–1992: A Review and Synthesis. *International Journal of Public Opinion Research* 5 (1993): 167–184.

64. Naomi Wolf, *The Beauty Myth: How Images of Beauty Are Used Against Women* (London: Vintage, 1991).

65. Kim Chernin, *The Obsession: Reflections on the Tyranny of Slenderness* (London: Harper Perennial, 1994).

66. Barrie Thorne, *Gender Play: Girls and Boys in School* (Buckingham, UK: Open University Press, 1993).

67. Mary Jane Kehily and Anoop Nayak, Lads and Laughter: Humour and the Production of Heterosexual Hierarchies, *Gender and Education* 9, no. 1 (1997): 69–87.

68. Catherine Driscoll, *Girls: Feminine Adolescence in Popular Culture and Cultural Theory* (New York: Columbia University Press, 2002), 97.

69. Rose, 1999.

70. Rose, 1999, p. 231.

71. Julia Davies, Negotiating Femininities Online, *Gender and Education* 16, no. 1 (2004): 35–50; Angela Thomas, Digital Literacies of the Cybergirl, *E-Learning* 1, no. 3 (2004): 358–382.

72. Thomas, 2004, p. 376.

73. Valerie Walkerdine, *Daddy's Girl: Young Girls and Popular Culture* (London: MacMillan Press, 1997), p. 188.

74. Currie, 1999.

75. McRobbie, 1991.

76. Marshall Sahlins, *Culture and Practical Reason* (London: University of Chicago Press, 1976).

77. Sue Widdicombe and Robin Wooffitt, *The Language of Youth Subcultures: Social Identity in Action* (Hemel Hempstead, UK: Harvester Wheatsheaf, 1995).

78. Harris, 2004.

79. Harris, 2004.

Questioning the Generational Divide: Technological Exoticism and Adult Constructions of Online Youth Identity

Susan C. Herring

Indiana University, School of Library and Information Science

The Internet Generation

Children born in the mid- to late-1980s and the 1990s have been labeled the "Internet Generation": the first generation to grow up in a world where the Internet was always present.[1] Surveys show that this generation (sometimes also called the "Net Generation," the "Net-Gen," "Generation i," the "Digital Generation," or the "Millenials") socializes more online, downloads more entertainment media, and consults the Web for a wider range of purposes than do present adults or young people of the previous generation.[2] As a result, members of the younger generation are often more Internet savvy than their teachers, parents, grandparents, and even older siblings. The age gap with respect to technology is referred to here as the generational digital divide, or simply the generational divide.[3]

The growing awareness of age-based differences in technology skill and use has given rise to rampant speculation about their nature and effects. As with other types of digital divide, the generational divide is typically interpreted to mean that people on one side of the gap—youth—have more access and a greater ability to use new technologies than those on the other side—the adults (and especially, older adults) who had the misfortune to be born before the advent of the Internet. Yet while there is little doubt that young people will determine the future of digital media, if only by virtue of growing older and replacing present day adults as decision makers, it is less clear what the effects of this will be. Will today's young trendsetters become conservative technology users over time, as what was new becomes outdated? Do their usage patterns reflect a life stage that they will outgrow, but that future generations will repeat? Or will they carry their present perspectives over into their adult usage, fundamentally transforming patterns of Internet use?

Neglected in most of this discourse[4] about the Internet Generation and its transformative potential is the continued presence and influence of adults in the larger digital landscape inhabited by young people. This influence is evident in various ways. Most obviously, adults create and regulate the media technologies consumed by young people, and profit financially from them. More insidiously, mainstream media commentators interpret new technologies and youth practices in normative, moral terms, a process that reinscribes youth as "other."[5] New media scholars also view the Internet through an adult lens, applying labels such as "unprecedented" and "transformational" from their historically situated perspectives in ways that exoticize technologically mediated communication and its youthful users. While the Internet may seem perfectly ordinary—even banal—to today's youth, it is not a native medium for most adults who write about it. Yet, with the exception of teen bloggers, it is adults who are doing most of the writing.

In this chapter, I present a view of the generational digital divide that shifts the focus from gaps in technology access and skill to the discrepancy between adult perspectives on new media and youth experiences, and consider the effects and implications of this discrepancy. In the process, I propose that the current so-called "Internet Generation" is in fact a transitional generation, in which young Internet users are characterized to varying degrees by a dual consciousness of both their own and adult perspectives. I further suggest that the birth of a true Internet Generation, which still lies some years in the future, will pave the way for changes in media attitudes and consumption that will be more thoroughgoing, normalized, and hence more difficult to question. It follows from this that we should take advantage of the present transitional moment to reflect across generations about technology and social change.

My argument is structured as follows. The first part characterizes some of the ways in which adults—including new media producers, commentators, and researchers—construct online youth. The second part considers to what extent young people actually orient toward adults in their online behavior, be it through acknowledgment of adult evaluations or through resistance to or subversion of adult proscriptions. I then move on to imagine what the first generation to be raised in a world in which Internet and mobile technologies are taken for granted by everyone will be like. Drawing on previous research on generational shifts in relation to television, I consider how the embedding in everyday life of digital technologies and practices such as computer-mediated communication and entertainment/information-on-demand may serve to naturalize them in ways that produce subtle social and cognitive effects.

The argument concludes by calling for a paradigm shift in research on youth and new media, one that tempers exoticism by moving away from a fascination with *technologies* to a focus on young *people* themselves and their communicative needs as they happen to be expressed through particular media. This proposed refocusing has methodological implications, both for how research on youth and new media can be done and what its findings can be interpreted to show. I suggest that current online youth practices have predictive value, but that these must be qualified by contextualized interpretations.

The chapter concludes with a consideration of the broader implications of the generational divide. I argue that this transitional juncture is historically significant and a potentially rich site for conversation about technological innovation, the forces behind it, and user choice, and that this conversation may serve to encourage young people to reflect on their media practices, rather than being swept along unreflectively on the technocultural tide.

Adult Constructions of Digital Youth

According to Neil Howe and William Strauss in their 2000 book *Millenials Rising*, the younger generation today is the most watched-over generation in memory. Parental expectations and school standards in the United States are up in comparison with Generation X,[6] the previous generation; children's time is more highly structured and their behavior is more closely monitored. This is presumably in part a reaction against the more laissez-faire styles of parenting favored by Baby Boomers[7] during the 1960s and 1970s, and in part a reflection of the availability of new technologies that enable increased efficiency, multitasking, and surveillance. To these historically specific reasons must be added the universal tendency for adult guardians, as more experienced and socially and economically powerful, to seek to protect and control children "for their own good."

Against this backdrop, other adult actors with a variety of motives ranging from crass self-interest to moral proscription to a thirst for knowledge publicly represent young people's experiences through television, movies, print, and—of course—digital media. The focus in this chapter is on adult constructions of youth identities and experiences as these involve the use of new digital media technologies, especially the Internet, the World Wide Web, and mobile technologies. Three forms of public discourse about "online youth" are presented as illustrations: media production, media commentary, and new media research.

Media Production and Advertising

It may seem obvious that adults, not youth, design and produce youth entertainment media. As Howe and Strauss write, "Today's movies and TV shows are the handiwork of Boomers and Gen Xers—not Millennials." The popular music that is a central component of youth experience, even when the artists are young, is also packaged and produced by the adult run music industry. Similarly, popular video games such as *Grand Theft Auto*, which features crime, assassinations, pimping, and violence against women, are designed and marketed to youth by adults. However, although these products are targeted for youth consumption, they do not necessarily reflect youth perspectives. Howe and Strauss assert that Millennials are, in fact, "the first youth generation in living memory to be actually *less* violent, vulgar, and sexually charged than the pop-culture adults are producing for them."[8]

Adults also profit financially from youth targeted media, and financially control young people's access. Computer and video games, for example, which are consumed primarily by children, adolescents, and young adults, generated 7.3 billion dollars in revenue for the gaming industry in the United States in 2004 alone, up from 7 billion in 2003.[9] While according to the theory of trickle-down economics, young people benefit from a healthy national economy that puts more money into their parents' pockets (and thence into children's allowances), most of this money is not spent *by* them, but rather *on* them, often in copurchases with parents.[10] For example, parents were present fully 92 percent of the time when computer games were purchased or rented in the United States in 2004,[11] in the process presumably monitoring, vetoing, advising, and setting rules about their children's game consumption.

Finally, adult advertisers target youth as consumer markets through new media. Marketing firms build and host website-based "online communities" designed to attract teens and preteens around themes such as sports, fashion, and dating, as vehicles primarily for youth-oriented advertising.[12] The products advertised through youth-targeted media are sometimes rather adult. One major U.S. beer company designs its website to appeal broadly to teens, with interactive features such as games and music, and downloadable alcohol branded items such as desktop wallpaper and instant messaging icons. The same company recently signed a deal with a leading provider of television content to cell phone users, many of whom are teens and preteens, to broadcast eighteen beer advertisements per hour.[13]

Intentionally or unintentionally, game designers provide role models on which young players may base their behavior and self-image. Advertisers seek to foster brand loyalty at an early age, and thus to construct youth identities (for example, as "street wise" and "independent") that depend for their performance on commercial products. In the words of youth and new media researcher David Buckingham, "However illusory it may be, the media increasingly offer children an experience of autonomy and freedom, a sense that they, and not adults, are in charge."[14] This experience, however, is mediated by adults and adult institutions, rather than arising from within the "Internet Generation" itself, whose members are not yet old enough to have attained positions of influence within the media production industry.

Media Commentary

If media producers construct the Internet Generation as self-reliant and "in charge," commentators in the mainstream media often represent young media users as vulnerable and in need of societal protection and direction. To a considerable extent, this discourse reflects what journalists perceive as the concerns of parents and educators about children who spend time on the Internet and the World Wide Web. For many, especially less technologically savvy, adults, the Internet is unfamiliar, intimidating, and potentially dangerous. Many adults are concerned about the risk of children being exposed to pornography or lured through interactions in online social spaces into offline encounters, and the occasional cases in which terrible things have happened to young Internet users do nothing to allay such fears. News reporting often sensationalizes these cases, occasionally giving rise to full-blown "moral panics" in which new media environments are represented as a threat to societal values and interests.

A recent example of a moral panic fueled by news media coverage involves MySpace.com, a social networking site popular with teenagers, in which members create mixed media profiles of themselves, check each other's profiles, and exchange messages.[15] Most profiles are public, and thus MySpace is attractive to sexual predators, as journalists often remind us. One recent article warns:

> As 90 million people use MySpace.com around the world, vulnerable users have fallen victim to predators, who have assaulted, abducted and, in some cases, murdered the people they meet online. In addition, thousands of teens and young adults have been led to moral corruption through the images and people they interacted with online.[16]

Other articles advise parents to "take action to ensure their children's safety" and prevent them from "be[coming] a victim" through their MySpace participation.[17] References to online youth as "vulnerable," "children," and "victims" are strikingly at odds with the constructions by media marketers of the "street-wise" Internet Generation. Both have in common, however, that they are produced by adults and reflect adult perspectives.

Another moral panic abetted by the media concerns the supposed widespread decline of young people's language skills, as manifested through what David Crystal in his 2001 book *Language and the Internet* termed "Netspeak"—the use of abbreviated and nonstandard spelling and typography in computer-mediated messages. These typing practices have given new impetus to the age-old fear of older generations that language in the mouths (or on the keyboards) of youth is in a state of rapid decay. As pointed out by communications scholar Crispin Thurlow, newspaper and other media reports not only often portray computer-mediated communication (starting with email, then chat, and most recently, instant messaging and text messaging) in a negative light, but also represent young people as communicatively inept. Thurlow cites as an example this 2001 headline from the *Vancouver Sun*:

> Online language has developed into a shorthand that all but obliterates the Queen's English. Our kids log on and catch the Webspeak virus. This new communicable disease spreads like jam on toast and, presto, Spell-Drek: The Next Generation.[18]

In some reports, the moral implications of youth's online communication practices extend beyond language. According to one article, "Text messaging . . . is posing a threat to social progress." Another warns, incredibly, that "civilization is in danger of crumbling."[19] Simultaneously, news reports tend to fetishize online communication, citing "humorous, tokenistic displays of text messaging" that are exaggerated or fabricated. In Thurlow's words, "That adults get away with misrepresenting young people on such a scale says a great deal about the relations of power that structure youth." Specifically, "the exaggeration of the distinctiveness of new media language . . . functions powerfully to 'other' young people by simultaneously exaggerating their differentness; this, in turn, serves to discipline youth and to elevate adulthood."[20]

Such media discourse arguably reflects not only (or even primarily) the perspective of individual journalists, but also the normative prescriptions of the larger society. Acting *in loco parentis*, it constructs youth's online behavior through the dual lenses of adult values and adult fears.

Media Research

The third discourse that constructs youth identities in relation to new media is produced by researchers in academic and other institutions. These are the experts whose words are (mis)quoted in news reports and whose recommendations may inform educational policy. Increasingly their writings are available on the Web, making them as accessible—if not yet as ubiquitous—as news media. Youth and new media researchers can be grouped into two types: those who write primarily for a scholarly audience and those who write for the general public. The writing of these groups differs in tone but has in common a tendency to exoticize the object of study by emphasizing its novelty, radical difference from what came before, and transformative potential.

One need not look far to find cases in point; exoticizing language is present in much of the literature I reviewed in writing this chapter, especially in introductory paragraphs, where it seems intended to demonstrate the value of the research through association with important phenomena such as technology and youth. Much of their importance apparently resides in their difference from what came before. Thus we are told that "the entire nature of the media system is undergoing dramatic change,"[21] and that "there's a revolution under way among today's kids."[22] Specifically, "they are different as a result of . . . exposure to and use of digital media;"[23] more precisely, "they are a new generation who, in profound and fundamental ways learn, work, play, communicate, shop, and create communities very differently than their parents."[24] Put simply, "technology has changed the Net Generation."[25] Some authors go further yet to assert uniqueness: "Millennials are unlike any other youth generation in living memory."[26]

In this discourse, the "Net Generation" is not only novel but powerful, indeed transformative. This generation is "already combining demographic muscle with digital mastery to become a force for social transformation."[27] Some warning bells are sounded, recalling mainstream media discourses: "New media culture holds both promise and peril for youth,"[28] and "there is a growing danger of exclusion and disenfranchisement."[29] However, most representations are upbeat. "The New Generation is exceptionally curious, self-reliant, contrarian, smart, focused, able to adapt, high in self-esteem, and has a global orientation,"[30] enthuses one writer. For Howe and Strauss, "the name 'Millennial' hints at what this rising generation could grow up to become—. . . a new force of history, a generational colossus far more consequential than most of today's parents and teachers (and, indeed most kids) dare imagine."[31]

Two points must be made about these acts of characterization, setting aside for the moment their tendency toward hyperbole. First, "exoticization" is a natural carryover of adult experiences and perspectives. For those of us who did not grow up with digital media, they are indeed new and different compared with our past experience, and for some, they have been genuinely transformative. Yet the experience gap between adults and youth can be problematic, given that adults control public discourses about youth. To paraphrase educational researchers Diana and James Oblinger, "having Baby Boomers talk about the Net Generation is not nearly as good as listening to young people themselves."[32]

Second, technology plays a strongly deterministic role in this discourse. Kids "are different as a result of . . . exposure to and use of digital media," "technology has changed the Net Generation," and "digital mastery" will make this generation "a force for social transformation." Thus at the same time that youth are represented as powerful—more even than "most kids dare imagine"—they are also shaped by technology, dependent on it *by definition* for their identity as a generation. Such constructions effectively represent contemporary youth as cyborgs, a merging of human and machine—exotic and "other."[33] Moreover, technological determinism is problematic in that it glosses over contextual factors and social motivations that shape human behavior. Peer groups and social relations are arguably more influential during youth than at any other life stage, and young people use and think about technology differently according to their cultural, economic, and family contexts.[34] Youth researchers know this, yet hyperbole about the power of technology to transform youth still permeates much of the research literature.

In short, many texts by "experts" contribute to constructing the Internet Generation as exotic. Their hyperbolic idealizations reflect the digital optimism of educated, presumably early adopter adults who tend to be pro-technology and committed to integrating technology into their educational vision for youth.

Youth Perspectives

The three forms of adult discourse described above are pervasive in contemporary society. In contrast, young people have fewer rights and opportunities to participate in public discourse. Youth voices as heard in interviews in the mass media and quoted in works of scholarship are mediated by adult institutions and contexts. When youth do speak out directly—such as in blogs on the Internet—their views lack the financial and institutional backing enjoyed by marketers, news producers, and academics, and thus carry less weight. Nonetheless, we must imagine that youth have different perspectives born of their own experiences. This section asks how the so-called Internet Generation views digital media, and to what extent young people's perspectives are affected by adult discourses.

Having raised these questions, I acknowledge that it is probably impossible for me as an adult to answer them in an "unadulterated" manner, and I do not claim to do so here. My interest is to problematize status quo understandings of the relationships among adults, youth, digital media, and the public sphere; it suffices for this purpose to cite evidence that calls previous assumptions into question. The evidence in this section is drawn from youth public discourse: published studies of youth and digital media that incorporate youth voices, transcripts of interviews with youth, and direct youth commentary publicly available on the Internet. In addition to being mediated to a greater or lesser extent by adult institutions, this material is necessarily partial and does not represent all youth, even in the Western, English-speaking contexts where most of it was generated. Nonetheless, it is indicative of the public discourses in which young people are currently allowed to speak about their relationships to digital media.

How Does the "Internet Generation" View Digital Media?

The available evidence suggests that youth perspectives on digital media differ from adult constructions in a number of respects. First, and most importantly, as Diana Oblinger and James Oblinger observe in their 2005 book, *Educating the Net Generation*, "if you ask Net Gen learners what technology they use, you will often get a blank stare. They don't think in terms of technology; they think in terms of the activity the technology enables." Nor are they inclined to marvel at the novelty of their world, drawing comparisons with pre-Internet times, about which they have limited knowledge. Young people's experiences necessarily lack a historical, comparative perspective. A consequence of this is that technology use in and of itself does not seem exotic to them; rather, it is ordinary, even banal.[35]

Young people use new technologies for social ends that are much the same as for earlier generations using old technologies. Young people instant message, text message, or email their friends much as my Baby Boomer generation talked on landline telephones. They abbreviate and use language creatively to signal their in-group identity, much as my friends and I wrote backwards (manipulating the affordances of the hand-written medium) and created special writing conventions to pass notes in class. They flirt online, while we flirted on the phone or in the hallways at school. They express their daily angst in blogs, whereas my generation kept hand-written diaries. They painstakingly craft their profiles in social networking sites to win the approval of their peers, while we dressed up to be "seen" hanging out at school dances and community youth events. Moreover, "search engines [function] as a library, . . . product-based sites as a mall, and downloadable movies and games as a theater or video arcade."[36] As was also true when I was young, the ends are more interesting and important to the participants than the technological means, especially if the means have been available all one's life.

Perhaps more surprising, many of what we consider new technologies (instant messaging, blogs, chat rooms, email, cell phones, search engines, etc.) are "transparent" to young users[37]—they do not consider them to be technologies, except in the broadest sense. In a recent survey, U.S. undergraduates defined technology as new or customizable; for example, a cell phone with standard features is not technology, but a cell phone with new features is.[38] For something to be "technology," in other words, it should be novel, challenging, and fun, not merely useful. (Analogously, in my youth, washing machines and telephones were not considered technology, but anything to do with computers was.)

Moreover, contrary to the stereotype that the digital generation is enamored of technology, for many youth, technology use may not be the most fun activity, but rather what is most available, a substitute for something they would rather do. In a recent survey of media use by six- to seventeen-year-olds in the U.K., a majority of teens said that they would rather go out to a movie or do something with friends than stay home and consume media,[39] and they complained that their neighborhoods did not provide enough activities for youth. Increasingly, parents are afraid to let their children go out for fear that they will not be safe, especially in urban areas. According to new media researcher Henry Jenkins, more elaborate indoor media environments have evolved to compensate for unsafe or otherwise inhospitable outdoor environments.[40] danah boyd, in her chapter in this volume, argues that social networking spaces such as MySpace.com substitute for traditional offline hangouts, whose numbers have dwindled dramatically in recent decades in the United States.

Youth also tend to be less techno-deterministic than adults. Whereas for my generation the Internet is powerful and the object of both fear and desire, young people understand that technology is not a solution to their problems. In the words of one young man, "I have access to 100,000 bands now [via the Internet], but that doesn't mean I'm going to wind up with good music. Technology isn't solving that problem, it just helps people who know what they're looking for, find it. So technology doesn't necessarily make the world a better place; it just makes it more efficient."[41] Kyle M., one of the teen winners of the 2006 Global Kids Digital Media Essay Contest sponsored by the MacArthur Foundation,[42] expressed a similar sentiment in his winning essay: "The Internet itself is nothing more than a way of speeding up communication, along with most other everyday activities."

Nor is technology to be feared. For fluent young users who know their way around a range of information and communication technologies, can use them simultaneously (multitask), and are able to learn new ones quickly, technology is at their service—they shape (customize) it, rather than it shaping them. As Dahye H., another Global Kids contest winner, wrote in his essay, "We own these new digital media. We shouldn't be their slaves. We have to be their masters and get all we can out of them."

In light of all this, the label "Internet generation" itself (and its variants such as "Net generation" and "digital generation") must be seen as reflecting the perspective of a demographic for whom the Internet and associated digital media are new and salient, not taken for granted as they are by many of today's youth. That is, it is an exonym—a name used to refer to a group by outsiders (in this case, adults)—rather than an endonym—a name chosen by the group to represent itself. Just as my generation did not self-identify in terms of the reproductive patterns of its parents' generation, but rather had the name "Baby Boomers" assigned to it, the current generation of young people does not self-identify in terms of the technology created by its parents' generation. Nor do most kids self-define primarily in terms of technology, although they acknowledge the prevalence of digital media in their lives.

Orientation to Adult Discourses

The "Internet Generation" is therefore an adult construct. But does this matter to youth? Do young people care how adult discourses construct them and their technology use, or more precisely, can one discern from their words and behavior that they are aware of and orient to adult evaluations? Adults have defined youth since time immemorial, yet children and adolescents often seem remarkably impervious to adult expectations for what they should do and become. Certainly young people often seem to tune the adult world out when they download and listen to music, play video games, IM their friends, and hang out in MySpace. At the same time, there is evidence that many young people are aware of adult representations of their generation and orient to them, while simultaneously orienting to their own experiences. I suggest that this double awareness or "dual consciousness" is particularly characteristic of the so-called Internet Generation.

Advertising Discourses As discussed in the chapter by Rebekah Willett in this volume, a consumer culture of music, games, product brands, and online sites saturates the digital media experiences of contemporary youth, providing resources for their identity construction and self-presentation. Yet advertising sends conflicting messages about what youth are like. While the explicit message is often that teens and preteens are independent minded, discriminating, racially tolerant, media savvy, and "cool" consumers, the underlying reality is that commercial interests seek to manipulate young people into requesting and buying certain products, thereby restricting their range of action and expression.

There can be no doubt that the Internet Generation is affected by advertising. Children are exposed to thousands of ads by the time they are five years old, contributing to what has been called "the urbanization of consciousness"[43] and a single global youth culture characterized by extensive new media consumption and Internet use. By all reports, youth consume advertised products (including alcohol, especially in the college years). But do young people also "buy" the pervasive marketing of youth identity?

There is a long tradition of antimaterialism and anticapitalism in youth culture. Most adolescents are aware of the manipulative nature of advertising, and react to it with attitudes ranging from overt rejection to apparent indifference to mitigated acceptance, where acceptance is mitigated by an awareness that advertising is designed to make money for the advertisers, and therefore is untrustworthy in principle. Nonetheless, critical public discourses initiated by youth about advertising appeared relatively infrequently in the research I conducted for this chapter. Here I am interested especially in young people's reflections on the accuracy of commercial representations of youth identity.

Despite the enormous sums spent annually on marketing research into what young people want, use, and consider to be the latest in cool, some teens consider marketing strategies to miss their target. An article in an online teen magazine produced in New Zealand warns that "[youth] culture is created, presented and sold to us every day. . . . This is a culture presented by marketers. It is inaccurate, it is often negative and it keeps changing."[44] A high school girl in a focus group in the United States, when asked to comment after watching a public television documentary on youth and marketing on the accuracy of advertising media's portrayal of her generation, is similarly dismissive: "I feel the problem is that we're not represented in our culture. We don't create it and it's not born of anything of us."[45]

Other teens are willing to admit that advertising representations have some basis in truth, but see them as distorted or exaggerated. "They're capitalizing on the fact that people want to be rebellious . . . but it's not rebelling at all," according to one boy in the same U.S. focus group. Another suggests, consistent with the observation of *Millennials* authors Howe and Strauss, that there is a generational gap in appreciation of sex and violence in the media: "The media's looking at the teenage generation, taking that image, and I think they're notching it up a step. They're making it that much more risqué, and then they're selling it back."

One girl in the group felt that advertising representations of teens were consistent with her own experience, but expressed discomfort with them: "I think it was accurate, but it wasn't me telling them. It was them telling me." These youth are uncomfortable with the idea of adult marketers telling them what they are like, even if they do not disagree entirely with the representations. Little wonder, then, that teens change their evaluations of what is "cool" as soon as today's latest trends hit the wider market. In part, they are seeking to distance and differentiate themselves from adult constructions that they consider manipulative or that they simply recognize as exogenous, and therefore inauthentic by definition.

For each of the critically reflexive teens quoted above, however, many more never overtly question commercial discourses. Moreover, even teens who critique traditional forms of advertising may fail to perceive the extent to which the Internet is a commercial space, despite the fact that two-thirds of all teenagers have either researched products or purchased products online, and marketing is increasingly targeting youth through social networking sites and youth-oriented Web "communities."[46] Many young people appreciate the opportunity to compare prices and get the best deal online, or, as in the case of music downloading, to get something at no cost. The teens in the focus group, especially the boys, tended to view the Internet as a means of empowerment, a way to escape the limitations on their choices imposed by marketing conglomerates. "What the Internet has done is to diversify the opportunities we have to find something we like," stated one boy, and another added: "I think the Internet is one outlet of independent-minded people."

The number of choices available to young people online is greater than in other domains, and thus the impression of the Internet as an empowering commercial space for youth is not entirely unfounded. However, as Willett points out, even independent choice can be exploited by marketers: youth are exhorted to make individual choices, yet in so doing, they conform to mainstream ideas about youth as individualistic (and about individualism as positively valued in a capitalistic society). According to this scenario, independent choice is an illusion, reminiscent of this lyric from a country-and-western song about a modern teenager in Dallas: "All her friends were non-conformists, so she became a non-conformist, too."[47]

To summarize, some youth publicly contest commercial representations of their generation, but such expressions are not common. More frequent are youth discourses celebrating the Internet as an environment in which consumer culture can be routed around or subverted. It is possible that increasing commercialization will eventually have the effect of making the Internet appear more constrained and less cool to a majority of young people, thereby accelerating its progress toward detechnologization—the inevitable future point at which the Internet will no longer be perceived as technology. However, this point has not yet been reached.

Mass Media Discourses Few preteens or teens could claim complete lack of awareness of adult views about online environments. To the extent that they abide by rules of Internet use set down by their parents, schools, or boys and girls clubs, they are orienting to adult concerns, although younger children may be only vaguely aware of the nature of those concerns. When a young person knowingly breaks a rule, moreover, awareness of adult perspectives is heightened, although it may be accompanied by dismissal or rationalization that the rule is misguided and unnecessary. Youth know from their own experience and that of their friends that the Internet is not as dangerous as the popular media make it out to be. They may go ahead and do whatever they are not supposed to—chat with strangers, use Netspeak, swear, post provocative photos, visit pornographic websites—hoping to keep below adult radar. Such behavior constitutes an implicit rejection of adult "moral panics" about youth online.

Rejection of moral panics may also be explicit. The Web is one public forum in which youth voices can be raised. For example, one young man posted a defense of "Internet chat and shorthand text" on his website, arguing that "in SMS and Internet chat, shorthand is the normal way to communicate," and that "criticizing people [for using Internet slang] in informal computer chat rooms, forums, usenet, other informal Internet areas or mobile media is misguided."[48] Youth are also weighing in on the moral panic about social networking. A male high school student recently blogged, "STOP BLAMING EVERYTHING ON MYSPACE! . . . America, give your children some credit. They're relatively intelligent, and they're pretty rebellious when they want to be. They will have their MySpace regardless of what you say, and by telling them they can't handle it, you're not helping the situation at all."[49]

However, orientation toward moral panics need not be rejecting; it may also take the form of explicit accommodation to and endorsement of adult perspectives. Young people generally look up to and want to please adults. Thus, accommodation is especially likely to occur in contexts in which adults set the larger agenda, such as interviews and contests, but it is also evident in open discourse on the Web. With regard to the examples of online activities discussed above, some youth are strongly critical of Netspeak, are critical and fearful of chat rooms, and are embarrassed about their online socializing, seeing it as a waste of time and something that they expect to outgrow. These attitudes echo the judgments of their parents' generation.

Youth endorsement of moral panics sometimes involves more rigid forms of self-policing than parents or teachers themselves would impose. Thus some websites created by youth for youth forbid the use of Netspeak,[50] and in other discussion forums, it is criticized as "abuse," "idiocy," and "illiteracy," as illustrated by the following comments: "To be honest, although I'm 21 and use IM a lot I avoid netspeak. I just can't bring myself to inflict such abuse on spelling and grammar." "I'm 19 and feel like I'm floating in a great ocean of idiocy (coupled with, obviously, illiteracy)." Some comments adopt an explicitly moral tone: "We should fight. its a good fight... I just see this as a 'moral victory' in which we, the fighters, will go out like the wild bunch, in a deluge of punkspeak, and wave after wave, of gibberenglish" (capitalization and punctuation errors original).[51]

Youth also speak out against MySpace, although not necessarily based on their own experience. A teenage girl in an essay posted to a website entitled, "MySpace: Danger or Fun?" states that although she has not herself joined and it sounds like it might be fun, MySpace is not suitable for teens, because "Youths are chatting with people who they don't know and never seen, which poses a danger. These strangers who pretend to be something their not are sick people who have the ability to lure these young people into grave situations." She concludes by calling for age limits or, rather extremely, "some kind of protection to prevent teens from chatting."[52]

This last example is striking for the dual, indeed self-contradictory, perspective it expresses: MySpace sounds like fun, but teens should be prevented from using it. The Global Kids essays manifest similar juxtapositions of positive evaluations (from the perspective of the authors and their peers) with negative societal evaluations. There are many good reasons for downloading music from the Internet, opines one boy, and I do it, but "people" should not do it. Chat rooms are a "great tool to enhance personal relationships," writes another, but "I am not going to condone such behavior."

Some essays point explicitly to the mass media as the source of their negative evaluations. One girl justified her negative assessment of MySpace—which she admitted to being "addicted to"—as follows: "I watch all sorts of thrillers where a killer finds a beautiful young girl in her prime by looking at her online journals. He stalks her, finds her, and kills her. They have to base these movies on real events and it scares me." Another girl wrote: "To paraphrase a recent ad I heard on the radio, the internet is a fun place to explore, but it can also be a dangerous jungle. . . . It's hard to ignore the talk of murders, rapes, sexual solicitation, and kidnappings associated with the internet." For every such comment that makes its way into a public space, there must be many others that are thought but not expressed.

To summarize, youth commentaries on issues involving youth and the Internet frequently reject adult moral panics. However, in a number of cases, a dual or ambivalent perspective is evident, suggesting that young people struggle to reconcile the concerns of mainstream media discourses, which are accessible to them directly as well as through parents, teachers, and adult community members, with their own and their friends' experiences of the Internet. It is also conceivable that youth voice negative opinions based on their own online experiences, but I found no examples of this in the contexts I surveyed.

Research Discourses While the pronouncements of most academic researchers never reach the eyes or ears of young people, some popular scholarship about youth does. Increasingly, with the availability of online discussion forums and the possibility for anyone to post book reviews on sites like amazon.com, youth can react to scholarship about them publicly. Two books published in recent years, one by Don Tapscott on the "Net Generation," the other by Howe and Strauss on "Millennials," have triggered a number of public responses, including from young people.[53] As with the other adult discourses discussed above, youth responses are varied, ranging from strong rejection to seemingly unquestioning acceptance, and mixed youth–adult perspectives are evident.

The visions of both Tapscott and Howe and Strauss are rejected by a number of young commentators on the grounds that they reflect adult "fantasies" rather than youth realities. One anonymous reviewer on amazon.com highlights the generational divide, writing that Tapscott "is looking at the internet as a man who is 100 years old—before the conception of the internet." Another accuses Tapscott of being "techno illiterate" and exaggerating the extent to which young people are "masters of the technology," characterizing youth instead as mostly "superficial users."

Howe and Strauss's book also comes in for criticism on the grounds of lack of realism. One young reviewer writes: "Although William Strauss and Neil Howe say they are proud of our generation, the only thing the book mentions any pride in is a mere phantastic chimera of how they WANT us to be." Another reviewer objects that "the kids at my high school are nothing like the book says we are. Kids do things whether their parents want them to or not." These young people see their generation as less obedient, trusting in authority, and clean cut than the book represents them as being.

At the same time, there are youth who appreciate the book's aspirations, focusing on what its positive effects might be, rather than its accuracy. One girl who gives the book a positive rating writes poignantly: "So many young people (myself included) are trying so hard to prove themselves in spite of unprecedented amounts of cynicism and elders who insist that 'today's youth are always the worst'—what we really need is for the general public to realize our potential and help us to cultivate it."

Still others appear to accept the authors' vision of what Millennials are like. One youth agrees, for example, that "our generation is savvy, mindful and understanding of the world" (a vision also promoted by some marketers, whom one suspects have read Tapscott's and Strauss and Howe's books). The younger the audience, the more likely it is to accept adult representations unquestioningly, especially when they seem to be pro-youth. One youth elevates the authority of the authors above his or her own experience, writing: "I am 15 and this book really did a great job at helping me know what my generation is about and telling me what expectations my generation has."

This last comment suggests a dual consciousness, in that the writer intimates that he or she is lacking in direct experience of what the book describes, but accepts it nonetheless. A similar willingness to accept the argument in the absence of direct experience is evident in this comment from a Global Kids essay winner: "The changing ways that kids think have three main points. They have a greater acceptance for diversity, are becoming more curious, and have great self-reliance and assertiveness. If this is truly the way minds are changing, I'm happy to be a part of it." I submit that the best way to understand this otherwise paradoxical juxtaposition of certainty and doubt is to see these two attitudes as emanating from different sources: what adults say to be true and the boy's own (lack of) experience. While he is not discussing the *Millennials* book per se, the concepts he invokes are related. Indeed, the book's claims have been widely disseminated in schools and universities in the United States; he could have heard about them from a teacher or classmates.

A similar phenomenon can be observed in undergraduate educational contexts. When invited to reflect on their generation in relation to technology, some older youth write in voices clearly influenced by adult academic discourses. For example, a recent scholarly book on education and technology includes three chapters by university undergraduates, the first of which begins:

I am a member of the Net Generation. The Internet and related technologies have had a major influence on my generation's culture and development. Many, if not most, Net Generation students have never known a world without computers, the World Wide Web, highly interactive video games, and cellular phones.[54]

With the exception of the first sentence, this sounds very much like the opening of many of the adult-authored works I reviewed for this chapter; the emphasis on the "major influence" of technologies on the generation (and the label "Net Generation" itself) especially suggests an exogenous, adult perspective. In scholarly publishing, students naturally look to adult models for how to write and what is appropriate to say. What some may find disturbing in this case is that students are not only being socialized into academic models of writing, but into ways of defining themselves. This example is not unique.

In this section I have argued that young people's public agreement or disagreement with adult discourses about youth and technology constitute evidence that they orient to those discourses, rather than being impervious to them. Moreover, a number of statements that are publicly available are ambivalent or even paradoxical, supporting the notion that the "Internet Generation" has a dual consciousness of both its own and adult perspectives. While this might be said for all young people who participate in youth subcultures while simultaneously inhabiting the larger adult world, the divide is greater as a result of Internet and mobile technologies, because of the extent to which they have changed communication and information access. Youth cannot easily comprehend the magnitude of this change, whereas adults cannot easily forget it. Both direct immersion in experience and a historical, comparative perspective are important, however, in moving into the future.

The Television Generation and the (True) Internet Generation

If today's youth straddle the digital generational divide, questions then arise as to when the first purely digital generation will come into being—that is to say, the first generation to be raised in a world in which Internet and digital technologies are taken for granted by *everyone*, because they were available to them since childhood—and what that generation will be like.

Strictly speaking, that generation should not arrive in my lifetime, since everyone presently alive who was born before approximately 1985 would need to be retired from active life in order to leave the field to younger generations. Babies born starting around the year 2050—the grandchildren and great-grandchildren of today's "Internet Generation"—will enter a world in which digital technologies will have been an integral part of life for all (although they will almost certainly take different forms), and in which the only reliable memories of pre-Internet life will be found in archives and historical accounts. However, this estimate is probably overly conservative. "Taken-for-grantedness" may come sooner when a technology diffuses rapidly, enters people's homes, or otherwise becomes a part of their everyday lives. The history of television, considered one of the most important technologies of the twentieth century prior to the invention of the Internet (together with the automobile and the airplane), illustrates this point.

In 1939, when television became commercially available in the United States, an estimated 2,000 sets were in use. By 1955, when I was born, television sets were a common fixture of middle-class homes, numbering in the tens of millions.[55] I entered the cultural scene as a member of the first "television generation" (roughly, 1945–60). My parents, as adults by the time television entered their lives, had had formative experiences with mass media (radio) that were very different from mine and my siblings'. But they shared television with us; viewing was a family activity, and after my siblings and I left home, my parents' viewing increased. At that point, it began to seem that theirs was the television generation, for as our viewing decreased as we went about establishing our adult lives, they went on to become early adopters of the remote control, VCRs, and cable TV, and the television was always on during my visits home. It seems fair to say that by the mid-1970s, television was fully taken for granted by my parents' generation and in American culture at large. This history suggests a time span of roughly thirty years from popular introduction to widespread taken-for-grantedness. By analogy, the Internet could attain this status by 2015. The process could even be further accelerated if, as some have claimed, technological innovation and change have been progressing at a more rapid rate since the introduction of the Internet.

Is it appropriate, though, to draw parallels between digital media and television? In his introduction to this volume, David Buckingham criticizes Tapscott's overly simplistic contrast between the television generation, characterized as passive, and the Net generation, characterized as interactive. Research has shown that television viewing engages some viewers actively, while not all Internet uses are equally interactive, calling into question this contrast and the techno-positivistic conclusions drawn from it regarding the empowerment of youth via the Internet. However, a number of important differences between the two media remain. First, unlike the television, which from the outset in the United States adopted an advertising model in order to provide "free" content to viewers,[56] Internet content is not (yet) driven by advertising nor (yet) subject to centralized control. While television restricts content provision to a set of government-regulated media providers, ordinary users can and do create Internet content. Moreover, the Internet is a metamedium that allows not only for broadcasting information and entertainment, as has traditionally been the case for television, but for two-way communication (like the telephone) as well as other activities that have no clear *technological* precedent, such as information searching and customized music access.[57]

Finally, the evolution of any technology takes place in a specific historical, cultural, and economic context. The rise of television in the United States took place during a period of economic expansion following World War II that saw a significant population shift to the suburbs and the cultural reification of the single-breadwinner nuclear family, on the one hand, and the Cold War and the nuclear arms race, on the other—both factors that significantly impacted my childhood awareness. The former created leisure time for wives and children to stay home and watch TV, and the latter arguably created a need for escapism from fears of impending annihilation (as I perceived it at the time).

The popularization of the Internet, in contrast, took place following a period of economic recession in the 1980s when it was common for both parents to work, and that was characterized by a growing cynicism about politics and corporate economics. Add to this the effects of television, including the blurring of news and entertainment, and the increasing tendency for TV content—more of which was by then being targeted at children—to be violent, sexualized, and commercialized. The grass roots values espoused by the inventors and early adopters of the Internet can be seen, in part, as a desire for an alternative to the centralized, commercialized, broadcast media that many of my generation (which was also the Hippie generation, it should be recalled) found offensive, manipulative, or simply trite.

Thus, television and the Internet are not straightforwardly comparable. Still, similarities can be noted, especially in the public discourses that have arisen about their effects. As observed by Buckingham in this volume, "Like television, digital media are seen to be responsible for a whole litany of social ills—addiction, antisocial behavior, obesity, educational underachievement, commercial exploitation, stunted imaginations . . . " (p. 13). In a more positive vein, both media have also been credited with promoting learning, creativity, democracy, and making the world a smaller place. What is certain is that both have seduced many people into spending large amounts of time sitting in front of flickering screens. Both have enjoyed unprecedented reach, and, as with any influential medium, both can be used to further pro-social as well as questionable agendas. Their prevalence and influence are such that both have been claimed to define entire generations.

What does the history of the television tell us about the likely future of the Internet and other digital media? In terms of social effects, societal transformation will be less radical than predicted, and children will not change fundamentally as social or thinking beings. The human race will not become smarter, kinder, or more just overall as a result of digital media, nor will it become dumber, more violent, or less moral. This is not to suggest that there will be no change. We can expect reactions against the practices and values of previous generations, as part of a larger process of historical flux. And some changes will reflect the affordances of the technology and the patterns of use that they support.

Research on television viewing has identified a number of physical, social, and cognitive effects, many of them controversial. The act of sitting and viewing a screen for extended periods of time has been claimed to lead to increased passivity, obesity, and other mental and physical health effects; frequent channel switching and the interruption of programming by advertisements have also been linked to shorter attention spans.[58] Screen size and viewing distance have been found to correlate with perceptions of social presence—people who view larger screens and view from closer distances identify more with television actors as social beings.[59] Finally, the content of programming has been found to affect children's mood and daydreaming—in one study, for example, viewing violent content led to angrier moods and more aggressive-heroic daydreaming, especially among boys[60]—and a tendency for viewers to perceive incorrectly the prevalence of particular professions, crime, and other features in the real world.[61]

There are so far more claims than empirical evidence as regards the effects of digital media. As early as 1984, it was claimed that personal computers would stimulate children's thinking.[62] John Seely Brown, former Chief Scientist of the Xerox Corporation, claims that the World Wide Web, due to its multimodal nature, supports multiple intelligences and requires new forms of literacy. Members of the digital generation are thought to be especially skilled at multitasking, or the rapid refocusing of attention from one activity to another, resulting in (or perhaps leveraging) already shorter attention spans. Multitasking can also be seen as a strategy for managing information overload, which is predicted to become increasingly important as the amount of information on the Internet continues to expand.[63] In a related fact, young people have been found to engage actively when using digital media, assembling diverse bits of content and communication practices in a kind of *bricolage*, defined by Seely Brown as "abilities to find something—an object, tool, document, a piece of code—and to use it to build something you deem important."[64] This activity crucially involves cognitive processes of selection and judgment.

These characterizations have little in common with television effects. Rather than being cognitively and perceptually affected by content that is broadcast at them, digital media users appear more likely to manage and create content and to be stimulated and challenged by these activities in multiple ways. Moreover, digital devices are becoming smaller as digital media become increasingly mobile, which means that their use does not require sitting in one place or even remaining indoors. The expected negative effects of smaller interfaces on perceptions of social presence may be offset by the highly social uses to which such devices (such as mobile phones) are put, as Gitte Stald's chapter in this volume suggests. However, caution should be exercised in generalizing these observations, since not all youth use digital media in the same ways, and some of the observed behaviors may be age-related, rather than conditioned by the media per se. I return to this point below.

By the time the first true digital generation comes into being, we may speculate that new technologies will be on hand, and some that are new at present will have become more widespread, such as artificial intelligence agents and devices for tracking the location of others and accessing information about them. Entertainment media may include customizable virtual realities, to go along with customizable music and news. It is likely that personal and social data will be increasingly shared on the Web. In addition to new media, the embedding in everyday life of computer-mediated communication and information-on-demand may serve to naturalize these practices in ways that produce subtle social and cognitive effects. With no predigital generations around to remind them of other ways of being, this future generation may think and behave in ways different from present generations—for example, as regards privacy, which many adults perceive as eroding dangerously, but which youth appear to manage with less concern. It is then that the effects of digital media may most accurately be assessed.

Implications and Conclusions

Research on Youth and Digital Media

The circumstances that I have termed in this chapter the generational digital divide—especially, the adult construction of "digital youth" as a generational identity—call for a rethinking of research on youth and new media. It is especially important that researchers seek to transcend the seemingly endless flux and change in new technologies and their affordances, as this can lead to exoticism—a fascination with what is new and different—at the expense of a more balanced view that recognizes continuities and trends.

Exoticism can be tempered by a shift from a focus on *technologies* to a focus on young *people* themselves and their communicative needs as they happen to be expressed through particular media.[65] Whereas ten years ago this was not yet the case,[66] we understand the effects of computer-mediated communication systems well enough now to move beyond them to a consideration of online practices as forms of discourse and social behavior. Rather than focus on the anonymity afforded by the medium, for instance, one might ask how anonymity functions in online youth culture. To what extent do young people mask their identity in different contexts of computer-mediated communication, and for what intended effects? This perspective may reveal more continuity than novelty in online youth practices, as well as providing nuanced understandings of present day youth's mediated experiences.

Two understandings are key in order to translate such a perspectival shift into research practice. The first is that if one wishes to understand the emic or "insider's" perspective of a group, it follows that one should observe and talk with its members. However, traditional ethnography may not succeed in breaking down structural hierarchies between the researcher and the researched in the case of age, where the hierarchies may seem natural and inevitable because of developmental differences. Any serious attempt to avoid cooptation of young people's experiences must therefore consider the more radical possibility of collaborating with youth in an attempt to break down those hierarchies, as suggested, for example, by sociolinguist Deborah Cameron and her colleagues, who provide examples of how this can be done in sociolinguistic research.[67]

The second is the importance of clearly conceptualized methods to tease apart the differences between transitory phenomena, life stage (including developmental) behaviors, and innovations leading to long-term change. These distinctions are crucial if we are to make informed predictions about the future of digital media and their social consequences on the basis of the current generation. Longitudinal studies of a cohort's use of specific media over time will provide the most direct indicators of change, but take years to carry out. Age-stratified cohorts can also be studied at a single point in time, and change can be inferred from the differences between the age groups, but this assumes that younger generations will grow up to resemble older generations, which would not be the case for life-stage-related behavior. Past research on youth may help to shed light on the kinds of behaviors that young people can be expected to outgrow. For example, sociological research has found that sociability is greatest among adolescents and young adults, and decreases over the life course.[68] All else being equal, this suggests that one should interpret observed differences in digital sociability between younger and older users as life-stage related, rather than as indicating an ongoing change in the direction of increased sociability for all digital media users. In this way, the digital media practices of contemporary youth can have predictive value, provided they are carefully interpreted.[69]

Finally, researchers should keep the broader social, cultural, and technological contexts of new media use ever in mind. My comparison of television and digital media hinted at the extent to which even temporally overlapping technologies are influenced by different factors and give rise to different cultures of use. It follows that one should not assume that mobile phones, video games, instant messaging, and music downloads, for example, are part of the same digital media culture, but rather sensitivity should be maintained to the norms and practices that characterize each. Cultures of childhood and youth also evolve, and form an important part of the backdrop to youth media use. In all of these practices, it is important that researchers maintain an awareness of their experiential bias and more powerful discursive position as adults, and make efforts to avoid reproducing the "othering" of youth that is prevalent in public, including scholarly, discourses.

Crossgenerational Conversation About New Media

The acuteness of the generational digital divide described in this chapter is likely to be transitory, in that today's new technologies will eventually be old for everyone. In the meantime, this transitional juncture is historically significant and a potentially rich site for crossgenerational conversation about technological innovation, the forces behind it, and user choice.

Different generations have different unique strengths to bring to this conversation. Youth necessarily lack a historical, comparative perspective. While this could be seen as limiting, it also potentially allows for genuinely new practices to evolve, free from the burden of excessive reflection and evaluation that often characterizes adult understandings. Adults—and especially older adults—have their own experiences of growing up with different technologies, and their perspectives on technology use (and nonuse) across the lifespan, to contribute.

Such an exchange would be an opportunity for learning. For youth, it could address what Henry Jenkins has called the "transparency problem," or the "challenges young people face in learning to see clearly the ways that media shape perceptions of the world;"[70] in this way, it could lead to the development of broader perspectives and more informed media use. It could also educate adults about the realities of youth cybercultures, which in turn might allay some of the fears and anxieties that feed moral panics, and modulate hyperbolic predictions about digitally empowered youth. Parents and offspring, educators and students, and researchers and researched alike might usefully participate in such exchanges, including via digital means.

Historically, commercial interests and the mass media have not behaved responsibly toward youth, and it is unlikely that their discourses will change to avoid the problems identified in this chapter. In contrast, educators and researchers, I would argue, have a moral imperative to respect youth. One form of respect is to take care not to define the younger generation in terms alien to its members or in terms that construct its members as alien. Definitions are never "just words," especially when the definers hold structural power over the defined, as is the case with adults and youth.

Notes

1. "Generation i." Microsoft. http://www.microsoft.com/issues/essays/11-01geni.asp (accessed August 3, 2006).

2. William H. Dutton, *Social Transformation in the Information Society* (Paris: UNESCO WSIS Publication Series, 2004); Susannah Fox and Mary Madden, *Generations Online*. Pew Internet & American Life Project. http://www.pewinternet.org/pdfs/PIP_Generations_Memo.pdf (accessed April 27, 2006); Amanda Lenhart, Mary Madden, and Paul Hitlin. 2005. *Teens and Technology. Youth Are Leading the Transition to a Fully Wired and Mobile Nation*. Pew Internet and American Life Project, July 27. http://www.pewinternet.org/pdfs/PIP_Teens_Tech_July2005web.pdf (accessed December 6, 2006).

3. See also Jane Kolodinsky, Michele Cranwell, and Ellen Rowe, Bridging the Generation Gap Across the Digital Divide: Teens Teaching Internet Skills to Senior Citizens. *Journal of Extension* 40, no. 3 (2002). http://www.joe.org/joe/2002june/rb2.html (accessed August 12, 2006); and Joy Mighty, Bridging the Generational Divide: Strategies for Engaging the Millennials. Closing Keynote at Dialogue '06. Queen's University, Kingston, CA, May 17–19. http://www.queensu.ca/admission/dialogue/newsletters/gendivide.ppt (accessed August 12, 2006).

4. I use the term "discourse" broadly to refer to "a group of statements . . . concerned with a particular subject area." Sara Mills, Discourse. *The Literary Dictionary*, 2005. http://www.litencyc.com/php/stopics.php?rec=true&UID=1261 (accessed December 28, 2006). The discourses of interest in this chapter are public in nature and both spoken (for example, on the radio or television) and written (for example, in newspapers, books, or on the World Wide Web).

5. Crispin Thurlow, From Statistical Panic to Moral Panic: The Metadiscursive Construction and Popular Exaggeration of New Media Language in the Print Media. *Journal of Computer-Mediated Communication*, 11, no. 3 (2006), article 1. http://jcmc.indiana.edu/vol11/issue3/thurlow.html (accessed April 27, 2006).

6. People born between 1962 and 1982. The generation that follows Generation X is sometimes called "Generation Y." Neil Howe and William Strauss, *Millennials Rising: The Next Great Generation* (New York:

Vintage Books, 2000). What I here refer to as the "Internet Generation" overlaps with Generation Y but begins several years later.

7. Baby Boomers were born between 1946 and 1961 (Howe and Strauss, 2000).

8. Howe and Strauss, 2000.

9. http://www.theesa.com/files/2005EssentialFacts.pdf (accessed August 12, 2006).

10. Howe and Strauss, 2000.

11. http://www.theesa.com/files/2005EssentialFacts.pdf (accessed August 12, 2006).

12. http://www.alloymarketing.com/media/teens/onlineadvertising.htm (accessed August 12, 2006).

13. http://www.marininstitute.org/alcohol_industry/booze_in_cyberspace.htm (accessed August 12, 2006).

14. David Buckingham, Media Education and the End of the Critical Consumer. *Harvard Educational Review* 73, no. 3 (2003): 309–328.

15. See the chapter by danah boyd in this volume for further discussion of MySpace.

16. http://www.christiantoday.com/news/life/xianzcom.the.christian.alternative.to.myspacecom/425.htm (accessed August 14, 2006). This article goes on to describe a Christian alternative to MySpace.com: Xianz.com, a "safe and pure environment."

17. See http://www.webmd.com/content/article/126/116289.htm and http://www.wcnc.com/news/topstories/stories/wcnc-ad-8_14_06-dbav.9a2b178.html (accessed August 14, 2006).

18. November 3, 2001. The Decline and Fall of Spellin' & Writin'. *Vancouver Sun*, p. 18, cited in Thurlow, 2006.

19. Both examples cited in Thurlow, 2006.

20. Thurlow, 2006.

21. Kathryn Montgomery, Youth and Digital Media: A Policy Research Agenda. *Journal of Adolescent Health* 27, 2 Suppl (2000a): 61–68.

22. Howe and Strauss, 2000.

23. Call for Papers for this series (Chicago: MacArthur Foundation, 2006).

24. Don Tapscott, *Growing Up Digital: The Rise of the Net Generation* (New York: McGraw-Hill, 1999).

25. Diana Oblinger and James Oblinger, eds. *Educating the Net Generation*. Educause. 2005. http://www.educause.edu/ir/library/pdf/pub7101.pdf (accessed August 14, 2006).

26. Howe and Strauss, 2000.

27. Tapscott, 1999.

28. Montgomery, 2000a.

29. Buckingham, 2003.

30. Tapscott, 1999.

31. Howe and Strauss, 2000.

32. Oblinger and Oblinger, 2005.

33. Donna Haraway, A Cyborg Manifesto: Science, Technology, and Socialist-Feminism in the Late Twentieth Century, in *Simians, Cyborgs and Women: The Reinvention of Nature* (New York: Routledge, 1991), 149–181.

34. Keri Facer, John Furlong, Ruth Furlong, and Ros Sutherland, *Screenplay: Children and Computing in the Home* (London: Routledge, 2003); Sarah Holloway and Gill Valentine, *Cyberkids: Children in the Information Age* (London: Routledge Falmer, 2003).

35. Susan C. Herring, Slouching Toward the Ordinary: Current Trends in Computer-Mediated Communication, *New Media & Society* 6, no. 1 (2004): 26–36.

36. Kathryn Montgomery, Children's Media Culture in the New Millennium: Mapping the Digital Landscape, The Future of Children, *Children and Computer Technology* 10, no. 2 (2000b): 145–166.

37. For a discussion of transparency with regard to old media such as television, see Sonia Livingstone and Moira Bovill, *Young People, New Media* (London: London School of Economics and Political Science, 2000). http://www.mediaculture-online.de/fileadmin/bibliothek/livingstone_young_people/livingstone_young_people.pdf (accessed August 14, 2006).

38. Oblinger and Oblinger, 2005.

39. Livingstone and Bovill, 2000. Similar findings have been reported by Facer et al., 2003 and Holloway and Valentine, 2003.

40. Henry Jenkins, Complete Freedom of Movement: Video Games as Gendered Play Spaces, in *From Barbie to Mortal Kombat: Gender and Computer Games*, eds. Justine Cassell and Henry Jenkins (Cambridge, MA: MIT Press, 1998), 262–297.

41. http://blogs.usatoday.com/gennext/2006/08/facebook_aint_h.html (accessed August 14, 2006).

42. The winning Global Kids essays are publicly available at http://www.digitallearning.macfound.org/site/c.enJLKQNlFiG/b.2148777/k.D6E4/Youth_Testimonials.htm (accessed November 20, 2006).

43. John Geraci, Peter Silsbee, Sarah Fauth, and Jennifer Campbell, Understanding Youth: What Works and Doesn't Work When Researching and Marketing to Young Audiences. Paper presented at Reinventing Advertising—The Worldwide Advertising Conference ESOMAR/ARF.2000. http://www.harrisinteractive.com/services/pubs/Youth_WhitePaper.pdf (accessed August 16, 2006).

44. http://www.justfocus.org.nz/articles/2006/01/26/identity-and-advertising/ (accessed August 16, 2006).

45. This and the following examples from the PBS teen focus group are available in a more complete transcript. http://www.pbs.org/wgbh/pages/frontline/shows/cool/teens/ (accessed August 16, 2006).

46. Federal Trade Commission. Children as Consumers of Entertainment Media: Media Usage, Marketing Behavior and Influences, and Ratings Effects. *Marketing Violent Entertainment to Children: A Review of Self-Regulation and Industry Practices in the Motion Picture, Music Recording & Electronic Game Industries: A Report of the Federal Trade Commission.* Appendix B. 2000. http://www.ftc.gov/reports/violence/Appen%20B.pdf (accessed August 16, 2006).

47. "Big Tex's Girl," by the Austin Lounge Lizards, Hank Card and Kristen Nelson (songwriters), *Small Minds* (album name), Watermelon Records, 1995.

48. http://www.vexen.co.uk/notes/text.html (accessed August 16, 2006).

49. http://schuylerhall.blogspot.com/2006/05/commentary-please-stop-invading.html (accessed August 16, 2006).

50. http://www.spankmag.com/content/about.cfm/cc.18/p.htm (accessed August 16, 2006).

51. http://www.haloscan.com/comments/cbyrneiv/115463639750549534/ (accessed August 16, 2006).

52. http://www.associatedcontent.com/article/47567/myspace_danger_or_fun.html (accessed August 16, 2006).

53. The comments in this section are drawn from reader reviews posted on amazon.com of Tapscott (1999) and Howe and Strauss (2000), all accessed August 16, 2006. For more youth views, see Fourthturning.com, a discussion forum for youth on the topic of Howe and Strauss's research on generations. Of course, as with most messages posted to public forums, we cannot know for certain that people who say they are youth really are.

54. Gregory R. Roberts, in Oblinger and Oblinger, 2005.

55. Raymond Williams, *Television: Technology and Cultural Form* (London: Fontana, 1974).

56. Stephen Kline, *Out of the Garden: Toys, TV, and Children's Culture in the Age of Marketing* (London: Verso, 1993).

57. Frank Biocca, New Media Technology and Youth: Trends in the Evolution of New Media, *Journal of Adolescent Health* 27, 2 Suppl (2000): 22–29.

58. John Murray, *Television and Youth: 25 Years of Research and Controversy* (Boys Town, NE: Boys Town Center for Youth Development, 1981).

59. Matthew Lombard, Direct Responses to People on the Screen: Television and Personal Space, *Communication Research* 22, no. 3 (1995): 288–324.

60. Patti Valkenburg and Tom H. A. van der Voort, The Influence of Television on Children's Daydreaming Styles: A 1-Year Panel Study, *Communication Research* 22, no. 3 (1995): 267–287.

61. Also known as first-order cultivation effects [L. J. Shrum, Assessing the Social Influence of Television. A Social Cognition Perspective on Cultivation Effects, *Communication Research* 22, no. 4 (1995): 402–429].

62. Milton Chen, Computers in the Lives of Our Children: Looking Back on a Generation of Television Research, in *The New Media: Communication, Research, and Technology*, ed. Ronald Rice (Beverly Hills, CA: Sage, 1984), 269–286.

63. Biocca, 2000.

64. John Seely Brown, Growing Up Digital: How the Web Changes Work, Education, and the Ways People Learn, *Change* 33, no. 3 (March/April, 2000): 11–20.

65. For an illustration of this approach, see Mary Gray, *Coming of Age in a Digital Era: Youth Queering Technologies in the Rural United States*. Unpublished doctoral dissertation (University of California, Los Angeles, 2004).

66. Susan C. Herring, Introduction, in *Computer-Mediated Communication: Linguistic, Social and Cross-Cultural Perspectives* (Amsterdam/Philadelphia: Benjamins, 1996), 1–10.

67. Deborah Cameron, Elizabeth Frazer, Penelope Harvey, Ben Rampton, and Kay Richardson, *Researching Language: Issues of Power and Method* (London: Routledge, 1992).

68. Michel Forsé, La sociabilité. *Economie et Statistique* 132 (1981): 39–48.

69. For further discussion of the paradigms for analyzing change mentioned in this paragraph, see Jack Chambers, *Sociolinguistic Theory: Linguistic Variation and Its Social Significance*, 2nd edition (Oxford, UK: Blackwell, 2002).

70. Henry Jenkins, *Confronting the Challenges of Participatory Culture: Media Education for the 21st Century*. White Paper on Digital Media and Learning. The MacArthur Foundation. 2006. http://www.digitallearning.macfound.org/atf/cf/{7E45C7E0-A3E0-4B89-AC9C-E807E1B0AE4E}/JENKINS_WHITE_PAPER.PDF (accessed December 8, 2006).

PART II: CASE STUDIES

Producing Sites, Exploring Identities: Youth Online Authorship

Susannah Stern

University of San Diego, Department of Communication Studies

> Millions of teens who grew up with a mouse in one hand and a remote control in the other now pour out their hearts, minds and angst in personal online diaries. And anyone with a connection—including would-be predators—can have a front-row view of this once-secretive teenage passion play. Welcome to teen America—on display at your nearest computer.[1]

So ran the lead sentences in a *USA Today* article in late 2005. Highlighting findings from a study by the Pew Internet & American Life Project, the story referenced the recent rise in online youth content creation. The study showed that more than half of online teens had shared some type of original content online, including poetry, artwork, music, witticisms, essays, and everyday musings. As more and more young people detailed their lives on the Internet, the news story explained, contemporary adults who grew up without the Internet were becoming increasingly perplexed about youth online expression and how to regard it.

A curious mix of intrigue, disdain, and apprehension continues to characterize many adults' sentiments about the creations young people place into the public eye on the Internet. Indeed, it is common to see journalists, educators, and parents oscillate between promoting youth Internet expression and denouncing it in practically the same breath. For example, it can be tempting for adults to dismiss teen blogs and personal home pages as the trivial and egocentric ruminations of self-indulgent, techno-frenzied kids. Yet, since stalkers and predators can harm youths who carelessly share their personal information, such outright dismissal often feels negligent. Then there is the question of creativity: many adults are impressed by the apparent ingenuity of young people's online content. But, on second thought, they wonder, aren't teens really just reproducing what the culture industries feed them? Inevitably, the train of thought arrives back at basic issues of time and value. That is, instead of wasting time playing around with online content creation, shouldn't teens be focusing their Internet use on more "worthwhile" purposes, such as education and career training?

At least part of the general bewilderment about youth online expression stems from the fact that public attention is disproportionately paid to *what* teens disclose and produce online, such as the words, text, images, and sounds that can be observed on the screen. Yet little consideration is typically given to understanding *why* young people express themselves in these ways or how their authorial experiences are meaningful to them. Even most scholarly critiques of youth online expression have been based on adults' impressions and analyses of the websites and postings they observe. Adults look at the intimate thoughts youths disclose and the cultural symbols they appropriate, and they decode them according to their own standards of evaluation. Although this type of textual analysis can be informative, we inevitably miss a crucial component when we allow our understanding of youth online cultural production to be shaped exclusively from this vantage point.

In this chapter, I provide a divergent perspective by exploring why young authors find value in expressing themselves online. My goal is neither to celebrate nor to critique youth online expression, but rather to illuminate the ways in which it is a meaningful form of cultural production, particularly during adolescence. Concentrating on the genres of personal home pages and blogs, in particular, I stay close to the producers themselves, asking: What do they see as the rewards of online expression? How do they make choices about the self-presentations they offer? What role do audiences play in their decision making? How is online expression valuable, and in what ways is it unfulfilling?

I draw not only from the growing body of literature exploring adolescent development, youth expression practices, and online publishing, but, centrally, from the interviews I have conducted over the past several years with hundreds of authors ranging in age from twelve to twenty-one years. Since there is no composite list of youth Internet authors or the works they publish online, it is impossible to draw a representative sample of such young people. Most of those I have interviewed have responded to a flyer at their school or in their community soliciting youth Internet authors. Many youth informants suggest that I speak to their friends as well. All of my conversations have taken place with young people who resided in the United States, chiefly in urban centers.

I begin this chapter by providing a general overview of development and identity, and then briefly describe the Internet genres under examination. Next, I use the evocative language of youth authors to ground discussions of the roles that online expression practices play in their lives. I note how authors' sentiments about their online practices reflect their engagement with important developmental tasks associated with adolescence. I conclude by discussing the ways in which personal sites provide young people with opportunities for learning about themselves and about self-presentation. My goal throughout this chapter is to illuminate how we might broaden the terrain for discussion about online youth expression practices, so that our public and popular discourse about young people is more meaningful and contextualized.

Adolescent Development and Identity

As Buckingham articulates in the introduction to this volume, identity is a concept both nebulous and contested. Adolescence, as a concept, arguably deserves the same characterization. Commonly, these concepts go hand in hand. That is to say, adolescence is often regarded (at least in technologically advanced, Western cultures) as a time when individuals are confronted with the task of defining their identity.[2] Indeed, this volume's focus on identity, youth, and digital media underscores a general acceptance of the notion that identity and adolescence are bound together in some way.

A multitude of explanations have been offered to describe the intersection between identity and adolescence. For example, some of the authors in this volume subscribe to a sociocultural approach to identity, which emphasizes the role society plays in creating the conditions that encourage young people to address the matter of identity. Through this lens, adolescence itself is viewed as a "by-product of social condition and historical circumstance," as well as of legal systems, educational institutions, economic structures, and the mass media.[3]

By contrast, this chapter is primarily informed by more developmental approaches, which interrogate transformations that occur *within* individuals as they age, although social circumstances are also thought to play a significant role. From a developmental perspective, identity generally refers to how one subjectively views oneself over time and across situations, and is typically believed to evolve throughout the life cycle as one's inner self changes. Identity is thus commonly viewed as a "process of qualitative stage reorganization rather than a mere unfolding of static personality characteristics."[4] The self can be considered as "a personal iconography of values, symbols, and identifications that answer the question, 'Who am I?'"[5] During adolescence, in particular, individuals typically begin to question and deconstruct how they think of their selves. This self-inquiry is not conducted in isolation, but rather in the context of, and through feedback from, meaningful others. As Erikson put it, "The process of identity formation depends on the interplay of what young persons at the end of childhood have come to mean to themselves and what they now appear to mean to those who become significant to them."[6]

The second decade of life is typically a time of significant physical and psychological change that has consequences for identity. Biologically, individuals experience puberty and subsequent bodily transformations. In consequence, young people start to feel different physically, and their view of themselves thus often shifts as well. Moreover, as children start to appear visually more adultlike, those around them begin to treat them differently. Social expectations often accompany these changes, as young people desire and are often encouraged to take more responsibility for their own decision making, to forge new relationships, and to practice greater autonomy.[7] Adolescents frequently begin to spend less time with families, more time with friends, and even more time alone.[8]

Cognitively, young people move through adolescence with an increasing preoccupation with how they appear to others. Trying to understand themselves and their role in a greater society (who am I?), adolescents frequently look to their social world for cues about what principles and traits to internalize, although the mixed messages they inevitably encounter can be bewildering as they figure out which to incorporate. With increasing experience and time, many of their self-doubts about beliefs and values are overcome, prompting late adolescents to focus more on their futures (who will I be?).[9]

These changes during adolescence provide a context in which online content creation can take on special meaning. In this chapter, I highlight some of the ways this occurs for the young people I have interviewed over the past several years. Indeed, listening to firsthand accounts of their online authorial experiences helps to explain why young people generate personal sites at more than twice the rate of adults.[10] Their comments and reflections demonstrate that online publications can provide important opportunities for managing the complex situations and shifting self-expectations that characterize adolescence. In descriptions of their decisions about what to reveal, exaggerate, and omit in their online communication, youth authors reveal a highly conscious process of self-inquiry. Adolescents consciously and conscientiously negotiate the boundaries of public and private spheres as they deliberate about who they are and who they want to be, within their local community and the larger culture. The Internet, young authors suggest, affords space and place for such complex identity work.

Personal Home Pages and Personal Blogs Defined

Although young people participate in a variety of self-publishing genres online, this chapter focuses exclusively on their experiences with personal home pages and blogs.

Personal home pages are web sites posted by individuals that generally include an array of multimedia features, including text, images, sounds, links, and audience response mechanisms, such as guest books and counters. Blogs, short for web logs, have been defined as "frequently modified web pages in which dated entries are listed in reverse chronological sequence."[11] Most popular and scholarly attention has been paid to political and journalistic blogging, but personal blogging actually appears to be the most common.[12] In the past decade, as computer prices have dropped and Internet connection times quickened, creating personal home pages and blogs has become increasingly popular. By 2005, more than one-fifth of online teens in the United States said they had kept a personal home page and nearly as many (19 percent) kept a blog or online journal.[13]

By most accounts, personal home pages and blogs are not altogether new genres for self-expression.[14] Rather, their authors appear to draw from a variety of preceding genres, including diaries, autobiographies, resumes, high school yearbook entries, personal letters, refrigerator doors, business cards, displays on bedroom walls or school lockers, and advertisements, among others.[15] Yet personal web pages and blogs differ notably from these predecessors, because they are not fixed or static, but rather allow for ongoing and alterable expression. Blogs, in particular, are expected to be unending and incomplete. Nonetheless, the fact that personal home pages and blogs can be self-published rather than filtered though a publishing company or other distributor has led to claims that they provide authors with their very own "publishing house, photo album, billboard, personnel file, sound studio, gallery, and social gathering place."[16]

Although blogs and personal home pages are distinct from one another in general appearance and composition, they share important commonalities. Both can be crafted by anyone with means (i.e., computer, Internet access, and skills to locate and employ appropriate composition software). Both are intentionally posted to a public forum. And both are explicitly and expectedly about their authors and their interests, as revealed by text, images, sounds, and links. Thus, although personal home pages and blogs may differ visually, the impetus to create them and the experience of maintaining them is presumably quite similar. Moreover, considering that both genres are much more commonly authored by online teens than online adults, it seems appropriate to proceed with a broad focus to explore what makes online expression in these genres compelling to youths, in particular. Hereafter, personal home pages and blogs are collectively referred to as "personal sites."

Social networking sites (SNS) provide what many people might consider to be the next generation of personal home pages; indeed, personal profiles on networking sites incorporate many of the expression features that traditional home pages have included, including blogs. In fact, it seems increasingly common for teens to keep social networking sites in lieu of personal home pages, because they allow for self-expression at the same time they provide opportunities for connection and relationship building. In comparison to personal home pages, social network site profiles are quite templated, although, as boyd (this volume) notes, opportunities for individuals to customize their personal SNS profiles abound. Altogether, it seems likely that many of the observations about self-expression on personal sites made in this chapter would naturally extend to self-expression on social networking sites as well. However, the unique affordances of networking sites render them a somewhat disparate genre, worthy of their own explicit analysis. boyd offers such an examination in the following chapter.

Listing to Youth Authors

Conversations with youth producers reveal that in order to understand their experiences, we must look beyond the artifacts they manufacture (e.g., the blog or home page as it is encountered on a screen), and focus as well on the practices of creating and maintaining these online works. The majority of this chapter is directed toward that end. I offer an interpretive perspective on youth online expression practices, illuminating the experiences of authors on their own terms and in their own words.

Critical scholars might fault this approach for overemphasizing youth authors' agency. For example, Willett (this volume) argues persuasively that online expression practices inevitably operate within cultural systems that influence how young people regard and express themselves. From this perspective, the belief that young people are simply free to express their emerging identities as they wish is considered illusory. Such critiques of the tensions between youth agency and external structural dynamics are necessary to consider as we seek to understand youth online expression.

However, the full story of youth online authorship is also incomplete when we fail to incorporate and respect the lived experiences of authors, despite the powers that might be operating around and upon them. When adults decide when and where expression is "pure" and how youths should engage in public address, they deny teenagers agency and neglect to consider the empowering possibilities their online expression experiences offer to them. In fact, recognizing youth authors as experts on their own experience is crucial if we hope to fully appreciate how online content creation, adolescence, and identity intersect. Accordingly, this chapter is devoted to describing young authors' perspectives and contextualizing them within adolescence. In so doing, I do not suggest that I offer the raw "truth" of youth authors' experiences. Indeed, the young authors with whom I have spoken no doubt deliberated about what to tell me based on how they wished for me to represent their authorship practices in my own research. To be sure, deliberate self-presentation occurs in offline spaces as well as online spaces. Although this practice can never be avoided, we are wise to bear it in mind as we endeavor to understand the experiences of others.

I begin by addressing why young people create personal sites, noting the variety of motivations that prompt site construction. The self-oriented benefits of personal site maintenance are then discussed, especially as they relate to self-reflection and self-inquiry. Next, the issue of audience is tackled. For whom do youth authors create their sites, and who do they imagine to be visiting them? Factors that influence their choices about self-presentation are explored next. The final section addresses the risks and rewards of audience feedback and its impact on authors' self-appraisals and online creations.

"It made my brain feel happy": Why Young People Create Personal Sites

Although much has been made of the opportunities personal sites offer for self-presentation and identity experimentation (discussed below), the reasons that young people initially choose to draft a personal site may be considered much more basic. Chiefly, young people are curious about what authorship entails, eager to take on the technological challenges presented by online authorship, and anxious to establish an online presence.

Most young authors learn about personal sites from other youths, or from accidental encounters with them online; less frequently, they hear about them in the popular media or from parents and teachers. Some young people become intrigued enough to want to learn more about them. In fact, "learning by doing" is the mantra that guides many young people to start drafting a personal site. As one young author put it, "I wanted to see what a personal home page was all about. So I figured the best way to do that was to just build one myself." Increasingly, schools introduce students to these genres as well, and so, by necessity, many young people are required to create personal sites to fulfill a class assignment. Some adolescents also create personal sites because their friends have: they desire to participate in their peer group through personal site creation, as well as simply share a common experience with their friends.

Many young people find unexpected pleasure and value in expressing themselves on their personal sites, and they subsequently continue the practice even after their initial curiosity has been satisfied or class assignment is fulfilled. Others, of course, do not: they abandon their site once they feel they have captured the essence of the experience. "Been there, done that" is the sentiment one author expressed as a way to signal his lack of interest in sustaining his publication. Oftentimes, young authors leave their personal sites posted online, even though they choose not to return to them. This phenomenon helps to explain why so many youth sites that persist online appear incomplete, rudimentary, and lacking in intimacy or information.

While some youths are driven to start Internet authoring because of curiosity, a school assignment, or peer pressure, others are compelled by their desire to master what they perceive to be the advanced technological skills necessary to construct a personal site. This motivation corresponds developmentally with adolescents' growing capacity to set goals and increasing desire to demonstrate autonomy and competence. As one home page author put it,

> Mostly I started it because I wanted to learn HTML and figuring out how to do that, like it made my brain feel happy, and I like learning new things, and I was very excited because I was like, woo, look at me, I'm the computer wiz.

Knowledge of HTML is no longer required for authors who wish to publish a personal site online, due to an assortment of templates on hosting services. Nevertheless, among those who have never created a personal site, the process appears to be technologically challenging. Thus, building a personal site can lead to a sense of pride and accomplishment that accompanies the mastery of something new.[17] Moreover, for many young people, the goal is not simply to construct a personal site, but to do so with careful attention to detail, navigation, and esthetic finesse. The product created becomes a visual and verifiable marker of what they have accomplished and the skill level they have achieved. Such perceived expertise increases feelings of self-worth, not least because young people believe these skills will be valuable assets in their future careers and education.

The desire to create an online presence additionally motivates a growing number of young people to construct personal sites. The term "online presence," often bandied about by marketers and communication consultants, has historically referred to the idea that companies must have web sites in order for their business to thrive. Web sites allow companies to advertise and sell wares and services directly to consumers, the logic holds, as well as establish a sense of credibility and quality in the minds of potential consumers. Of late, this logic has trickled down to young people, some of whom suggest that establishing an online presence "proves" that they exist in a world that otherwise pays them little attention. As one youth blogger put it, "Anybody who is anybody has a web site." Indeed, for many, online presence is synonymous with authentic presence.

This sentiment is promoted, if not exploited, by companies keen on capturing the lucrative teen market. Indeed, recognizing how eager teens are to speak out and be heard, corporations enlist them as participants in viral online marketing campaigns, and they design ad campaigns promoting the idea of consumption *as* production. Moreover, commercial software packages are available that offer "new opportunities" for youth expression as a way to reap greater profits. By making expression easier through fill-in-the-blank templates and hosting clearing houses that promise wide exposure for personal expression, such companies nurture the idea that youths are autonomous producers at the same time as they place constraints on the types of creations that youths can produce. Social networking sites, perhaps even more than personal home page and blog sites, increasingly operate in this way. For instance, young people are incited to provide specific information (e.g., name, age, relationship status, favorite musicians), although such disclosure is often experienced as self-expressive, personalized, and customized.

Some young people identify web authorship as a way to deal with these and other pressures that demand that they exploit all avenues of public address. A trend consultant recently quoted in the *New York Times* proclaimed that young people these days are "fabulous self-marketers. . . . They see celebrities expressing their self-worth and want to join the party."[18] Indeed, mainstream media (e.g. *Entertainment Tonight*, *Us*, *People*) divulge ever-more detail about the lives of pop stars, and some ordinary people are elevated to the status of celebrity simply by their apparent willingness to provide such details about themselves (as seen on, for example, *The Real World* and *Laguna Beach*). Virtually all "real" and "wanna-be" stars have web pages and blogs, not to mention that many have fan sites devoted to them as well.

In this context, some young people view personal sites as avenues to participate in, or respond to, a culture that valorizes publicity as an end in itself. Indeed, they feel that personal sites can serve as symbols to others and themselves that they belong to and in the public culture. This does not mean that young authors uncritically buy into the dominant messages about celebrity and pop culture that persist in mainstream media, but rather that many have recognized the cultural value of self-promotion and are motivated to publish online in consequence.

"Laying it all out": Online Expression for Self-Reflection, Catharsis, and Self-Documentation

Despite the various reasons that motivate young people to create a personal site, it is only after having done so that many teens deliberate whether or not online expression is particularly valuable or potentially functional for them. This sequence of events appears to be different for adults, who generally reflect on the expected utility of online expression *before* commencing to author a personal site.[19] Because the benefits that youth authors derive from their personal sites are often unanticipated, they tend to be appreciated all the more.

In particular, nearly all of those who sustain these works for any length of time identify their utility for self-reflection, releasing pent-up feelings, and witnessing personal growth. In this sense, personal sites are reminiscent of private diaries, which have frequently been considered as objects for self-examination and engagement. They appear to be particularly meaningful during adolescence, when young people consciously search for a sense of who they are and how they fit in within their social worlds. Time is often devoted to mapping out personal beliefs and values, questioning taken-for-granted truths, and navigating ever-more complex relationships. Because personal sites are made public, many critics often overlook this internal focus that such creative works can activate. Ironically, this internal focus is often the most revered aspect of online expression for adolescents.

Self-reflection is, perhaps, the most commonly cited reward of maintaining a personal site among youth authors. The site serves as an impetus to look inward, to pause amidst life's busyness to think things through. The excerpts below are typical of the ways that young people speak about their blogs and home pages:

> [My home page] helped me lay out what just all of my beliefs and values and thoughts are. And a lot of nothing that I didn't even put up on the page, but just—it just helped me lay it all out.

> My blog has helped me to center my feelings and realize that I need to take things one step at a time. It forces me to think about who I am, what I like, and who I want to be. I can think about one of the problems I am going to face, but writing about it allows me to work through the problem and start to look at solutions.

Remarks like these signal that despite what ends up on the site, the very process of self-inquiry provides meaning and value. As Blood puts it, "The blogger, by virtue of simply writing down whatever is on his mind, will be confronted with his own thoughts and opinions."[20] This process may be particularly valuable for young authors, since adolescence is thought to mark the arrival of formal operational skills. These skills allow individuals to "construct more abstract self-portraits, to distinguish between their real and ideal selves, and to begin the process of resolving discrepancies between multiple aspects of themselves."[21] Later in adolescence, teens become preoccupied with their futures, their religious and political beliefs, and their standards for behavior. Expressing oneself online becomes a way for them to explore their beliefs, values, and self-perceptions, and thereby to help them grapple with their sense of identity. Indeed, youth authors indicate that personal sites provide both a space and a stimulus to participate in this internal dialogue.[22]

Ownership of a personal site, for many young authors, seems to be accompanied by a sense of obligation: the blog needs to be updated, the home page must be modified. The pressure to maintain these sites demands that teen authors engage with questions about their own identities as they determine what or what not to post. Some welcome this sense of obligation: they admit that without their personal sites, they wouldn't otherwise make the time to reflect seriously on themselves and their lives. Others feel a burden to update, and enter into the self-reflection process less eagerly, sometimes even bitterly. Nonetheless, these young authors suggest, they emerge from their self-examination with greater clarity, and are thus grateful for the push their personal sites provided. One author remarked,

> My blog is forcing me to sit down and think about my life and what is going to happen . . . And even though I don't like that most of the time, I know it's going to be more beneficial to me in the end.

Many young online authors also appreciate how personal sites provide forums for a cathartic release of pent-up feelings.[23] When they have a lot on their minds, many say, it is helpful to express themselves, whether through writing or adding music, art, or images. "Getting it all out," as one author put it, restores a sense of calm and often helps put a problem or emotion in context (e.g., "it's often not as bad as I thought"). A surprising number of youth authors use the word "therapeutic" to describe how it feels to express themselves online after experiencing stress, grief, anger, or betrayal. Clinical psychologists have long noted the therapeutic value of writing, often encouraging people to keep journals to help them express their emotions and concerns.[24] For some young people, personal sites provide comparable spaces for such practices.[25]

Documenting emotional ups and downs, experiences, convictions, and preferences is another self-oriented role that personal sites play for adolescent authors. In this way, personal sites may serve as a point of stability during a period of flux. "My blog keeps tabs on me," one blogger explained: it helps her to chronicle who she is, what she has done, and how she feels about it. Similarly, on personal home pages, images and music can symbolize moments in time or capture emotions and experiences. For example, photo galleries capture actual events in authors' lives, such as school dances or trips with friends. Images of celebrities, performers, and/or cultural icons symbolize connections, sometimes fleeting, with particular subcultures or lifestyles. Artwork denotes cultural preoccupations as well as current aesthetic preferences and levels of skill. In these ways and others, personal sites allow adolescents to record their current self-impressions for consumption now and reconsumption later. Like written diaries, as Kitzmann has observed, "It is reasonable to conclude that [they] are constructed around the premise that they will serve as records or artifacts of the present for the future."[26]

In large part, the interest in self-documentation reflects many young authors' desire to witness their own personal growth. Envisioning a time when they will look back at their online expression, they yearn to capture the present so that comparisons in the future will reveal how far they have advanced. Such sentiments are subtly expressed by these late adolescent authors:

> I just wanted to write . . . Seeing how my year went even if only for my personal benefit I can go back and see. It'll kind of be a timeline of change, maybe in some areas. And that's all you can really hope for, some kind of change from the beginning to the end. Some kind of growth. That's all that you can hope.

> I'm praying that, like, when I look at my blog at the end of the year, that I can read through it and see, like, the beginning stages of thinking about what I'm going to do. And I'm crossing my fingers that in May, like, I'll have some semblance of an idea of where I'm going . . . and so hopefully I won't be at the same level for six months, and I'll, like, move up a step or two.

Comments like these signal how adolescents frequently accept the characterization of adolescence as an in-between stage or a state of becoming: that is, they expect themselves to change. This expectation can likely be tied to a variety of sources, including the psychological tendency for middle and late adolescents, in particular, to speculate about their future and ideal selves; environmental pressures on teens to plan for their futures (e.g., as frequent recipients of questions such as "What do you plan to be when you get older?"); and cultural messages that belittle the teen experience and glorify the freedom and independence of young adulthood. Expectations of change may also be explained by Giddens' concept of the "project of the self," as briefly described by Buckingham in the introduction to this volume. Giddens argues that in modern times, people feel obligated to continuously work and rework themselves, as they seek to weave a story of their own personal identity. In this context, the self is viewed as evolving and flexible. Each of these explanations underscores why adolescents view change as both forthcoming and largely desirable. Not surprisingly, then, youth authors indicate that the satisfaction they garner from documenting their lives online is twofold: current and anticipated.

"My page is for me": Conceptualizing the Audience

Despite the inwardly focused rewards that online authorship has for adolescents, it is impossible to ignore the fact that personal sites are not exclusively self-oriented. Knowing—and hoping—that others will encounter their online expression is the fundamental appeal of publishing (literally "making public") personal sites for young authors. Of course, this is true for anyone, not just adolescents. However, the ability to address the public is, perhaps, more momentous for adolescents than we might otherwise consider. Adolescents have historically had few opportunities for public address, and, like other disenfranchised groups, they have received little encouragement toward this end. In fact, young people recognize from an early age that adults' voices are more culturally valued than their own. This uncomfortable reality is evidenced by the paucity of widely disseminated or published works authored by young people, by the adult designation of "appropriate" youth expression venues (e.g., diaries and bedrooms), and the stigmatization of many public youth expression practices (e.g., body art, graffiti).

Of course, many young authors today have never known a time when it was not possible to address potentially vast numbers of people online. Consequently, they rarely view their personal home pages and blogs as rebellious attempts to claim space in the way that, for example, urban graffiti artists did in the 1970s.[27] Nonetheless, it is quite clear that Internet self-expression genres, like zines in the 1990s, provide young people with some of the only opportunities to voice themselves in a media environment heavily dominated by adults and corporate interests.[28] Youth authors are distinctly aware of the relative shortage of spaces for them to publicize their thoughts and lives amidst an increasingly mediated culture. Yet simultaneously, they feel entitled to engage in public address. In fact, for some youth authors, personal sites symbolize their worth as public communicators. Consider, for example, the comments of a youth author who had recently taken down her blog:

> I felt like as long as I had the blog, I had an audience—and having an audience made me feel as if what I was saying was important. Without it, I don't feel anyone is listening to what I say anymore.

Youth authors' desire to address the public is not simply about actually being heard (or read) by many people, but also about feeling empowered by the mere prospect of mass reception. Much has been made of the "blurring boundaries" between conceptions of public and private in the digital age. And young authors do, in fact, seem to have reconfigured these concepts in ways that pre-Internet folk find confusing. For example, people have traditionally considered their communication to be private when it is encountered exclusively by a limited and targeted individual or individuals. But some youth authors think of their communication as private when the people they know in real life do not see, hear, or read it, regardless of who else does. This understanding of privacy is illuminated by the words of a female teen, who shared the following on her personal home page: "I totally butchered my leg . . . I don't want sympathy from it . . . that's why I'm not telling anyone."[29]

Not all young authors feel this way, of course. Many of those with whom I have spoken demonstrate a keen awareness of who can and might be in the audience, including both "known and unknown, welcome and unwelcome readers alike."[30] But knowing that their personal sites are publicly accessible does not lead most young people to envision a broad audience for their online works. And, despite their recognition that virtually anyone with Internet access can pore over their sites, most adolescents, by and large, cannot imagine why "some random stranger" would be interested in doing so (unless, of course, he is a "creeper"—a stalker or pedophile—about whom most young authors tend to demonstrate awareness and dismissal in equal measure).

Rather, the typical audience that young authors visualize as they deliberate what to post online are those people that they know actually visit their sites (based on online or offline comments) and those whom they have directed to visit their sites, despite a lack of confirmatory evidence that such visits actually occur. Thus, for many authors, the types of people they picture are quite various: offline friends, online friends, school acquaintances, people with similar interests (e.g., skateboarding, rap) or lifestyles (e.g., homosexual, disability), parents, teachers, siblings and any combination thereof. Generally speaking, these people comprise a group of significant others, from whom adolescents conscientiously seek to learn about themselves and the appropriateness of the identities they project onto their personal sites.

Authors promote their sites not only by telling people about them in direct communication, but also by posting the address for their home page or blog in their instant message profiles, email signatures, and social networking site profiles. Of course, most authors do not tell everyone they know: many intentionally avoid telling family members, especially parents, people they don't like, and those they know would disapprove of their online expression. Meanwhile, some try to increase traffic beyond those whom they know, for example, by registering their blogs with online communities and joining web rings.

Still other young people do not deliberately tell anyone about their sites, but wait, instead, for their pages to be "found." For some, the idea of promoting their sites feels arrogant and too much like advertising. "It's so vain to think that anyone would actually care to learn more about me and my life," one author put it, preferring just to put his site "out there and see what happens." Alternatively, some authors do not tell anyone about their sites because they want the freedom to say whatever they want, without fear of repercussion. Both sentiments are interesting, considering that they are held by young authors who bother to make their works public. Authors reconcile this apparent inconsistency by acknowledging their desire for their sites to be visited by others, but not at the risk of damaging their image or inviting trouble. Moreover, they indicate, those people who do actually visit their sites can be seen as more authentically interested, because they are there of their own accord.

In this discussion of audience, it is important to emphasize that despite, and in some cases, because of their awareness of multiple intended and anonymous external audiences, nearly all young authors adamantly identify *themselves* as their principal audience. Many consider their online presentations to be most appealing to, most beneficial for, and most frequently consumed by themselves. Accordingly, their works *feel* self-directed above all. Comments from three youth authors exemplify this perspective:

> My page is for me. I don't really care who else sees it or what they think. I see it, and I'm who matters. I focus on what I want, and I don't do anything for anyone else.

> I write, first and foremost, for myself. I am my own best and worst critic, my best and worst friend.

> It is hard to be honest with yourself when you look at all of the different audiences. That is why I try my hardest to forget about them and pay attention to me.

At the same time, it seems that at least part of the insistence on the self-directedness of their online creations derives from young authors' desire to appear modest. They imply that constructing a blog or personal page for oneself is a much more noble enterprise than crafting one for others' consumption and pleasure. Paradoxically, such a perspective reveals a substantive concern for how others think of them. Indeed, although many young authors contend they give little thought to their audiences as they deliberate what to post online, when pressed, they generally reveal an intense awareness of how their personal sites—and by extension, they themselves—might be perceived by their online site visitors.

"A nice shiny me": Presenting Selves Online

Because the audience is never far from their minds, young authors demonstrate considerable awareness of how they project their "real," internal sense of themselves into their online self-presentations. Generally, they view their public selves not as fabrications, but as "touched-up" versions of themselves. A key task of adolescence involves bringing the actual self more in line with the ideal self, and in moving away from distinct, nonoverlapping facets of identity. The online "touching up" that youth authors reference may thus function as an "as-if" exercise—a way of trying out new ways of being and attempting to incorporate their ideal selves into their actual selves.[31]

> I think my homepage is a little more wittier . . . well, not wittier, but I put more thought into what I am saying rather than just like spewing off the top of my head the way I do in real life. But other than that, it's basically the same thoughts that I have and the same take on life that I have, more or less. So I think it does an accurate job of representing me. I mean, all shined up and polished. A nice shiny me.

These words, conveyed by a teenage home page author, capture what many online users, both young and old alike, value about the Internet: the opportunity to put their best face forward. This opportunity seems especially welcome during adolescence, when individuals increasingly make decisions regarding self-presentation based on their newfound capacity to imagine the variety of responses they might receive from others.

While not addressing youth expression in particular, most literature examining blogs and personal home pages has focused on this issue of self-presentation, invoking the theories of Cooley and Goffman, among others.[32] In their own way, these theorists have each emphasized the idea that our decisions about how to present ourselves to others are rarely haphazard. On the contrary, we typically deliberate about who our audience is and how we wish to be received. More than a century ago, Cooley coined the idea of the "looking glass self," encapsulating the notion that we tend to take the role of the other toward ourselves.[33] Extending this years later, Goffman, perhaps the most recognized authority on the subject, characterized all self-presentation as performative, in the sense that we play roles in our interactions, much like actors in the theater. Such role taking allows us to take others' perspectives and thus to consider how we appear to them. Consequently, we can strategically adapt our self-presentations to best achieve our desired outcomes.[34] As Buckingham notes in the introduction to this volume, Goffman has been criticized for failing to consider the possibility that all interactions can be viewed as performances and for neglecting other forces that operate on individuals as they survey themselves and construct their self-presentations.

Despite these differences in approach, many current scholars and journalists have noted that ideas about self-presentation take on new meaning within the context of the Internet. The strategy and intentionality behind self-presentation is illuminated in online settings, because communicators must consciously *re*-present themselves online (via text, images, etc.). In the absence of audible or visual cues, they often feel less inhibited, a sensation heightened by the experience of crafting messages in front of a computer screen, frequently in the privacy of one's own room or other personal space. Moreover, the possibilities for strategic self-presentation, it is argued, are expanded online. Authors possess more control over the impressions they give than they do in offline spaces, since they make all the decisions about what to reveal, omit, embellish, or underplay,[35] although they are, of course, limited by their design skills and the software itself.

These affordances are not lost on youth authors, who candidly offer dozens of examples of tactical choices they have made about what to post online in an effort to manage others' impressions and to gain social approval. For example, one youth author explained how she wanted people who visited her personal home page to understand how important music was in her life. Even though, in person, she identified her interest in a range of musical genres from pop to country to classical to reggae, she wished to project a counterculture, antiestablishment image on her home page, and thus strategically picked which groups and songs to reference there. Another youth author described how his blog was aimed at showing his "deeper, introspective side," and thus he intentionally avoided what he perceived to be trivial or irrelevant information in discussion of his daily life on his blog.

These examples not only demonstrate that youth authors care deeply about the image they project online, but also that their personal sites are, like all productions, informed by the larger culture. Although youth authors may see themselves as unique and their works as original, the choices they make about how they present themselves online are still informed by a society that relies heavily on acceptance and "fitting in." As they fashion themselves for self and others, what they highlight is often informed by what the media and culture industries tell them is "cool" about being young or teen-aged. Even the most "alternative" teenagers have learned the codes of their subculture through the lens of various forms of commodified popular culture. Thus, the self-presentations that youth authors offer on their personal sites must be viewed as constructions, not mirrors, of teens' emerging sense of self.

Of course, highlighting those aspects of themselves that they believe will leave the best or "right" impression with site visitors is endemic to any online self-presentation. But a relatively unique self-presentational ability that online genres offer some young authors is the chance to present the kind of identity or self-image they feel they cannot present in other spaces. For example, some female online authors address taboo or unsavory personal topics, such as depression, self-mutilation, and lesbian sexual desire. Young males sometimes share music, post images, and disclose concerns that address homosexuality, violence, fear, and rejection. Adolescents of both sexes lament their inability to broach these kinds of issues in offline conversations with friends and family for fear of social or parental reprisals, and, given their age and relatively limited ability to travel freely, they can rarely locate many physical places where encounters with strangers regarding these topics would be possible or safe. Consequently, they are grateful that the Internet provides at least one nonprivate space to explore these personal issues. Of course, these kinds of self-presentations are most common among authors who feel little threat of being linked physically to their virtual representations, and hence these young authors tend to use pseudonyms and other disguises to safeguard their anonymity online.

These types of self-presentational practices might be described as "identity experimentations" in the sense that young people use their personal sites to test out different versions of their current and possible identities. Youth authors are, in fact, the first to acknowledge how they use their personal sites to broadcast aspects of themselves in order to see what kind of reception they receive. For example, several young authors have described how they consider themselves to be humorous, but they rarely show their comical side to friends and peers because they fear rejection. Online, however, they have the time to craft their comedy and worry less about negative responses because they are removed from the moment of its reception. Similarly, studies of queer youth online have found that young people consider the Internet as a "space and time to safely rehearse the coming-out process."[36]

Interestingly, however, young people often reject the characterization of these types of practices as "experimentation," because, they argue, this term suggests that what they put online is somehow not true or real. Indeed, it is worth noting that social scientists who have tried to empirically measure "identity experimentation" among online adolescents have operationalized this concept as "pretending to be someone else."[37] Rather, most young authors see themselves trying to capture who they are—albeit in a palatable fashion for the audience—rather than trying out entirely new and different identities. In nearly all cases, young authors perceive the identities they present online to be authentic, even if "shined up" and "polished." In fact, some youth authors see their online self-presentations as even more representative of their "real" selves than their offline self-presentations, a phenomenon other scholars have also noted.[38] Two youth authors described the experience this way:

> I think this is a real, honest portrayal of me that I don't give in everyday life. Because I can be a very guarded person, and I like to come off as being more confident than someone who is so utterly confused about everything in their life. And so [on my blog] you see that real side of me.

> In my day to day interactions with people, I don't think I really show who I am. I try to hide behind triviality and a 'life is good' image. Not so on my home page.

Youth authors can therefore use their personal sites to explore ways to present in public versions of themselves that may be stifled—for various reasons—in other settings. Especially during adolescence, when the social ramifications for speech and symbolic behavior can be severe in most offline spaces, online genres provide relatively safe opportunities for youth authors to present what feels like an authentic self-presentation, even when it conflicts with or departs from their "everyday" self. Indeed, it seems that personal sites provide youth authors with somewhat protected spaces for reconfiguring actual, possible, and ideal selves in various arrangements, all of which are central to their self-image.

"Doing a freak show online?": Online Authorship and Social Validation

One of the main reasons young people concern themselves so much with authenticity in their self-presentations on their personal sites is because, ultimately, they seek social validation from their audience. Thus, they indicate, if their self-presentations are inauthentic, feedback from site visitors is irrelevant, if not meaningless. The desire for meaningful feedback is particularly acute during adolescence, when individuals increasingly crave social and self-acceptance. Social acceptance is desired as adolescents frequently view and value themselves based on how they are viewed and valued by others. They are especially hungry for social approval because they begin to focus more on peer group acceptance and conformity than ever before. In fact, peer approval becomes increasingly predictive of adolescents' sense of self-worth. Adolescents' concerns about self-acceptance also motivate them to seek feedback that reassures them that they are not alone in their thoughts, feelings, and experiences. Validation thus relieves their fear about being different or abnormal.[39] In this context, it is not surprising that receiving audience feedback constitutes most youth authors' primary objective when posting a personal site on the Internet.

In their quest for validation, youth authors are not shy about directly soliciting feedback. They pepper their blogs and personal home pages with requests for comments, through guest books, comment boxes, user surveys, and requests for email or instant messages. They also commonly insert counters on their web sites, to provide a measure of how many times their sites have been visited. Their attitudes about counters are generally negative, however: they would rather receive qualitative than quantitative feedback, and they are often suspicious of the accuracy of the numbers reflected by the counters. Nonetheless, such feedback mechanisms do, as Kitzman says, serve to create a kind of "economy of recognition," signaling popularity not only to youth authors themselves, but also to their site visitors.[40]

Not surprisingly, the comments youth authors value most of all are those that suggest empathy and identification, as one author explained:

> The most meaningful comment is when someone writes in and says that they understand what my problem is and that they can relate to it. And it just makes me feel good to know that I'm not just out there doing this freak show online, that people actually do feel the same way I do.

Yet even for those who do not share problems or issues, the sense of validation that stems from comments simply signaling a shared interest or appreciation of a talent is powerful. Indeed, the drive for connection and validation is what impels many young authors to share so much of themselves in online spaces. The potential reward of being praised by unknown others is compelling, particularly in those instances in which young people share personal information that they hide in offline, public settings. Such exposure and consequent vulnerability makes the yearning for audience feedback particularly strong, as these authors express:

> I cannot imagine how much I want everyone to read it. I never would have thought so.

> I didn't realize how much I would come to care about this, because I really have. I really love what I'm doing. I love being up online. I love people reading it. I love people commenting to me, and the comments that I have gotten about it have been just as genuine as I have been. The people who have written into me have completely matched what I said to them, and that just felt so good.

Comments like these illustrate youth authors' own acknowledgement that audience response is, at base, a form of validation for themselves. By contrast, they rarely suggest that they offer their comments, art, and insight on the Internet as a way to contribute to the greater social, political, or artistic world. Rather, their offerings are in large part directed at audiences so as to solicit feedback about the appropriateness or value of their own experiences, ideas, and lifestyles. Such feedback, either offline or online, is crucial for identity achievement.

Not only do youth authors try to elicit comments through direct solicitations, but they also try to compel feedback by attending to their audiences in much the same way that mainstream media producers do. They implement design elements like frames and "back" buttons to make navigation easier, they adjust color schemes to facilitate easy reading, and they use first person address (e.g., "I'd like to welcome you to my site!"). Like the broadcast networks during sweeps week, they also include images of and references to sensational topics, celebrities, and social events. Sometimes they make personal and intimate disclosures reminiscent of confessionals commonly used in reality programming, because they know this might "hook people in." By appropriating music and images and incorporating links to retail and media sites, they indicate that consumer culture provides accessible and appealing tools not only for self-presentation and subcultural affiliation, but also for entertaining their audience. And they try to keep content new and fresh in order to keep audiences coming back for more, considering frequent updates a sign of a good page or blog. They even deliberate how much content is too much, or not enough, as one author explained:

> I'm always conscious of, like, what if it's too long... will people read it? If it's not long enough, will people just think, you know, that I sat down and did it just so I could have the day marked off as having done it?

Altogether, many youth authors take innumerable steps to increase the chances that their site visitors will respond. Their earnestness in this regard testifies to the importance of validation by others in the process of forming and developing identity.

"Hey, this is who I am!": Self Realization through Online Expression

Beyond simply confirming that their voices have been heard and valued, site visitor comments can also be powerful instigators for changing how youth authors think of themselves, and in some instances, how they behave in offline spaces. For instance, positive audience reactions can prompt the integration of online self-presentations into offline self-presentations. Take the example of Lisa, a late adolescent whom I followed for a year after she decided to keep a blog. My initial conversations with Lisa revealed that she originally viewed her blog much like a newspaper column, and she saw herself as a Carrie Bradshaw–type character from the HBO series *Sex & the City*. She spent hours trying to make her entries sound witty and sarcastic, and painted a picture of herself as simultaneously stylish, neurotic, adorable, and ambitionless. However, after a few months of blogging, she declared, "I'm moving further and further away from creating a character and closer and closer towards being myself." In fact, with each subsequent interview over the course of a year, Lisa described her growing realization that she *was* the character she portrayed online—she simply hadn't admitted it before. She explained,

> Right from the start I was more honest in the blog than I ever was in real life. And since it's gone on, I've kind of become more honest to catch up with it in my own life, 'cause I figured, "hey, if I can do this online, why can't I do this all the time?" So I've kind of been catching up with that and opening up a lot more. And I feel as though sometimes my blog has gotten even more honest because of that. I mean, I just don't feel like I'm hiding anything anymore.

According to Lisa, what was most fundamental to her transformation was that her audience didn't reject the person she presented online. In her blog, she had disclosed weaknesses such as her lack of direction, her desire simply to find a husband and become a "soccer mom," and her laziness about finding a job—all traits that she feared others would despise about her. She also disclosed her insecurities about friendships, growing up, and final exams. But sharing these sentiments online, she said, allowed her to accept herself as she never could before, and to show her vulnerability in "real" life, which she had previously attempted to conceal:

> [My blog has] made me more comfortable with myself. . . . Instead of having to do things to please other people, to put on different masks for everyone, it's sort of made me say, "Hey!, This is who I am! And you want to write in your comments, go ahead, but read this—This is me. Either you like it or you don't . . .
>
> And from having to do that online, it's really made me fit it in to my own life. The truth is, I just never thought people would be interested in knowing the real me . . . because it sounds like a sad thing to say, but I just—I just never thought so, and that's why the blog has really helped me, and made me that much more confident. It showed me I can be myself and people like that, and they actually prefer it.

This is just one example of how some youth authors perceive the impact of their online self-presentation on their offline lives. Other young people have described the opposite situation, in which their self-presentations were so poorly received online that they decided to change some aspect of themselves in their offline lives. Naturally, one cannot simply alter many aspects of one's real-life persona, such as one's sex or race, simply in reaction to online audience feedback. Nonetheless, it seems a common experience among youth authors to rework their self-image or self-presentation at least in part due to reactions to their online presentations.

"It's more of a Picasso": The Risks and Disappointments of Online Expression

Simply because youth authors seek validation from their audiences does not guarantee that they receive it, however. In fact, most youth authors express their biggest frustration with their personal sites as the dearth of comments, especially substantive ones. Lack of feedback is especially disheartening to those who disclose what they consider to be highly intimate information, as well as those who put considerable effort into the appearance of the personal home page or the language of the blog. The feeling that one has been heard, that one matters in a greater context, is impeded when authors receive no or little response, youth authors explain. One lamented:

> I thought I'd get more feedback from who's reading it . . . I like to hear what they have to say. Because that's part of why I wanted to do it, to put my story out there to have others tell me their stories so I could learn as well. It wouldn't just be 'me me me' all the time.

Although many youth authors are disappointed that more people aren't responding to their web sites, they are also not uniformly pleased with the feedback they do receive. Some youth authors, for example, are frustrated that site visitors chastise them for the content of their personal sites. In response to a site visitor who complained that her personal home page was too depressing, one author replied on her page:

> if u wanted to bitch me out with the reason that I write so damn negative on my page, then ur fuckin' lame cause that's the most dumbest fuckin' A stupidest reason in the world. its as if my page was not negative, would u compliment me on being such a wonderful person? bitch me out for being negative, compliment me for being positive. Uh huh yea ok. please seriously. Ur telling me i have problems but who's the one wasting his fucking time 'trying' to bitch out a girl who's never even done anything to u, and we'd never meet anyways.

The anger evident in this response likely stems from the tendency for most authors to view their sites as their own private spaces, even though they exist within a public forum. Although they desire feedback from others, they also desire respect. Negative comments are felt almost as invasions of privacy. In her discussion of blogging, (which could easily extend to other kinds of personal sites online), boyd explains this seeming contradiction poignantly: ". . . [E]ven in the the public world of blogging, there is an understanding of a private body. By entering a public square, we do not expect to be molested; likewise, in blogging, we do not expect to be attacked simply because we are in public. We view our bodies as private space in public, just as we view our blogs. And yet, the relationship between private and public is quite blurred, particularly considering that the public square of the blogosphere is not ephemeral, but across space and time."[41]

Other youth authors describe situations in which their self-presentations online had been interpreted too literally or narrowly. They express frustration that audience members would essentialize their entire characters as being one way, simply because they chose to relay these aspects of themselves online. For example, one author explained:

> Sometimes I have thrown a crazy whim into my blog, and suddenly people assume that it must be something incredibly important. One of my online friends asked me if she should be concerned that I do so much drinking. She missed the entire point of what I was writing. I am not writing a blog about drinking; it is a blog about me and that sometimes is a part of it. Even though it is my blog, it is still not

all of myself. I think it needs to be taken on face value. Just because you read my blog does not mean you know me.

The final words of this excerpt are particularly poignant, as many youth authors are very adamant that people cannot "know" them based on their pages. This conviction is somewhat paradoxical, given that, in large part, their sites are devoted to making themselves known to others. The fear, however, is that blogs and home pages cannot fundamentally capture them as a whole person:

I mean if you read someone's poetry, you might be able to get to the deeper side of that person, but then you won't know the sense of humor in that person. I guess what I mean is that on my home page, you get sort of the surface of who I am, and the very deep part of who I am, but you don't get the middle.

In his studies of adult bloggers, Reed found similar sentiments. He explained, "While journal bloggers are happy to assert that 'my blog is me', they also insist that 'I am not my weblog'."[42] Youth authors use words like "snapshot" and "two-dimensional" to describe how their home pages and blogs, while honest, do not capture everything that they are. As one author put it, his self-portrait online is "more of a Picasso," because it is neither a fabrication nor an identical rendering of himself. What disappointed him most, he explained, was when people interpreted it as more or less than he himself did.

"I'm only a first draft": Self and Site in Process

Fortunately, however, youth authors take considerable solace in the knowledge that their personal home pages and blogs are not static entities. They appreciate their ability to update, revise, delete, or otherwise alter their sites for any reason at almost any time. Upon recognition, for example, that site visitors seem to be getting the wrong impression from their sites, they change the offending material, add new entries or content, or even post comments warning audience members to "back off" and "respect that this is a page for me, not for you." Perhaps Chandler and Roberts-Young put it best when they explained, "Homepages are unlikely to be updated as often as we "update' our internal conceptions of ourselves—in fact, this is an incentive to revise them. But they have the potential to be closer to the fluid self than any other textual form whilst also being very public."[43]

The relationships youth authors share with their living documents is thus complex and constantly in flux. The following conversation with a youth author reveals this intricacy:

Participant: My webpage is a mirror . . . I have a relationship with it . . . . I sort of see myself reflected there. You know that old adage? People know you better than you know yourself sometimes.

Interviewer: Yes, but you created this website, right?

Participant: Right, I created the page and when I lose myself, if I ever lose myself, I go back to the webpage, and I think, oh, here's something to hang onto, a foundation . . . But I can also improve myself, my good qualities, my not so good qualities . . . That's what I mean when I say that I'm only a first draft. Because I myself am incomplete, the page will always be evolving.

Views of themselves as incomplete and evolving are commonly voiced among youth authors. The opportunity to revise one's site as one revises one's self-conception is thus appealing, especially since such changes are not only anticipated, but frequently desired. Personal sites operate as visual artifacts of the self-evolution that young authors endure as they grow older. Indeed, the unfixed, malleable, and evolving nature of personal sites is not at all unlike identity itself: an enduring process, rather than a fixed state. Other scholars in this volume, including Buckingham and Weber and Mitchell, articulate just such a vision of identity, as a project that is always under construction. Technologies like the Internet become part of the environment from which identity choices are selected and in which identity choices are projected and reprojected.

Conclusion

The predominant perceptions of youth online content creation that circulate in popular media and in academic research are based almost exclusively on analyses of and encounters with the actual artifacts themselves. It may thus be unsurprising that such works are often dismissed as superficial or exalted as transcendental. When taking into account the perspectives and the actual lived experience of the producers of these online publications, a more complicated picture emerges.

Youth authors use their personal sites to engage with their culture and to practice ways of being within it. They concern themselves simultaneously with how they appear to themselves and to their audiences. Although this process is not unique to *online* self-presentation, the deliberate nature of the construction magnifies the experience. Indeed, if, as has been argued, all presentation is performative and we constantly evaluate ourselves from the perspective of the "other," then moments of self-appraisal and self-presentation meld into one another, especially online.

The youth authors with whom I have spoken welcome this self-conscious intersection of public and private identities, because they are eager to complete the identity work that they understand to be part of growing up. As part of a larger society that constantly reminds them that they are no longer children but not yet adults, they tend to view themselves as drafts that can be retooled in response to both internal and external evaluations. Performing and playing with their identities in online public spaces is especially gratifying, because it is viewed as less risky but potentially more validating than experimentation in other arenas.

In these ways and others, personal sites appear to be used by young authors to engage directly with the challenges of identity formation that are common to adolescence in Western cultures. During adolescence, many young people move beyond their stable and secure sense of themselves as nurtured by their families and begin to develop their own, more personalized vision of themselves and their potential. Emotions are experienced intensely and are often more negative than earlier in life.[44] Personal sites, for some authors, provide a point of stability in this time of change, at the same time that they facilitate the very types of personal growth that constitute the identity formation process.

In some ways, maintaining personal home pages and blogs serve the same functions that traditional media consumption, especially music listening, has served for adolescents for decades. For example, it has long been established that media consumption helps adolescents identify with a youth culture and "feel connected to a larger peer network, which is united by certain youth-specific values and interests."[45] In an online context, authors work toward feelings of connection not simply by consuming youth culture (via particular websites, for example) but also by appropriating and integrating youth cultural symbols into their personal sites. Their sites thus not only broadcast their cultural affiliations to other youths, but also serve as signals to themselves. It has also been argued that young people intentionally use their private media experiences, such as music listening, "to directly engage with issues of identity." Listening to music during solitary time provides "a fantasy ground for exploring possible selves. . . . The images and emotions of popular music allow one to feel a range of internal states and try on alternate identities, both desired and feared."[46] On their personal sites, youth authors suggest this type of identity play can be taken farther, because it can be manifested virtually on the screen for others to see and comment upon. Identities are thus not simply imagined, but reconstituted visually and publicly for self and others, even as youths sit in the private confines of their bedrooms or other personal spaces.

In these ways and others, personal sites offer a variety of informal learning experiences. Most importantly, youth authors tell us, learning about themselves and genuine introspection are the major rewards and rationale for online authorship. As they consider if and how they will draft themselves into existence online, they are forced to reflect on who they are and how they wish to be viewed by others. Despite what ends up on their personal sites, the requirement for active and deliberate self-presentation mandates that youth (and other) authors evaluate how their self-as-presented matches the self they envision to be at their own core. Identity development and self-learning thus operate in tandem, and personal sites not only archive but also propel this process forward.

Another type of learning is at work here as well: learning about effective self-presentation. Like any message producers, youth authors who produce personal sites gradually learn how to create the identities and images they want others to see. They learn how to use cultural symbols for their own purposes, while at the same time they learn the technological skills necessary to create these representations. In so doing, they make choices that will reflect on how others view them, and thus are pushed to think critically about what kind of self-statements they offer through their personal sites. In some cases, the presentations they offer are met with poor reception by site visitors (as, for example, described in the preceding section). Instances of audience rebuke push young authors to consider how the acts of encoding and decoding messages can diverge from one another, and reveal how message creators in any context must work to insert meaning into their texts strategically. By trying to appeal to audiences and solicit feedback, they learn how to negotiate an image-driven culture. This is increasingly important as the world is more and more media dominated, and fewer and fewer physical spaces exist in which to connect and explore shared cultural concerns.[47]

The Internet has certainly not pioneered youth expression, but it does manifest youth expression more abundantly, conspicuously, and collectively than ever before. Consequently, we find before us a heightened opportunity to engage with youth cultural production. As Buckingham, Herring, and Willett (this volume) implore, we should hesitate to exoticize youths' practices or products at such a moment, though this is certainly tempting when so many of us lack the drive to construct the types of creative expression we witness among youths online. But we must also pay serious attention to youth online expressions, as sites of meaning making and identity production. When young people are telling us that they find fulfillment in and even personal transformation from the experiences they have expressing themselves online, we must recognize these practices as significant, despite or perhaps in light of the contexts in which they occur. Listening to what young people have to say about their experiences of cultural production yields a valuable—and irreplaceable—perspective as we endeavor to understand the changing role of new technologies in contemporary adolescence.

Notes

1. Janet Kornblum, Teens Wear Their Hearts on Their Blog. *USA Today*/October 30, 2005. http://usatoday.com (accessed November 2, 2005).

2. Jane Kroger, *Identity in Adolescence: The Balance Between Self and Other* (New York: Routledge, 1989), 2.

3. Kroger, 1989.

4. Ibid.

5. Reed Larson, Secrets in the Bedroom: Adolescents' Private Use of Media, *Journal of Youth and Adolescence* 24, no. 5 (1995): 535–551.

6. Erik Erikson, *Toys and Reasons: Stages in the Ritualization of Experience* (New York: W.W. Norton, 1977), 106.

7. Peter Arnett, Adolescents' Uses of Media for Self-Socialization, *Journal of Youth and Adolescence* 24, no. 5 (1995): 519–534.

8. Larson, Secrets in the Bedroom, 1995.

9. Susan Harter, *The Construction of the Self: A Developmental Perspective* (New York: Guilford Press, 1999).

10. Amanda Lenhart and Mary Madden, *Teen Content Creators and Consumers* (Washington, DC: Pew Internet and American Life Project, 2005).

11. Susan Herring, Lois Ann Scheidt, Sabrina Bonus, and Elijah Wright, Weblogs as a Bridging Genre, *Information, Technology & People* 18 (2005): 142–171.

12. Herring et al., 2005.

13. Lenhart and Madden, 2005.

14. It is worth noting here that not everyone agrees that blogs and home pages should be considered genres. boyd, for example, argues that the blog is better understood as a medium than as a genre. See danah boyd, A Blogger's Blog: Exploring the Definition of a Medium, *Reconstruction* 6, no. 4 (November 2006). http://reconstruction.eserver.org/064/boyd.shtml (accessed December 18, 2006).

15. See, e.g., Daniel Chandler and Dilwyn Roberts-Young, *The Construction of Identity in the Personal Homepages of Adolescents*. 1998. http://www.aber.ac.uk/~dgc/strasbourg.html (accessed July 21, 1999); Joseph Dominick, Who Do You Think You Are? Personal Home Pages and Self-Presentation on the World Wide Web, *Journalism & Mass Communication Quarterly* 76 (1999): 646–658; John Killoran, The Gnome in the Front Yard and Other Public Figurations: Genres of Self-Presentation on Personal Home Pages. *Biography: An Interdisciplinary Quarterly* 26 (2003): 66–84; Hugh Miller and Russell Mather, The Presentation of Self in WWW Home Pages, Paper presented at the IRSS Conference in Bristol, U.K. (March 1998), 25–27; and Weber and Mitchell, this volume.

16. Malcolm Parks and Tonjia Archey-Ladas, *Communicating Self Through Personal Homepages: Is Identity More Than Screen Deep?* Paper presented at the International Communication Association, San Diego, CA (May 2004), 3.

17. John Suler, *Adolescents in Cyberspace: The Good, the Bad, the Ugly*. (2005). http://www.rider.edu/suler/psycyber/adoles.html (accessed July 2, 2006).

18. Alex Williams (2006, Feb. 19) "Here I am taking my own picture." *New York Times*. http://www.nytimes.com (accessed February 20, 2006).

19. For example, Aviva Rosenstein (1999) found that critical events spurred the authors she studied to create their personal home pages (*Contradictory Social Contexts of the World Wide Web: The Paradoxical Implications of the Personal Home Page*. Paper presented at the ICA Annual Conference [May 1999]).

20. Rebecca Blood, *Weblogs: A History and Perspective*. (2000). http://www.rebeccablood.net/essays/weblog_history.html (accessed September 25, 2003).

21. Duane Buhrmester and Karen Prager, Patterns and Functions of Self-Disclosure During Childhood and Adolescence, in *Disclosure Processes in Children and Adolescents,* ed. Ken Rotenberg (New York: Cambridge University Press, 1995), 10–56 (quote on page 37).

22. Daniel Chandler and Dilwyn Roberts-Young, 1998.

23. Duane Buhrmester and Karen Prager, 1995.

24. Deborah Sosin, The Diary as a Transitional Object in Female Adolescent Development, *Adolescent Psychiatry* 11 (1983): 92–103.

25. This appears to hold true for adults as well, as discussed in Adam Reed, 'My Blog Is Me': Texts and Persons in U.K. Online Journal Culture (and Anthropology), *Ethnos* 70, no. 2 (2005): 220–242.

26. Andreas Kitzmann, That Different Place: Documenting the Self Within Online Environments, *Biography* 26 (2003): 48–65.

27. See, for example, Jeff Ferrell, Urban Graffiti: Crime, Control and Resistance, *Youth & Society* 27 (1995): 73–93; Ivor Miller, Guerilla Artists of New York City, *Race and Class* 35 (1993): 27–41.

28. Julie Chu, Navigating the Media Environment: How Youth Claim a Place Through Zines, *Social Justice* 24 (1997): 71–85.

29. First quoted in Susannah Stern, Virtually Speaking: Girls' Self-Disclosure on the WWW. *Women's Studies in Communication* 25, no. 2 (2002): 223–253.

30. Madeleine Sorapure, Screening Moments, Scrolling Lives: Diary Writing on the Web, *Biography* 26, no. 1 (2003): 1–23 (quote on page 11).

31. Susan Harter, 1999.

32. See, for example, Dominick (1999); Parks and Ladas (2004); Katherine Walker, "It's Difficult to Hide It," The Presentation of Self on Internet Home Pages, *Qualitative Sociology* 23 (2000): 99–120; and Sherry Turkle, *Life on the Screen: Identity in the Age of the Internet* (New York: Touchstone, 1995).

33. Charles Cooley, *Human Nature and the Social Order* (New York: Scribner's, 1902).

34. Erving Goffman, *The Presentation of Self in Everyday Life* (University of Edinburgh Social Sciences Research Centre, 1959).

35. Joseph Walther, Anticipated Ongoing Interaction versus Channel Effects on Relational Communication in Computer Mediated Communication, *Human Communication Research* 20 (1994): 473–501; Martin Lea and Russell Spears, Love at First Byte? Building Personal Relationships over Computer Networks, in J. T. Wood and Steve Duck, eds. *Understudied Relationships: Off the Beaten Track* (Beverly Hills, CA: Sage, 1995), 197–233.

36. Joanne Addison and Michelle Comstock, Virtually Out: The Emergence of a Lesbian, Bisexual, and Gay Youth Subculture, in *Generations of Youth: Youth Cultures and History in Twentieth-Century America,* eds. J. Austin and M. Nevin (New York: New York University Press, 1998), 367–378.

37. See, for example, Elisheva Gross, Adolescent Internet Use: What We Expect, What Teens Report, *Journal of Applied Developmental Psychology* 25, no. 6 (2004): 633–649; Patti Valkenburg, Alexander Schouten, and Jochen Peter, Adolescents' Identity Experiments on the Internet, *New Media & Society* 7 (2005): 383–402.

38. See, for example, Daniel Chandler and Dilwyn Roberts-Young (1998) and Joseph Tobin, An American Otaku (or a Boy's Virtual Life on the Net.), in *Digital Diversions: Youth Culture in the Age of Multimedia,* ed. J. Sefton-Green (London: UCL Press, 1998).

39. Duane Buhrmester and Karen Prager, 1995.

40. Andreas Kitzmann, 2003.

41. danah boyd, 2006, op. cit.

42. Adam Reed, 2005.

43. Daniel Chandler and Dilwyn Roberts-Young, 1998.

44. See Reed Larson, Secrets in the Bedroom, 1995.

45. Peter Arnett, 1995.

46. Reed Larson, 1995. (Quote on page 547.)

47. See also, danah boyd, this volume; and Mats Lieberg, Teenagers and Public Space, *Communication Research* 22 (1995): 720–744.

Why Youth ♥ Social Network Sites: The Role of Networked Publics in Teenage Social Life

danah boyd

University of California, Berkeley, School of Information

If you're not on MySpace, you don't exist —Skyler, 18, to her mom[1]

I'm in the 7th grade. I'm 13. I'm not a cheerleader. I'm not the president of the student body. Or captain of the debate team. I'm not the prettiest girl in my class. I'm not the most popular girl in my class. I'm just a kid. I'm a little shy. And it's really hard in this school to impress people enough to be your friend if you're not any of those things. But I go on these really great vacations with my parents between Christmas and New Year's every year. And I take pictures of places we go. And I write about those places. And I post this on my Xanga. Because I think if kids in school read what I have to say and how I say it, they'll want to be my friend —Vivien, 13, to Parry Aftab during a "Teen Angels" meeting[2]

During 2005, online social network sites like MySpace and Facebook became common destinations for young people in the United States. Throughout the country, young people were logging in, creating elaborate profiles, publicly articulating their relationships with other participants, and writing extensive comments back and forth. By early 2006, many considered participation on the key social network site, MySpace, essential to being seen as cool at school. While not all teens are members of social network sites, these sites developed significant cultural resonance amongst American teens in a short period of time. Although the luster has since faded and teens are not nearly as infatuated with these sites as they once were, they continue to be an important part of teen social life.

The rapid adoption of social network sites by teenagers in the United States and in many other countries around the world raises some important questions. Why do teenagers flock to these sites? What are they expressing on them? How do these sites fit into their lives? What are they learning from their participation? Are these online activities like face-to-face friendships or are they different, or complementary? The goal of this chapter is to address these questions and explore their implications for youth identities. While particular systems may come and go, how youth engage through social network sites today provides long-lasting insights into identity formation, status negotiation, and peer-to-peer sociality.

This work could not have been done without the support of and conversations with numerous people and groups. In particular, I would like to thank Peter Lyman, Mimi Ito, Marc Davis, and Cori Hayden for their advice and unbelievable amount of support. I would also like to thank everyone on the Digital Youth Project and especially Dan Perkel for sharing amazing insights into teen life. I would also like to thank Irina Shklovski, Fred Stutzman, Nicole Ellison, and Tom Anderson for long nights spent discussing social network sites and youth practices. Finally, I am forever grateful to the Berkeley School of Information and the USC Annenberg Center for Communications for giving me a home in which to think crazy thoughts.

To address the aforementioned questions, I begin by documenting the key features of social network sites and the business decisions that lead to mass adoption, and then seek to situate social network sites in a broader discussion of what I call "networked publics." I then examine how teens are modeling identity through social network profiles so that they can write themselves and their community into being. Building on this, I investigate how this process of articulated expression supports critical peer-based sociality because, by allowing youth to hang out amongst their friends and classmates, social network sites are providing teens with a space to work out identity and status, make sense of cultural cues, and negotiate public life. I argue that social network sites are a type of networked public with four properties that are not typically present in face-to-face public life: persistence, searchability, replicability, and invisible audiences. These properties fundamentally alter social dynamics, complicating the ways in which people interact. I conclude by reflecting on the social developments that have prompted youth to seek out networked publics, and considering the changing role that publics have in young people's lives.

Methodology and Demographics

The arguments made in this chapter are based on ethnographic data collected during my two-year study of U.S.-based youth engagement with MySpace. In employing the term ethnography, I am primarily referencing the practices of "participant observation" and "deep hanging out"[3] alongside qualitative interviews. I have moved between online and offline spaces, systematically observing, documenting, and talking to young people about their practices and attitudes.

While the subjects of my interviews and direct observations are primarily urban youth (differing in age, sex, race, sexuality, religion, ethnicity, and socioeconomic class), I have also spent countless hours analyzing the profiles, blogs, and commentary of teenagers throughout the United States. Although I have interviewed older people, the vast majority of people that I have interviewed and observed are of high school age, living with a parent or guardian. There is no good term to reference this group. Not all are actually students (and that role signals identity material that is not accurate). Vague terms like "youth," "young people," and "children" imply a much broader age range. For these reasons, and in reference to the history of the term "teenager" in relation to compulsory high school education,[4] I have consciously decided to label the relevant population "teenagers" even though the majority of individuals that I have spoken with are between the age group of fourteen to eighteen. While strictly speaking, there are teenagers who are not in high school, the vast majority of those fourteen to eighteen are high school students; I will focus primarily on that group.

In examining the practices of teenagers on social network sites, I focus primarily on MySpace. This will be my primary case study, although my discussion of these sites is applicable more broadly; I will reference other sites as appropriate. I should note that prior to studying teen practices on MySpace, I did a two-year ethnographic study of Friendster, another social network site. While it is unlikely that MySpace will forever be the main destination site for teenagers, I use this site because its mass popularity offers critical insight into participation patterns that do and will exist on other sites.

Although news media give the impression that all online teens in the United States are on MySpace, this is not the case. For this reason, I want to take a moment to discuss who is not participating. In 2004, PEW found that 87 percent of teenagers aged twelve to seventeen have some level of Internet access.[5] In a study conducted in late 2006, they found that

55 percent of online teens aged twelve to seventeen have created profiles on social network sites with 64 percent of teens aged fifteen to seventeen.[6] While these numbers are most likely low,[7] it is very clear that not all high school students participate in online communities that require public content creation like social network sites.

Qualitatively, I have found that there are two types of nonparticipants: disenfranchised teens and conscientious objectors. The former consists of those without Internet access, those whose parents succeed in banning them from participation, and online teens who primarily access the Internet through school and other public venues where social network sites are banned.[8] Conscientious objectors include politically minded teens who wish to protest against Murdoch's News Corp. (the corporate owner of MySpace), obedient teens who have respected or agree with their parents' moral or safety concerns, marginalized teens who feel that social network sites are for the cool kids, and other teens who feel as though they are too cool for these sites. The latter two explanations can be boiled down to one explanation that I heard frequently: "because it's stupid." While the various conscientious objectors may deny participating, I have found that many of them actually do have profiles to which they log in occasionally. I have also found numerous cases where the friends of nonparticipants create profiles for them.[9] Furthermore, amongst those conscientious objectors who are genuinely nonparticipants, I have yet to find one who does not have something to say about the sites, albeit typically something negative. In essence, MySpace is the civil society of teenage culture: whether one is for it or against it, everyone knows the site and has an opinion about it.

Interestingly, I have found that race and social class play a little role in terms of access beyond the aforementioned disenfranchised population. Poor urban black teens appear to be just as likely to join the site as white teens from wealthier backgrounds, although what they do on there has much to do with their level of Internet access. Those who only access their accounts in schools use it primarily as an asynchronous communication tool, while those with continuous nighttime access at home spend more time surfing the network, modifying their profile, collecting friends, and talking to strangers. When it comes to social network sites, there appears to be a far greater participatory divide than an access divide.

Gender also appears to influence participation on social network sites. Younger boys are more likely to participate than younger girls (46 percent vs. 44 percent) but older girls are far more likely to participate than older boys (70 percent vs. 57 percent). Older boys are twice as likely to use the sites to flirt and slightly more likely to use the sites to meet new people than girls of their age. Older girls are far more likely to use these sites to communicate with friends they see in person than younger people or boys of their age.[10] While gender differences do exist and should not be ignored, most of what I discuss in this article concerns practices that are common to both boys and girls.

Fundamentally, this chapter is a case study based on ethnographic data. My primary goal is simply to unveil some of the common ways in which teenagers now experience social life online.

The Making of Social Network Sites

Although a handful of sites predated it, Friendster popularized the features that define contemporary social network sites—profiles, public testimonials or comments, and publicly articulated, traversable lists of friends. Launched in 2002 as a newfangled dating site, Friendster quickly became popular amongst mid-twenty/thirty-something urban dwellers living in the United States. Although some used the site for its intended purpose of meeting potential partners, others engaged in a wide array of activities, ranging from tracking down high school mates to creating fictional profiles for entertainment purposes.[11] By the summer of 2003, some San Francisco-based bands realized that they could leverage the site to connect to their fans and promote their gigs.[12] Word spread in the relevant music scenes, although Friendster forbade this practice and began deleting bands' profiles (along with any profile deemed "fake"). When MySpace launched in the fall of 2003, they welcomed bands online, quickly attracting the attention of indie rock musicians from the Silverlake neighborhood of Los Angeles.

Music is cultural glue among youth. As the bands began advertising their presence on MySpace, mid-twenty/thirty-something club goers jumped on board in the hopes of gaining access to VIP passes or acquiring valuable (sub)cultural capital.[13] While fans typically have to be twenty-one plus in the United States to get into the venues where bands play (because of alcohol laws), younger audiences are avid consumers of music and the culture that surrounds it. When young music aficionados learned that their favorite bands had profiles on MySpace, they began checking out the site. Music junkies loved the fact that they could listen to and download music for free while celebrity watchers enjoyed writing to musicians who were happy to respond. A symbiotic relationship between bands and fans quickly emerged on the system as bands wanted to gather fans and fans wanted to be connected to their favorite bands. Given the degree to which youth are active participants in music subcultures, it is not surprising that MySpace attracted young fans.

While the first wave of young participants learned of the site through their interest in music and musicians, they also invited their less musically engaged peers to join the site. Many began participating because of the available social voyeurism and the opportunity to craft a personal representation in an increasingly popular online community. Just like their older counterparts, teenagers loved the ability to visualize their social world through the networked collection of profiles. At the same time, younger participants adopted different participation strategies from those of earlier, older participants. While many adults find value in socializing with strangers, teenagers are more focused on socializing with people they knew personally and celebrities that they adore.

By mid-2005, MySpace was a popular destination for high school students throughout the United States but teenagers from other countries were on a variety of other social network sites. Friendster had lost its grip on twenty/thirty-something urbanites but it had become popular amongst teenagers in Singapore, Philippines, Indonesia, and Malaysia. Social network sites like Orkut and Hi5, which were initially popular among adults in Brazil and India, began attracting the attention of younger audiences in those countries. Facebook, a United States site for college students, opened its door to high school students in September 2005. In other regions, new social network sites were launched explicitly to attract the attention of teens. Sites like Tagworld, Bebo, Piczo, Faceparty, and Mixi all launched with youth in mind and took off in places like the United Kingdom, New Zealand, Australia, and Japan. Preexisting community sites like Black Planet, Asian Avenue, and MiGente implemented social network site features, although this did not help them regain the teens that they had lost to MySpace. In China, an instant messaging service called QQ added social network site features, as did the popular Korean community site Cyworld; both are popular across all age groups in China and South Korea.

Most of the social network sites were brewed by venture-backed startups, but there are a few exceptions to this. Cyworld is a property of SK Telecom, the largest mobile phone operator in South Korea. Orkut began as a side project by a Google employee but, shortly before launch, Google decided to attach its name to the site so that it launched as a Google project. Microsoft, Yahoo!, AOL, and Wal-Mart have all created social network sites, but these have not been particularly successful. In 2005, Fox Interactive Media (a division of Murdoch's News Corporation) purchased MySpace for US $580 million. Unfortunately, not much is currently known about the long-term effects of corporate participation in social network sites. While there has been tremendous speculation about what Fox's ownership of MySpace will mean, there have been few changes made since the site was acquired. Of course, broader concerns about the impact of consumer culture on young people's agency[14] in online participation are completely applicable to social network sites.

While there are dozens of social network sites, participation tends to follow cultural and linguistic lines. Few sites successfully support groups from different nation-states; although Orkut is popular in both India and Brazil, Cyworld has large audiences in China and South Korea, and MySpace is trying to grow globally. Cyworld has completely separate domains that segregate the Koreans from the Chinese. On Orkut, the Indians and Brazilians share the site but barely interact with one another. Furthermore, the Indian participants have segmented themselves within the system along caste lines.[15] Even on MySpace where there is a strong American culture, there is an intense division along race and age lines. While cultural forces clearly segment participation, there are many structural similarities across the sites. Fundamentally, social network sites are a category of community sites that have profiles, friends, and comments.

Profiles, Friends, and Comments

Social network sites are based around profiles, a form of individual (or, less frequently, group) home page, which offers a description of each member. In addition to text, images, and video created by the member, the social network site profile also contains comments from other members and a public list of the people that one identifies as Friends within the network.[16] Because the popularized style of these sites emerged out of dating services, the profile often contains material typical of those sites: demographic details (age, sex, location, etc.), tastes (interests, favorite bands, etc.), a photograph, and an open-ended description of who the person would like to meet. Profiles are constructed by filling out forms on the site. While the forms were designed to control the layout of the content, MySpace accidentally left open a technological loophole and their forms accepted (and then rendered) HTML and CSS code. Capitalizing on this loophole, participants can modify the look and feel of their profiles. By copying and pasting code from other websites, teens change their backgrounds, add video and images, change the color of their text, and otherwise turn their profiles into an explosion of animated chaos that resembles a stereotypical teenager's bedroom. The default profile is publicly accessible to anyone, but most social network sites have privacy features that allow participants to restrict who can see what. For example, MySpace allows participants to make their profiles Friends-only (and sets this as the default for those who indicate they are fourteen or fifteen years old) while Facebook gives profile-access only to people from the same school by default.

After creating a profile, participants are asked to invite their friends to the site by supplying their email addresses. Alternatively, they can look at others' profiles and add those people to their list of Friends.[17] Most social network sites require approval for two people to be linked as Friends. When someone indicates another as a Friend, the recipient receives a message asking for confirmation. If Friendship is confirmed, the two become Friends in the system and their relationship is included in the public display of connections on all profiles.[18] These

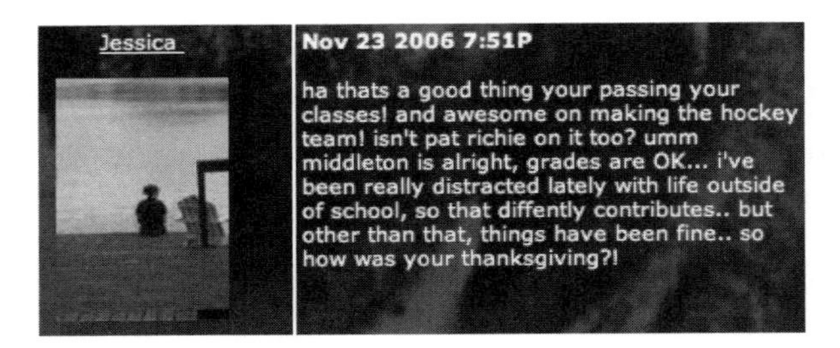

Figure 1
Conversation as MySpace comment.

displays typically involve photos and nicknames that link to their profile. By clicking on these links, visitors can traverse the network by surfing from Friend to Friend to Friend.

In addition to the content that members provide to create their own profiles, social network sites typically have a section dedicated to comments by Friends. (On Friendster, this section is called Testimonials; on Facebook, it is called The Wall.) Because Friendster implemented this feature to encourage people to write testimonials about their friends for strangers to read, early adopters used this feature to write single messages about the person represented in the profile. Over time, reciprocity motivated people to write creative testimonials back and forth, creating a form of conversation[19]; this was particularly popular amongst people using Friendster for playful activities (see Figure 1). For example, a profile representing table salt wrote long love odes about pepper on the profile representing pepper; pepper reciprocated and this went back and forth for weeks.

As teenagers began joining Friendster, they also used this section to write to the profile owner, even though the testimonials were public. When MySpace implemented the same feature and called it Comments instead of Testimonials, writing to the person became status quo, particularly amongst younger participants (see Figure 1). The following comments highlight the difference:

Mark is a man among boys, a razor sharp mind towering over the general sludge. (Testimonial on Friendster Profile of Mark, 27)

Are we still gonna go paintballing? (Comment on MySpace Profile of Corey, 14)

In essence, Corey's friend is writing a purportedly private message to him in a public space for others to view. Corey will reply to the comment in kind, writing the answer on his friend's profile. By doing this, teens are taking social interactions between friends into the public sphere for others to witness.

Although many sites include other common features,[20] the practices that take place through the use of the most prevalent three—profiles, friends, and comments—differentiate social network sites from other types of computer-mediated communication. Furthermore, what makes these three practices significant for consideration is that they take place in public: Friends are publicly articulated, profiles are publicly viewed, and comments are publicly visible.

Networked Publics

Defining the term public is difficult at best.[21] As an adjective, it is commonly used in opposition to private. When referring to locations, public is used to signal places that are accessible to anyone (or at least anyone belonging to a privileged category like adults). In reference to actions or texts, public often implies that the audience is unknown and that strangers may bear witness.

As a noun, public refers to a collection of people who may not all know each other but share "a common understanding of the world, a shared identity, a claim to inclusiveness, a consensus regarding the collective interest."[22] In some senses, public is quite similar to audience as both refer to a group bounded by a shared text, whether that is a worldview or a performance.[23] These words often collide conceptually because speaking to the public implies that the public is acting as an audience.

When talking about the public, one must ask if there is only one public. When United States' President Bush addresses the public, he is not conceptualizing the same public as Zimbabwe's President Mugabe would. Likewise, it is not the same audience that hears both presidents. If, instead, we talk about a public, it is possible to recognize that there are different collections of people depending on the particular situation.[24] Talking about a public also implies that there must be multiple publics separated by social contexts. What then constitutes the boundaries of a given public?

In this article, I move between these many different meanings of public. Social network sites allow publics to gather. At the same time, by serving as a space where speech takes place, they are also publics themselves. The sites themselves also distinguish between public and private, where public means that a profile is visible to anyone and private means that it is Friends-only.

The types of publics that gather on social network sites and the types of publics that such sites support are deeply affected by the mediated nature of interaction. For these reasons it is important to distinguish these sites as publics, not simply public, and networked publics, not simply publics. While this latter term has been used to reference "a linked set of social, cultural, and technological developments that have accompanied the growing engagement with digitally networked media,"[25] I am primarily talking about the spaces and audiences that are bound together through technological networks (i.e. the Internet, mobile networks, etc.). Networked publics are one type of mediated public; the network mediates the interactions between members of the public. Media of all stripes have enabled the development of mediated publics.

The reason for differentiating networked publics from mediated and unmediated publics has to do with fundamental architectural differences that affect social interaction. In unmediated environments, the boundaries and audiences of a given public are structurally defined. Access to visual and auditory information is limited by physics; walls and other obstacles further restrain visibility. Thus when I say that I embarrassed myself in public by tripping on the curb, the public that I am referencing includes all of the strangers who visually witnessed my stumble. The audience is restricted to those present in a limited geographical radius at a given moment in time. The public that I conceptualize might also include all of those who might hear of my accident through word of mouth, although the likelihood of others sharing the event is dependent on my status in the public and the juiciness of the story. While I might think that the whole world must know, this is not likely to be true. More importantly, in an unmediated world, it is not possible for the whole world actually to witness this incident; in the worst-case scenario, they might all hear of my mishap through word of mouth.

Mediating technologies like television, radio, and newsprint change everything. My fall could have been recorded and televised on the nightly news. This changes the scale of the public. Rather than considering all of the people who did witness me visually, I must also consider all of the people who might witness a reproduction of my fall. The potential audience is affected by the properties of the mediating technologies, namely persistence, replicability, and invisible audiences. Networked publics add an additional feature—searchability—while magnifying all of the other properties. While broadcast media take advantage of persistence, it is not as if anyone could go to the television and watch my fall whenever they wish, but if my fall is uploaded to YouTube or MySpace Video, this is possible.

These four properties thus fundamentally separate unmediated publics from networked publics:

1 Persistence: Unlike the ephemeral quality of speech in unmediated publics, networked communications are recorded for posterity. This enables asynchronous communication, but it also extends the period of existence of any speech act.

2 Searchability: Because expressions are recorded and identity is established through text, search and discovery tools help people find like minds. While people cannot currently acquire the geographical coordinates of any person in unmediated spaces, finding one's digital body online is just a matter of keystrokes.

3 Replicability: Hearsay can be deflected as misinterpretation, but networked public expressions can be copied from one place to another verbatim such that there is no way to distinguish the "original" from the "copy."[26]

4 Invisible audiences: While we can visually detect most people who can overhear our speech in unmediated spaces, it is virtually impossible to ascertain all those who might run across our expressions in networked publics. This is further complicated by the other three properties, since our expression may be heard at a different time and place from when and where we originally spoke.

In short, a mediated public (and especially a networked public) could consist of all people across all space and all time. Of course, in reality, it probably will not, even when a person desperately wishes to have such attention. Still, the bounding forces of networked publics are less constrained by geography and temporal collocation than unmediated publics. Because people are not accustomed to socializing when they do not know the audience or the context, interactions in networked publics are often peculiar to newcomers who get frustrated when what they intended is not what is interpreted.

These properties affect both the potential audience and the context in which the expression is received. We will address this further in the next section as we consider young people's engagement with social network sites more specifically.

Participation

When I ask teenagers why they joined MySpace, the answer is simple: "Cuz that's where my friends are." Their explanation of what they do on the site is much more vague: "I don't know . . . I just hang out." Beneath these vague explanations is a clear message: the popularity of MySpace is deeply rooted in how the site supports sociality amongst preexisting friend groups. Teens join MySpace to maintain connections with their friends.[27]

While socializing drives certain kinds of engagement with the site, teens with Internet access at home offer another plausible explanation for the long hours they spend there: "because I was bored."

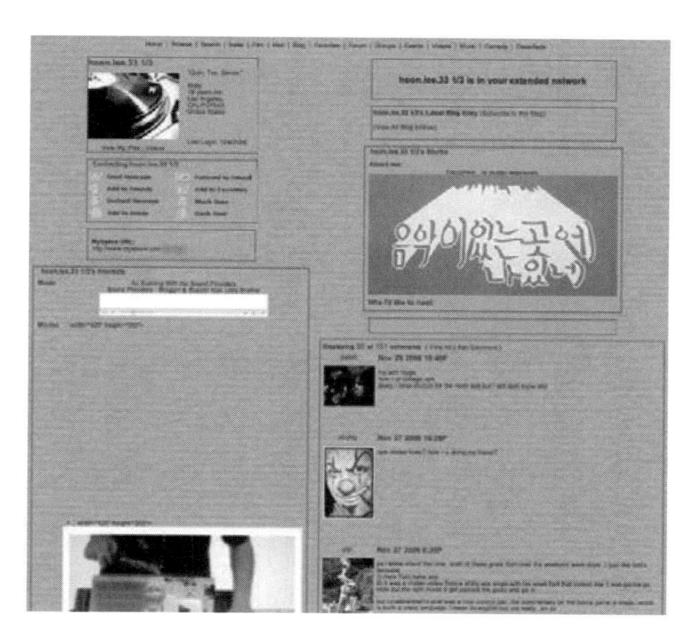

Figure 2
Example profile featuring modified background and multimedia.

Just because I'm on the computer at 2:30 am, doesn't mean I'm up to no good. Like last night (my mom) comes in and yells at me to go to bed. When I don't, she is all 'well what are you doing, show me what you're doing.' Of course I was lurking MySpace profiles, cause there is nothing better to do, but that's annoying to explain, she wouldn't understand. —Pam, 17

Teens often turn to sites like MySpace for entertainment; social voyeurism passes time while providing insight into society at large.

In the next three sections, I examine three different aspects of teenage practices on MySpace. First, I discuss the profile construction process in light of how teens are working through impression management and identity issues. I then turn to consider teens' conceptions of public, private, and context. Finally, I discuss changing historical constructions of youth publics, in order to shed light on why so much critical social development is taking place online in sites like MySpace.

Initiation: Profile Creation

Teenagers typically learn about MySpace through their friends—they join because a friend invites them to join. After creating an account, they begin setting up their profile by filling in forms on the site (see Figure 2 for an example profile). This generates a generic profile with content like "favorite books" and "about me." Before writing anything of depth, teens tend to look at others' profiles, starting with the friend who invited them. In viewing that profile, they are offered links to their friends' MySpace Friends, and so they can spend countless hours surfing the network, jumping from Friend to Friend. By looking at others' profiles, teens get a sense of what types of presentations are socially appropriate; others' profiles provide critical cues about what to present on their own profile. While profiles are constructed through a series of generic forms, there is plenty of room for them to manipulate the profiles to express themselves. At a basic level, the choice of photos and the personalized answers to generic questions allow individuals to signal meaningful cues about themselves. While the ability to identify oneself through such textual and visual means is valuable, MySpace profiles also afford another level of personalization (see Figure 2).

Experimenting with the generic forms, a few early adopters discovered that MySpace had failed to close a security hole. While most other sites blocked HTML, CSS, and Javascript in their forms, MySpace did not. Early adopters began exploiting this hole to personalize their pages by adding code to the form fields that changed the background and added multimedia to their pages. There is no simple way to make these modifications[28]; individuals must figure out what CSS or HTML goes in what form. While the site itself does not offer support, numerous other websites (most initially created by teenagers) emerged to provide code and instructions for modifying every aspect of a MySpace page. Individuals choose a desirable layout and then they are instructed to copy and paste the code into the appropriate forms. This code inevitably includes links back to the helper page.[29] A copy/paste culture emerged, as teens began trafficking in knowledge of how to pimp out[30] their profiles. Although most teens' profiles are altered, it is important not to assume technological literacy[31]—few teens hand-code their pages; most use a helper site or beg friends to do it for them.

Building an intricate profile is an initiation rite. In the early days of their infatuation, teens spend innumerable hours tracking down codes, trading tips, and setting up a slick profile. Through this process, they are socialized into MySpace—they learn both technological and social codes. While technological information gives them the wherewithal to craft a profile, the interpretation and evaluation of this performance is dictated by social protocols. MySpace profiles become yet another mechanism by which teens can signal information about their identities and tastes.

Identity Performance

In everyday interactions, the body serves as a critical site of identity performance. In conveying who we are to other people, we use our bodies to project information about ourselves.[32] This is done through movement, clothes, speech, and facial expressions. What we put forward is our best effort at what we want to say about who we are. Yet while we intend to convey one impression, our performance is not always interpreted as we might expect. Through learning to make sense of others' responses to our behavior, we can assess how well we have conveyed what we intended. We can then alter our performance accordingly. This process of performance, interpretation, and adjustment is what Erving Goffman calls impression management,[33] and is briefly discussed in the introduction to this volume. Impression management is a part of a larger process where people seek to define a situation[34] through their behavior. People seek to define social situations by using contextual cues from the environment around them. Social norms emerge out of situational definitions, as people learn to read cues from the environment and the people present to understand what is appropriate behavior.

Learning how to manage impressions is a critical social skill that is honed through experience. Over time, we learn how to make meaning out of a situation, others' reactions, and what we are projecting of ourselves. As children, we learn that actions on our part prompt reactions by adults; as we grow older, we learn to interpret these reactions and adjust our behavior. Diverse social environments help people develop these skills because they force individuals to reevaluate the signals they take for granted.

The process of learning to read social cues and react accordingly is core to being socialized into a society. While the process itself begins at home for young children, it is critical for young people to engage in broader social settings to develop these skills. Of course, how children are taught about situations and impression management varies greatly by culture,[35] but these processes are regularly seen as part of coming of age. While no one is ever a true master of impression management, the teenage years are ripe with opportunities to develop these skills.

In mediated environments, bodies are not immediately visible and the skills people need to interpret situations and manage impressions are different. As Jenny Sundén argues, people must learn to write themselves into being.[36] Doing so makes visible how much we take the body for granted. While text, images, audio, and video all provide valuable means for developing a virtual presence, the act of articulation differs from how we convey meaningful information through our bodies. This process also makes explicit the self-reflexivity that Giddens argues is necessary for identity formation, but the choices individuals make in crafting a digital body highlight the self-monitoring that Foucault describes.[37]

In some sense, people have more control online—they are able to carefully choose what information to put forward, thereby eliminating visceral reactions that might have seeped out in everyday communication. At the same time, these digital bodies are fundamentally coarser, making it far easier to misinterpret what someone is expressing. Furthermore, as Amy Bruckman shows, key information about a person's body is often present online, even when that person is trying to act deceptively; for example, people are relatively good at detecting when someone is a man even when they profess to be a woman online.[38] Yet because mediated environments reveal different signals, the mechanisms of deception differ.[39]

Writing Identity and Community into Being

A MySpace profile can be seen as a form of digital body where individuals must write themselves into being. Through profiles, teens can express salient aspects of their identity for others to see and interpret. They construct these profiles for their friends and peers to view. (We will complicate the issue of audience in the next section.) While what they present may or may not resemble their offline identity, their primary audience consists of peers that they know primarily offline—people from school, church, work, sports teams, etc. Because of this direct link between offline and online identities, teens are inclined to present the side of themselves that they believe will be well received by these peers.

The desire to be cool on MySpace is part of the more general desire to be validated by one's peers. Even though teens theoretically have the ability to behave differently online, the social hierarchies that regulate "coolness" offline are also present online. For example, it is cool to have Friends on MySpace but if you have too many Friends, you are seen as a MySpace whore. These markers of cool are rooted in the social culture of MySpace. One of the ways that coolness is articulated is through bulletin posts meant to attack those who have status online and offline. One such post is a satirical Top 10 list of "How To Be Cool On MySpace," which includes material like "Your MySpace name MUST contain symbols and incorrect spelling" and "All your blogs have to be about how bad your day was." While this post is meant to dismiss these common practices, when these posts are spread around, they simultaneously reinforce these norms in the process of mocking them.

Part of what solidifies markers of cool has to do with the underlying Friend network. MySpace Friends are not just people that one knows, but public displays of connections.[40]

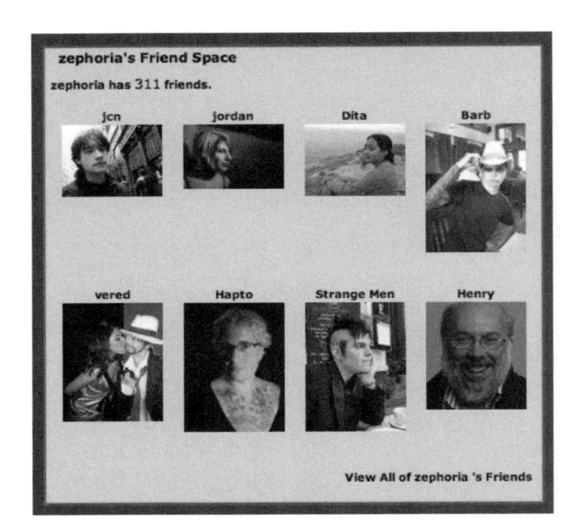

Figure 3
Example Top 8.

While teens will typically add friends and acquaintances as Friends, they will also add people because it would be socially awkward to say no to them, because they make the individual look cool, or simply because it would be interesting to read their bulletin posts. Because Friends are displayed on an individual's profile, they provide meaningful information about that person; in other words, "You are who you know."[41] For better or worse, people judge others based on their associations: group identities form around and are reinforced by the collective tastes and attitudes of those who identify with the group. Online, this cue is quite helpful in enabling people to find their bearings (see Figure 3).

The best indicator of an individual's close friends is their Top Friends (see Figure 3); these are displayed directly on an individual's profile, while the rest of their Friends require an additional click. Individuals can choose which Friends will be displayed. While the Top Friends feature allows members to quickly get to and show off the profiles of their closest friends, the public nature of this display tends to complicate relationships. In short, the Top Friends feature is considered pure social drama:

> Myspace always seems to cause way too much drama and i am so dang sick of it. im sick of the pain and the hurt and tears and the jealousy and the heartache and the truth and the lies . . . it just SUCKS! . . . im just so sick of the drama and i just cant take it anymore compared to all the love its supposed to make us feel. i get off just feeling worse. i have people complain to me that they are not my number one on my top 8. come on now. grow up. its freaking myspace." —Olivia, 17

The reason that the Top Friends feature wreaks social havoc on teens' lives is because there are social consequences in publicly announcing one's friends, best friends, and bestest friends. Feelings are hurt when individuals find that someone that they feel close with does not reciprocate.

> As a kid, you used your birthday party guest list as leverage on the playground. 'If you let me play I'll invite you to my birthday party.' Then, as you grew up and got your own phone, it was all about someone being on your speed dial. Well today it's the MySpace Top 8. It's the new dangling carrot for

gaining superficial acceptance. Taking someone off your Top 8 is your new passive aggressive power play when someone pisses you off. —Nadine, 16

Yet, for all of the social discomfort, these Friends help provide group structure, further indicating the meaningful identity markers of the individual. In choosing Friends, teens write their community into being, which is precisely why this feature is so loved and despised.

As discussed in the introduction to this volume, identity can be seen as a social process that is fluid and contingent on the situation.[42] On MySpace, an individual's perceived audience frames the situation. While others might be present, the markers of cool are clearly dictated by an individual's friends and peers. What teens are doing here is conceptualizing an imagined audience.[43] While this may seem peculiar, it is a practice that is commonplace for people like writers and actors who regularly interact with the public through mediating technologies. Without having cues about who will witness a given expression, an imagined audience provides a necessary way of envisioning who should be present. The size and diversity of this imagined community depends on the individual; some imagine acquiring fans while others imagine a community that is far more intimate. As Stern discusses earlier in this volume, youth's views on audience are quite nuanced.[44] While some value the possibility of a wide audience, actually attracting such an audience can introduce complications. At the same time, wanting a large audience does not mean that a large audience will appear; online, everyone is famous to fifteen people.[45]

Regardless of desires, it is impossible to see the actual audience across all space and all time. At the same time, it is necessary to understand the scope of one's audience to properly present oneself. By imagining an audience, regardless of its accuracy, teens are able to navigate the social situation required in crafting a profile. Because of the intricate connection between offline and online social worlds, the audience that teens envision online is connected to their social world offline, or to their hopes about the possible alternatives online. Yet, their audience online may not be who they think it is.

Privacy in Public: Creating *MY* Space

My mom always uses the excuse about the internet being 'public' when she defends herself. It's not like I do anything to be ashamed of, but a girl needs her privacy. I do online journals so I can communicate with my friends. Not so my mother could catch up on the latest gossip of my life. —Bly Lauritano-Werner, 17.[46]

For Lauritano-Werner, privacy is not about structural limitations to access; it is about being able to limit access through social conventions. This approach makes sense if you recognize that networked publics make it nearly impossible to have structurally enforced borders. However, this is not to say that teens also do not try to create structural barriers.

Teens often fabricate key identifying information like name, age, and location to protect themselves (see Figure 4). While parents' groups often encourage this deception to protect teens from strangers,[47] many teens actually engage in this practice to protect themselves from the watchful eye of parents.

Fabricating data does indeed make search more difficult, but the networked nature of MySpace provides alternate paths to finding people. First, few teens actually lie about what school they attend, although some choose not to list a school at all. Second, and more problematically, teens are not going to refuse connections to offline friends even though that makes them more easily locatable. Parents simply need to find one of their child's friends; from there, it is easy to locate their own kid. While teens are trying to make parental

Figure 4
The formal data she provides MySpace says she is sixty-seven and from Zimbabwe; in her self-description, she indicates that she is actually fourteen and goes to high school in Texas.

access more difficult, their choice to obfuscate key identifying information also makes them invisible to their peers. This is not ideal because teens are going online in order to see and be seen by those who might be able to provide validation.

Another common structural tactic involves the privacy settings. By choosing to make their profile private,[48] teens are able to select who can see their content. This prevents unwanted parents from lurking, but it also means that peers cannot engage with them without inviting them to be Friends. To handle this, teens are often promiscuous with who they are willing to add as Friends on the site. By connecting to anyone who seems interesting, they gain control over the structure. Yet, this presents different problems because massive Friending introduces a flood of content with no tools to manage it.

Another structural approach intended to confound parents is creating mirror networks. When Stacy's mom found her profile, she was outraged. She called the moms of two of Stacy's friends—Anne and Kimberly. All three parents demanded that their kids clean up their profiles and told them to tell their friends the same or else more parents would be called. Steamed by the prudish response of their parents, Stacy, Anne, and Kimberly reluctantly agreed to change their profiles. Then, they each made a second account with fake names and details. Here, they linked to each other's second profile and uploaded the offending material, inviting their friends to do the same. In doing so, they created a network that completely mirrored the network that their parents had seen. Their parents continued to check their G-rated profiles and the girls continued to lead undercover lives.

While deception and lockdown are two common structural solutions, teens often argue that MySpace should be recognized as my space, a space for teenagers to be teenagers. Adults typically view this attitude as preposterous because, as they see it, since the technology is public and teens are participating in a public way, they should have every right to view this content. This attitude often frustrates teenagers who argue that just because anyone can access the site does not mean that everyone should.

When teens argue for having my space in a networked public, they are trying to resolve the social problems that emerge because the constructions of public and private are different online and offline. In unmediated spaces, structural boundaries are assessed to determine who is in the audience and who is not. The decision to goof off during lunch is often made with the assumption that only peers bear witness. In mediated spaces, there are no structures to limit the audience; search collapses all virtual walls.

Most people believe that security through obscurity will serve as a functional barrier online. For the most part, this is a reasonable assumption. Unless someone is of particular note or interest, why would anyone search for them? Unfortunately for teens, there are two groups who have a great deal of interest in them: those who hold power over them—parents, teachers, local government officials, etc.—and those who wish to prey on them—marketers and predators. Before News Corporation purchased MySpace, most adults had never heard of the site; afterwards, they flocked there either to track teenagers that they knew or to market goods (or promises) to any teen who would listen. This shift ruptured both the imagined community and the actual audience they had to face on a regular basis. With a much wider audience present, teens had to face a hard question: what is appropriate?

This problem is not unique to social network sites; it has been present in all forms of mediated publics. Consider Stokely Carmichael's experience with radio and television.[49] As an activist in the 1960s, Carmichael regularly addressed segregated black and white audiences about the values and ideals of the burgeoning Black Power movement. Depending on the color of his audience, he used very different rhetorical styles. As his popularity grew, he started attracting media attention and was invited to speak on TV and radio. This opportunity was also a curse because both black and white listeners would hear his speech. As there was no way to reconcile the two different rhetorical styles he typically used, he had to choose. By maintaining his black roots in front of white listeners, Carmichael permanently alienated white society from the messages of Black Power. Faced with two disjointed contexts simultaneously, there was no way that Carmichael could successfully convey his message to both audiences.

Teenagers face the same dilemma on MySpace. How can they be simultaneously cool to their peers and acceptable to their parents? For the most part, it is not possible. While most adults wish that kids would value what they value, this is rarely true. It is easy to lambaste teens for accepting the cultural norms of the "in" crowd, but social categories[50] and status negotiation[51] are core elements in teen life; this is part of how they learn to work through the cultural practices and legal rules that govern society. The behaviors that are typically rewarded with status in school are often resistant to adult values. On MySpace, teens are directly faced with peer pressure and the need to conform to what is seen to be cool. Worse, they are faced with it in the most public setting possible—one that is potentially visible to all peers and all adults. The stakes are greater on both sides, but the choice is still there: cool or lame?

Unfortunately, the magnified public exposure increases the stakes. Consider a call that I received from an admissions officer at a prestigious college. The admissions committee had planned to admit a young black man from a very poor urban community until they found his MySpace. They were horrified to find that his profile was full of hip-hop imagery, urban ghetto slang, and hints of gang participation. This completely contradicted the essay they had received from him about the problems with gangs in his community, and they were at a loss. Did he lie in his application? Although confidentiality prevented me from examining his case directly, I offered the admissions officer an alternative explanation. Perhaps he needed to acquiesce to the norms of the gangs while living in his neighborhood, in order to survive and make it through high school to apply to college?

Situations like this highlight how context is constructed and maintained through participation, not simply observation. When outsiders search for and locate participants, they are ill prepared to understand the context; instead, they project the context in which they relate to the individual offline onto the individual in this new online space. For teens, this has resulted in expulsions, suspensions, probations, and being grounded.[52] In Pennsylvania, a student's parody of his principal was not read as such when the principal found this profile on MySpace; the student was removed from school and lawsuits are still pending.[53] Of course, not every misreading results in the punishment of youth. Consider the story of Allen and his daughter Sabrina. Because Sabrina thinks her dad is cool, she invited him to join her on MySpace. Upon logging in, Allen was startled to see that her profile included a quiz entitled "What kind of drug are you?," to which she had responded "cocaine." Confused and horrified, Allen approached his daughter for an explanation. She laughed and explained, "it's just one of those quizzes that tells you about your personality . . . but you can kinda get it to say what you want." She explained that she did not want to be represented by marijuana because the kids who smoked pot were lame. She also thought that acid and mushrooms were stupid because she was not a hippie. She figured that cocaine made sense because she heard that people did work on it and, "besides Dad, your generation did a lot of coke and you came out OK." This was not the explanation that Allen expected.

Teens are not necessarily well prepared to navigate complex social worlds with invisible audiences, but neither are adults. While Allen was able to talk with his daughter about other possible interpretations of her choice in presentation, he recognized that her profile was not meant for such audiences. How could he teach her how to engage in identity presentation while navigating multiple audiences? While MySpace is public, it is unlike other publics that adults commonly face. This presents a generational divide that is further complicated by adults' misreadings of youth participation in new media.[54]

But Why There? The power that adults hold over youth explains more than just complications in identity performance; it is the root of why teenagers are on MySpace in the first place. In the United States, the lives of youth—and particularly high school teenagers—are highly structured. Compulsory high school requires many students to be in class from morning to midafternoon; and many are also required to participate in after-school activities, team sports, and work into the evening. It is difficult to measure whether today's high school teens have more or less free time than previous generations, but the increased prevalence of single working parent and dual-working parent households implies that there are either more latchkey kids or more after-school programs watching these kids.[55] Given the overwhelming culture of fear and the cultural disdain for latchkey practices, it is likely that teens are spending more time in programs than on their own. Meanwhile, at home in the evenings, many are expected to do homework or spend time with the family. While the home has been considered a private sphere where individuals can regulate their own behavior, this is an adult-centric narrative. For many teens, home is a highly regulated space with rules and norms that are strictly controlled by adults.

Regardless of whether teens in the United States have the time to engage in public life, there are huge structural and social barriers to their doing so. First, there is an issue of mobility. While public transit exists in some urban regions, most of the United States lacks adequate transportation options for those who are unable to drive; given the suburbanization of the United States, teens are more likely to live in a region without public transit than one with public transit. There is a minimum age for drivers in every state, although it varies from sixteen to eighteen. A license is only one part of the problem; having access to a car is an entirely separate barrier to mobility. This means that, for many teens, even if they want to go somewhere they are often unable to do so.

American society has a very peculiar relationship to teenagers—and children in general. They are simultaneously idealized and demonized; adults fear them but they also seek to protect them.[56] On one hand, there has been a rapid rise in curfew legislation to curb teen violence[57] and loitering laws are used to bar teens from hanging out on street corners, in parking lots, or other outdoor meeting places for fear of the trouble they might cause. On the other hand, parents are restricting their youth from hanging out in public spaces for fear of predators, drug dealers, and gangs. Likewise, while adults spend countless hours socializing over alcohol, minors are not only restricted from drinking but also from socializing in many venues where alcohol is served.

Moral entrepreneurs have learned that "invoking fears about children provides a powerful means of commanding public attention and support."[58] This ongoing culture of fear typically overstates the actual dangers and obfuscates real risks in the process.[59] Yet, the end result of this is that youth have very little access to public spaces. The spaces they can hang out in are heavily controlled and/or under surveillance:

> My [guardian] is really strict so if I get to go anywhere, it's a big miracle. So I talk to people on MySpace . . . I know she means well, I know she doesn't want me to mess up. But sometimes you need to mess up to figure out that you're doing it wrong. You need mistakes to know where you're going. You need to figure things out for yourself. —Traviesa, 15

Many adults believe that these restrictions are necessary to prevent problematic behaviors or to protect children from the risks of society. Whether or not that view is valid, restrictions on access to public life make it difficult for young people to be socialized into society at large. While social interaction can and does take place in private environments, the challenges of doing so in public life are part of what help youth grow. Making mistakes and testing limits are fundamental parts of this. Yet, there is a pervading attitude that teens must be protected from their mistakes.

At the beginning of this chapter, I explained that I would use the term teenagers to refer to youth of high school age living at home. In doing so, I glossed over how problematic any definition of youth or teenager is.[60] Yet, it is precisely the construction of teenager/youth in opposition to adult that creates the power dynamic upon which most of the challenges stated earlier hinge. The term teenager did not exist a century ago. It was most likely coined in the 1920s or 1930s, and it first appeared in print as a marketing term in 1941.[61] The notion of a young adult did exist and it primarily referenced young people who were entering the workforce. By about fourteen, most young people began laboring outside the home; they continued to live with their parents and their income helped the family pay its costs. The workforce was a critical site of socialization into adulthood for young people; very few went to high school or college. This changed in the United States during the Great Depression. With too few jobs and too many adults needing employment, the labor movement joined social reformers who had been urging the government to require high school attendance for young people. While social reformers believed that young people were not mature enough to be entering the workforce, the labor movement was more interested in keeping young adults out of the work force (and off the streets). Together, they were able to convince Congress to pass compulsory education and child labor laws.

While the appropriateness of this move can be debated, its effect was clear: young people were neatly segregated from adults in all aspects of their lives. Through funding structures, schools were encouraged to consolidate into large institutions that could support at least 100 students per year and provide activities and sports that kept youth from mixing with adult laborers in leisure as well as work. The school reform that took place during this era created the iconic American high school imagery that Hollywood popularized around the world during the second half of the twentieth century. Idealists viewed high school as a place where youth could mature both intellectually and socially, but age segregation meant that young people were being socialized into a society that did not include adults. While peer socialization is obviously valuable and important, it is fundamentally different from being socialized into adult society by adults themselves; generations emerge and norms change rapidly per generation. By segregating people by age, a true dichotomy between adult and teen emerged.

The development of an age-segregated group also created a target demographic for marketers. Following World War II, organizations and corporations began explicitly targeting teens directly, appealing to the tastes and values generated in teen culture. Spaces like dance halls, roller rinks, bowling alleys, and activity centers began offering times for teens to socialize with other teens. (These spaces, once vibrant in the United States, are virtually extinct now.) Businesses welcomed middle- and upper-class teens with open arms because of their perceived consumer power. Products began to be designed explicitly for teens. This consumer process similarly reinforced separate youth and adult publics.

By late-twentieth century, shopping malls became the primary "public" space for youth socialization.[62] While shopping malls once welcomed teens, now they are primarily seen as a nuisance. Shopkeepers are wary of teens because of shoplifting and they are often ejected for loitering. While the public spaces built around consumerism have become increasingly hostile to teenagers, they still rabidly market to them. In other words, teens are still a marketable demographic for products, even if there is little interest in providing services for them.

This dynamic, while overly simplified for brevity's sake, does not properly convey the differences across different social groups within the American society. It is primarily the story of white, middle class, suburban teens. Poor teens and people of color were never given access to these types of spaces in the first place. That said, commercialism has moved on to coopt the spaces that these groups do traverse. The corporatization and glorification/demonization of hip-hop and "the 'hood" is one example of this.[63] As we move toward a more global market, multinational corporations are expanding on their desire to target niche groups of teens, simultaneously supporting the attitude that teens are both angels and demons.

Collectively, four critical forces[64]—society, market, law, and architecture—have constructed an age-segregated teen culture that is deeply consumerist but lacks meaningful agency. The contradictions run deep—we sell sex to teens but prohibit them from having it; we tell teens to grow up but restrict them from the vices and freedoms of adult society.[65] Teenagers have navigated and challenged this hypocrisy over decades. Changes in society, market, and law have shifted the perception and treatment of youth. What emerged with the Internet was a radical shift in architecture; it decentralized publics.

While the jury is still out on whether or not the Internet is democratizing, online access provides a whole new social realm for youth. Earlier mediated communication devices—landline, pager, mobile—allowed friends to connect with friends even when located in adult-regulated physical spaces. What is unique about the Internet is that it allows teens to participate in unregulated publics while located in adult-regulated physical spaces such as homes and schools. Of course, this is precisely what makes it controversial. Parents are seeking to regulate teens' behavior in this new space; and this, in turn, is motivating teens to hide.

A few of my friends won't even dare to tell their parents about their MySpace cause they know they'll be grounded forever. I know two kids who got banned from it but they secretly got back on. —Ella, 15

Yet, putting aside the question of risk, what teens are doing with this networked public is akin to what they have done in every other type of public they have access to: they hang out, jockey for social status, work through how to present themselves, and take risks that will help them to assess the boundaries of the social world. They do so because they seek access to adult society. Their participation is deeply rooted in their desire to engage publicly, for many of the reasons we have discussed earlier. By prohibiting teens from engaging in networked publics, we create a participation divide,[66] both between adults and teens and between teens who have access and those who do not.

Conclusion

Publics play a crucial role in the development of individuals for, as Nancy Fraser explains, "they are arenas for the formation and enactment of social identities."[67] By interacting with unfamiliar others, teenagers are socialized into society. Without publics, there is no coherent society. Publics are where norms are set and reinforced, where common ground is formed. Learning society's rules requires trial and error, validation and admonishment; it is knowledge that teenagers learn through action, not theory. Society's norms and rules only provide the collectively imagined boundaries. Teenagers are also tasked with deciding how they want to fit into the structures that society provides. Their social identity is partially defined by themselves and partially defined by others. Learning through impression management is key to developing a social identity. Teenagers must determine where they want to be situated within the social world they see, and then attempt to garner the reactions to their performances that match their vision. This is a lifelong process, but one that must be supported at every step.

In today's society, there is a push toward privacy. It is assumed that people are public individuals who deserve the right to privacy rather than the other way around. With an elevated and idealized view of privacy, we often forget the reasons that enslaved peoples desperately wished for access to public life. By allowing us to have a collective experience with people who are both like and unlike us, public life validates the reality that we are experiencing. We are doing our youth a disservice if we believe that we can protect them from the world by limiting their access to public life. They must enter that arena, make mistakes, and learn from them. Our role as adults is not to be their policemen, but to be their guides.

Of course, as Hannah Arendt wrote long before the Internet, "everything that appears in public can be seen and heard by everybody and has the widest possible publicity."[68] What has changed with the emergence of new tools for mediating sociality is the scale and persistence of possible publicity. For most people in history, public life was not documented and distributed for the judgment of others who were not present. Only aristocrats and celebrities faced that type of public because structural and social forces strongly limited the "widest possible publicity." Not everything could be documented and spreading information was challenging. Only the lives of the rich and famous were deemed important enough to share.

The Internet has irrevocably changed this. Teens today face a public life with the possibility of unimaginably wide publicity. The fundamental properties of networked publics—persistence, searchability, replicability, and invisible audiences—are unfamiliar to the adults that are guiding them through social life. It is not accidental that teens live in a culture infatuated with celebrity[69]—the "reality" presented by reality TV and the highly publicized dramas (such as that between socialites Paris Hilton and Nicole Richie) portray a magnified (and idealized) version of the networked publics that teens are experiencing, complete with surveillance and misinterpretation. The experiences that teens are facing in the publics that they encounter appear more similar to the celebrity idea of public life than to the ones their parents face.

It is not as though celebrities or teenagers wish for every conversation to be publicly available to everyone across all time and space, but mediated publics take the simplest public expressions and make them hyperpublic. Few adults could imagine every conversation they have sitting in the park or drinking tea in a café being available for such hyperpublic consumption, yet this is what technology enables; there is an ethos that if it is possible to access a public expression, one should have the right to do so.

While we can talk about changes that are taking place, the long-term implications of being socialized into a culture rooted in networked publics are unknown. Perhaps today's youth will be far better equipped to handle gossip as adults. Perhaps not. What we do know is that today's teens live in a society whose public life is changing rapidly. Teens need access to these publics—both mediated and unmediated—to mature, but their access is regularly restricted. Yet, this technology and networked publics are not going away. As a society, we need to figure out how to educate teens to navigate social structures that are quite unfamiliar to us because they will be faced with these publics as adults, even if we try to limit their access now. Social network sites have complicated our lives because they have made this rapid shift in public life very visible. Perhaps instead of trying to stop them or regulate usage, we should learn from what teens are experiencing. They are learning to navigate networked publics; it is in our better interest to figure out how to help them.

Notes

1. Quote posted by her mother Kathy Sierra: http://headrush.typepad.com/creating_passionate_users/2006/03/ultrafast_relea.html (accessed January 9, 2007).

2. Part of a conversation from December 2004 that motivated Parry Aftab (Executive Director of Wired Safety) to help teens use social network sites safely; story shared by one of her "Teen Angels" (http://www.teenangels.com).

3. Clifford Geertz, *The Interpretation of Cultures* (New York: Basic Books, 1973).

4. Thomas Hine, *The Rise and Fall of the American Teenager* (New York: Bard, 1999).

5. Amanda Lenhart, Mary Madden, and Paul Hitlin, Teens and Parents Survey, *PEW Internet and American Life Project* (October–November 2004).

6. Amanda Lenhart, Social Networking Websites and Teens: An Overview, *PEW Internet and American Life Project* (7 January 2007).

7. In conducting phone interviews, PEW first speaks with the parent and then the child. It is quite likely that the child's answers are influenced by the presence of their parents. With social network sites, the overwhelming disapproval of most parents suggests that teens are more likely to say "no" if affected by the presence of their parents. Furthermore, this does not account for the number of teens who have had profiles made for them and my qualitative experience has shown that teens who formerly had a profile

will often say "no" when asked if they ever created a profile. That said, PEW is unlikely to be off by more than 10 percent.

8. In a private message, Mary Gray (Indiana University) shared that her research in Kentucky shows that rural teens have no access to MySpace because they access the Internet at schools and libraries, where MySpace is banned.

9. There is nothing to confirm that the person being represented is the person behind the profile. Teens are most notorious for maliciously creating fraudulent profiles to bully the represented, but it is equally common for teens to create profiles for their friends. Because one's friends are made visible on one's profile, teens complain that their profile is ruined if their best friend does not have a profile that can be listed as a Friend on the site.

10. Amanda Lenhart, Social Networking Websites and Teens, 2007.

11. danah boyd (in press), None of This Is Real, in *Structures of Digital Participation*, ed. Joe Karaganis. Social Science Research Council, in press.

12. danah boyd, Friendster and Publicly Articulated Social Networks, *Proceedings of Conference on Human Factors and Computing Systems (CHI 2004)* (Vienna: ACM, 2004).

13. Sarah Thornton, *Club Cultures: Music, Media, and Subcultural Capital* (Middletown, CT: Wesleyan University Press, 1996).

14. See Rebekah Willett in this volume.

15. There is no published documentation of the caste segmentation in Orkut although there is a discussion about the issue on the "I, Me, and Media" blog (http://differentstrokes.blogspot.com/2006/09/caste-communities-on-orkut.html), and I was able to confirm this dynamic with Orkut's product manager. (Accessed January 10, 2007).

16. Defining a category through articulated boundaries is problematic (see George Lakoff, *Women, Fire, and Dangerous Things* [Chicago: University of Chicago Press, 1987]). My effort to do so is to distinguish what is unique to this new style of site from previous types of social software. Although this definition brings some clarity, newer social software is beginning to implement these features into sites that are predominantly about video sharing (YouTube), photo sharing (Flickr), music tastes (Last.FM), etc. The social network sites that I discuss here are first and foremost about the friends' network, while these newer sites are primarily about media sharing or discovery.

17. For legibility, when I am referring to the Friends feature on MySpace, I capitalize the term. When I am referring to people that individuals would normally talk about as their friends, I do not.

18. For a more detailed analysis on the Friending process, see danah boyd, Friends, Friendsters, and MySpace Top 8: Writing Community Into Being on Social Network Sites, *First Monday* 11, no. 12 (2006). http://www.firstmonday.org/issues/issue11_12/boyd/ (accessed January 10, 2007).

19. danah boyd and Jeffrey Heer, Profiles as Conversation: Networked Identity Performance on Friendster, in *Proceedings of the Hawai'i International Conference on System Sciences (HICSS-39), Persistent Conversation Track* (Kauai, HI: IEEE Computer Society, January 4–7, 2006).

20. Most social network sites support private messaging so that people can contact other members directly. Some sites support blogging and posting of videos. MySpace and Friendster have a bulletin feature where participants can post messages that all of their Friends can read. Other features that appear on social network sites include instant messaging, teacher ratings, message boards, groups, and classified ads. Exactly how these features are implemented differs by site.

21. For a primer on some of the key debates concerning "public" and "public sphere," see Craig Calhoun, *Habermas and the Public Sphere* (Cambridge, MA: MIT Press, 1992).

22. Sonia Livingstone, "Introduction" and "On the Relation Between Audiences and Publics," in *Audiences and Publics: When Cultural Engagement Matters for the Public Sphere*, ed. Sonia Livingstone, 9–14 (Bristol, UK: Intellect, 2005).

23. Op. cit.

24. Michael Warner, The Mass Public and the Mass Subject, in *Habermas and the Public Sphere*, ed. Craig Calhoun (Cambridge, MA: MIT Press, 1992), 377–401.

25. Mizuko Ito (in press), Introduction, in *Networked Publics* (Cambridge, MA: MIT Press).

26. Nicholas Negroponte, *Being Digital* (New York: Vintage, 1996).

27. The power of technology to support *always-on intimate communities* is articulated in Mizuko Ito, Daisuke Okabe, and Misa Matsuda, *Personal, Portable, Pedestrian: Mobile Phones in Japanese Life* (Cambridge, MA: MIT Press, 2005).

28. While MySpace recognized this hole within hours, they did not close the loophole nor did they begin supporting the practice. They allowed it to exist as an underground copy/paste culture. They have banned the specific code that puts the site and participants at risk. For example, they block Javascript to make it harder for scammers to prey on members.

29. While the original copy/paste sites were created by teenagers, it is not clear who runs the thousands of code sites currently operating. Most make money off of advertising, so it is likely to be a business venture. Scammers looking to exploit participants' willingness to copy/paste anything probably run some as well.

30. "Pimp out" is a slang term that basically means "make cool" (by teen standards). Pimped out profiles usually involve heavy modifications to the templates and numerous multimedia components. What looks pimped out to a teen is typically viewed as horrifyingly chaotic to adults. Technologists complain that the design resembles that of early homepages with blink tags and random colors. The best way that I've found to describe what these profiles look like is a highly decorated teenage bedroom wall or locker.

31. Dan Perkel, Copy and Paste Literacy: Literacy Practices in the Production of a MySpace Profile—An Overview, in *Proceedings of Informal Learning and Digital Media: Constructions, Contexts, Consequences* (Denmark, September 21–23, 2006).

32. Fred Davis, *Fashion, Culture and Identity* (Chicago: University of Chicago Press, 1992).

33. Erving Goffman, *The Presentation of Self in Everyday Life* (Edinburgh: University of Edinburgh, 1956).

34. Erving Goffman, *Behavior in Public Places* (New York: The Free Press, 1963).

35. Jean Briggs, *Inuit Morality Play: The Emotional Education of a Three-Year-Old* (New Haven, CT: Yale University Press, 1999).

36. Jenny Sundén, *Material Virtualities* (New York: Peter Lang Publishing, 2003).

37. See David Buckingham's introduction to this volume for a greater discussion of this.

38. Joshua Berman and Amy Bruckman, The Turing Game: Exploring Identity in an Online Environment, *Convergence* 7, no. 3 (2001): 83–102.

39. Judith Donath, Identity and Deception in the Virtual Community, *Communities in Cyberspace*, eds. Marc Smith and Peter Kollock (London: Routledge, 1999).

40. Judith Donath and danah boyd, Public Displays of Connection, *BT Technology Journal* 22, no. 4 (October 2004): 71–82.

41. Like "guilt by association," this phrase is logically fallible, but people still judge others based on those around them (see Irving David Shapiro, "Fallacies of Logic: Argumentation Cons," *ETC.: A Review of General Semantics* 33, no. 3 [Fall 1996]: 251–265).

42. See David Buckingham's Introduction to this volume, 2007.

43. Benedict Anderson coined the term "imagined community" to discuss nationality. In talking about "imagined audiences," I am drawing on his broader point about how communities can be socially constructed and imagined by those who see themselves as members (Benedict Anderson, *Imagined Communities* [New York: Verso, 1991]).

44. To follow this thread, see Susannah Stern's chapter in this volume.

45. This riff on Andy Warhol's infamous comment has circulated the web; I am not sure where to properly locate its origin.

46. Bly Lauritano-Werner, 2006. Reading My LiveJournal. Youth Public Radio. http://youthradio.org/society/npr060628_onlinejournal.shtml (accessed June 28, 2007).

47. Kevin Farnham and Dale Farnham, *MySpace Safety: 51 Tips for Teens and Parents* (Pomfret, CT: How-To Primers, 2006).

48. Private profiles in MySpace are visible to Friends only. When strangers visit their page, they are shown the primary photo, name, location, age, and a saying. They must become Friends with that person to see the rest of the content.

49. Joshua Meyrowitz, *No Sense of Place* (New York: Oxford, 1985).

50. Penelope Eckert, *Jocks & Burnouts: Social Categories and Identity in the High School* (New York: Teacher College Press, 1989).

51. Murray Milner Jr., *Freaks, Geeks, and Cool Kids: American Teenagers, Schools, and the Culture of Consumption* (New York: Routledge, 2004).

52. Alex Koppelman, 2006. MySpace or OurSpace? *Salon.* http://www.salon.com/mwt/feature/2006/06/08/my_space/ (accessed June 8, 2007).

53. Kevin Poulson, 2006. Scenes from the MySpace Backlash, *Wired News,* February 27, 2006. http://www.wired.com/news/politics/1,70254-0.html (accessed January 10, 2007).

54. To follow this thread, see Susan Herring's chapter in this volume.

55. Julia Overturf Johnson, Robert Kominski, Kristin Smith, and Paul Tillman, Changes in the Lives of U.S. Children 1990–2000. *Working Paper No 78, United States Census Bureau* (November 2005).

56. Joe Austin and Michael Nevin Willard, Introduction: Angels of History, Demons of Culture, *Generations of Youth: Youth Cultures and History in Twentieth-Century America*, eds. Joe Austin and Michael Nevin Willard (New York: New York University Press, 1998), 1–20.

57. William Ruefle and Kenneth Reynolds, Curfew and Delinquency in Major American Cities, *Crime and Delinquency* 41 (1995): 347–363.

58. David Buckingham, *After the Death of Childhood* (Oxford: Polity, 2000), 11.

59. Barry Glassner, *The Culture of Fear: Why Americans Are Afraid of the Wrong Things* (New York: Basic Books, 2000).

60. See David Buckingham's introduction in this volume.

61. The history in this paragraph is well documented and cited in Thomas Hine, *The Rise and Fall of the American Teenager*, 1999.

62. Margaret Crawford, The World in a Shopping Mall, *Variations on a Theme Park: The New American City and the End of Public Space*, ed. Michael Sorkin (New York: Hill and Wang, 1992), 3–30.

63. Murray Forman, *The 'Hood Comes First: Race, Space, and Place in Rap and Hip-Hop* (Middletown, CT: Wesleyan University Press, 2002).

64. Lawrence Lessig, *Code and Other Laws of Cyberspace* (New York: Basic Books, 1999).

65. The contradictions and challenges of youth as a social construct are well articulated in David Buckingham, *After the Death of Childhood*, 2000.

66. Henry Jenkins, Confronting the Challenges of Participatory Culture: Media Education for the 21st Century, White Paper for MacArthur Foundation, 2006.

67. Nancy Fraser, Rethinking the Public Sphere: A Contribution to the Critique of Actually Existing Democracy, *Habermas and the Public Sphere*, ed. Craig Calhoun (Cambridge, MA: MIT Press, 1992), 125.

68. Hannah Arendt, *The Human Condition* (Chicago: University of Chicago Press, 1958), 50.

69. Jake Halpern, *Fame Junkies: The Hidden Truths Behind America's Favorite Addiction* (Boston: Houghton Mifflin, 2007).

Mobile Identity: Youth, Identity, and Mobile Communication Media

Gitte Stald

IT University of Copenhagen, Department of Innovative Communication

Parents usually don't know how important a tool the mobile has become in young people's lives. They only think about the communicative function, not the social meaning.[1]
(sixteen-year-old girl)

The girl who is quoted above expresses an immediate understanding of the mobile phone's dual, but interdependent qualities for young people. One quality is the communicative function, which is facilitated by the technological device: it is about the mobile as a tool and a channel for the exchange of information. The other quality is the social meaning, which develops from the communication. Rich Ling describes the mobile phone as being doubly articulated, that is, it is a physical device but it is also a medium through which we communicate and through which we maintain social contact.[2] In short, the meaning of the mobile goes beyond its practical function. The quote also indicates the young girl's perception of the mobile as holding a specific meaning for young people as compared to adults: that is, the value of the mobile depends on contextual uses and experiences.

The focus of this article is on the meaning of the mobile in young people's lives, specifically in relation to questions of identity. In the crossover between this volume's three key themes—youth, learning, and identity—other issues might well have been included, for example the use of mobile platforms in education and formal learning,[3] or organized projects on how to explore and exploit mobile digital platforms for creative and innovative purposes. My aim, however, is to take a closer look at the mundane and everyday uses of this medium by young people in relation to identity and learning. Because of the always there, always on status of the mobile and the pace of exchange of information, and because the mobile is the key personal communication device for so many young people, it becomes important in establishing social norms and rules and in testing one's own position in relation to the peer group.

My title, "Mobile Identity," has a double meaning. On the one hand, supported by the subtitle, it includes the idea that young people's identity is influenced by their use of media, in particular personal communication media such as the mobile phone. On the other hand, it also implies a view of adolescent identity as mobile, changing and developing moment by moment and over time, as very sensitive to changes in the relations between friends and families, and to the emotional and intellectual challenges experienced and mediated through the use of the mobile phone (among other factors). The notion of mobile identity suggests that identity is fluid and that adolescents are constantly negotiating who they are, how they are that identity, and with whom they are that identity. The mobile phone facilitates this mobility of identity, as it is ubiquitous in youth cultural contexts as a medium for constant updating, coordination, information access, and documentation. At the same time, the mobile is an important medium for social networking, the enhancing of groups and group identity, and for the exchange between friends which is needed in the reflexive process of identity construction. The mobile has become the ideal tool to deal with the pace of information exchange, the management of countless loose, close or intimate relations, the coordination of ever-changing daily activities,[4] and the insecurity of everyday life. Hence the mobile becomes a learning tool for dealing with living conditions in modern society for young people, while at the same time it adds to the conditions they are trying to deal with.

This chapter addresses four broad themes. The first theme is *availability*—the fact that the mobile is always on, which makes the users always available with no or few communication- and information-free moments. The second theme is the experience of *presence* during mobile communication, that is, the experience of social presence in public space being invaded by ongoing mobile communication. The third theme is the importance of the mobile as a *personal log* for activities, networks, and the documentation of experiences, a role that has implications both for relations between the individual and the group and for emotional experience. These discussions lead to analysis of the mobile as a tool for *learning social norms*. Before I proceed with the discussion of these themes, however, I offer a short discussion of the concept of mobile media and a broader account of the role of the mobile phone in the context of contemporary youth culture.

The main empirical basis for my analysis is quantitative and qualitative findings from a series of studies of fifteen- to twenty-four-year-old Danes and their mobile phone use.[5] These studies, which were conducted in 2004 and 2006, included questionnaire surveys, individual interviews, observations, and (in one case) high school essays on "My Mobile and Me." As even younger groups of children have their own mobiles, the fifteen- to twenty-four-year-olds cannot necessarily be seen as representative of young Danish mobile phone users in general. However, other studies and surveys[6] indicate that the general findings from these studies also reflect some of the main uses and meanings of younger children's mobile phone use, as well as experiences in other national and cultural settings.

The Mobile Phone and Mobility

The most obvious characteristic of the mobile phone is precisely that it is mobile, that it can be transported. Compared to the first transportable phones, which were huge machines, then very heavy telephones, both built into cars, and then heavy but portable telephones,[7] mobile phones today are so small, flat and light that they can fit into a pocket and effectively disappear in the hand and at the ear. Especially when connected with a light headset, the mobile seems to be part of the user's body—which may remind the reader of McLuhan's discussions of media as the "extensions of man," but which also points to the fact that it is so easy to take the mobile everywhere and to have it near and ready to hand that the user hardly notices it, until it isn't there, when it doesn't alert the user with a new message or call.

But what are the specific potentials of mobiles? How are they different from landline phones? And how does the use of mobiles differ from PCs and traditional Internet? The German sociologist Hans Geser states that "Seen in this very broad evolutionary perspective, the significance of the mobile phone lies in empowering people to engage in communication, which is at the same time free from the constraints of physical proximity and spatial immobility."[8] This general and yet simple notion is expanded by Rich Ling, who describes the social changes resulting from the adoption of the mobile in everyday life: "The mobile telephone shifts ideas about where and when we can travel, how we organize our daily life, what constitutes public talk, and how we keep track of our social world. In addition, our use, or refusal to use, says something about us as individuals."[9] But even this is not quite enough to describe the duality of function and meaning of the mobile. Within a decade, the typical mobile available on the popular market has developed from being a portable telephone to being a handheld computer with enough data and speed capacity to facilitate mobile Internet access, MP3 music, photography, video, graphically advanced games, and tools such as a calculator, diary, notebook, alarm, clock, GPS, and more. These multiple functions change the role of the mobile from being only a medium for interpersonal communication to incorporate multiple forms of information exchange at a user level as well as at a technological level: peer (mobile) to peer (mobile/Internet/Messenger), citizen to institution and vice versa, mobile to PC/Internet and vice versa, employer to workplace and vice versa. These expanded technological potentials facilitate a much more extensive range of uses and hence of meanings. However, the mobile largely remains a "personal, portable, and pedestrian"[10] medium that is primarily used for interpersonal communication via calls or text messages.

Mobility and Young People

Young people in many parts of the world are on the move in their local context, and some are on the move in a global context when they travel. They are on the move within and between physical locations but also in virtual spaces, in well-known (as well as foreign) areas. They are processing, digesting, and exchanging information, deliberating what to do, what to choose, what to think. The portability of the mobile phone makes it possible for the user to access and exchange information independent of place, of physical location, while being on the move. We are mobile, the device is mobile with us, but above all information is mobile, meaning that it is available independent of time and space, accessible from wherever you are with your mobile transmitter and receiver.

However, the Swedish scholar Alexandra Weilenmann states that even if we use the mobile to carry our social and personal life with us as we move, mobile technologies have not made people independent of place. According to her, "place" and "the local" are still important in the mobile world[11] because we are constantly negotiating our mutual understanding of the situation in which we find ourselves. We usually regard mobile technology as being private and personal; but the act of sharing mobile content and communication in public spaces and in shared social situations, voluntarily or not, must be included in our understanding of the nature of the mobile and of mobility. This shall be explored further in the following sections of this chapter.

In the same way, we should consider the meaning of "mobile" as going beyond movement in physical space. The additional meaning of "mobility" is about being ready for change, ready to go in new directions. One of the sixteen-year-old participants who wrote high school essays about *My Mobile and Me* as part of our research combines these two levels of understanding. She had been considering the ontological meaning of "mobile" and looked it up in her mother's dictionary (which was published in 1968). She found that it said: "Movable, agile, able to be moved or transported easily and fast; ready to march, ready for battle." She was somewhat surprised by the last two translations of "mobile," and concluded that in fact that is exactly what she is with her mobile at hand: "I am easily accessed and I am movable; I am agile and transport myself easily and quite fast; I am always ready to receive a message or a call; but best of all I am ready to march, ready for battle! So, if 'mobile' means the same today as it did in 1968, then I am mobile, mobile I am." This girl interprets mobile as more than a matter of physical movement between locations, she thinks of herself as physically on the move, supported by her mobile, but at the same time she applies the military terminology to her own situation and her interest in moving forward in life and battling for herself in more than physical terms. The mobile facilitates her social mobility and readiness to communicate. Exchange between friends is an important part of the development of identity, because it supports the testing of cultural, social, and individual codes and makes ongoing, mutual reciprocity possible. In this context, being movable, agile and ready to march means being ready to move as a person, too.

The Mobile Phone in Contemporary Youth Culture

I think it is nice.[12] It is such an easy way to communicate. "They" made it so easy for us. (Dea, seventeen-year-old-girl)

The question is if it has deprived us of the possibility of being "offline"? (Boy, sixteen years old)

There have been numerous studies of mobile phone users, and adolescent users in particular. As Taylor and Harper point out, these studies almost all deal with the same issues and problems and reach the same conclusions: "With mobile devices, we are told, we will be always available to those who love us or need us; we will always be capable of accessing the information we need and desire whether it be work related or to do with our personal affairs; we will be able to work wherever we want since information will be accessible anywhere; and though we may be apart from colleagues and friends, the mobile network will keep us in touch."[13] There are, as Taylor and Harper point out, many other interesting aspects of mobile phone use, such as the use of the mobile in face-to-face settings, for example, "giving" each other photos and text messages from the personal mobile phone. (See also Weber's and Mitchell's discussion of the meaning of photo sharing in their chapter in this volume.) Research also raises questions about risk and trust, and about the use of the mobile as a new tool for citizenship. When it comes to young people in particular, however, there is an important difference in the fact that young users unanimously discuss the importance and meaning of the mobile in a social context. Within the time that has passed since the mobile phone first became visible in Danish youth cultures, it has developed from being a rare and exciting object for the privileged few to becoming one of the most important popular and obvious tools for communication, information, and entertainment. As the quotes from young users shall demonstrate, the mobile is a ubiquitous, pervasive communication device which young people find it difficult to be without, whether they like it or hate it, or feel something in between.

Adolescents in Denmark, who are generally very well equipped with digital media such as PCs and Internet, DVD players, MP3–players, and mobile phones,[14] cannot imagine not being able to get in touch with friends and family around the clock, or not being able to choose between multiple entertainment programs, games, music recordings, and news programs on the platform which best suits their needs at that moment.[15] Stories about the media biographies of their parents seem to be referring to a different era. Some of the oldest informants in our research do remember when they had only landline telephones, but just like the younger informants they cannot imagine not having their mobiles, not being constantly in contact, contactable, and informed. Seventeen-year-old Thorbjørn says: "The mobile makes everyday life a little easier I think. Well, they managed all right before the mobile but it kind of belongs to the times we live in. It is as if you can hardly walk out into everyday life without your mobile." "They" refers to everyone who, unlike Thorbjørn and people younger than him, has not grown up with the mobile but has had to find other channels for communication and personal networking, for coordinating everyday life, and for the exchange of emotional, intimate content.[16] (See also Susannah Stern's chapter in this volume for a discussion of the meaning of intimacy in exchanges on personal websites.)

The Importance of The Mobile

Thorbjørn's phrase "walk out into everyday life" is a typical yet illuminating example of young people's perception of the uses of media in everyday life. It has a double meaning: you need to bring your mobile when you leave home and your PC/Messenger, and in order to manage life in general in this historical era, the mobile is indispensable or at least close to it.

Our survey[17] showed that seven out of ten young people rated the importance of the mobile between eight and ten on a scale from zero to ten. Only around 4 percent did not find the mobile very important, giving it a rating of three or below. The mobile seemed to be rated as more important among the older than among the younger informants. The oldest have moved away from home and very few have a landline telephone, which makes the mobile and the Internet the only available channels for fast communication. Another explanation we found from interviews is that the mobile becomes increasingly important for coordination not just of social relationships, but also of work/study-related appointments, communication with institutions (bank, library, etc.) and as the lifeline to family and lovers. (Shelley Goldman et al. in their chapter include examples of the use of mobiles for coordination of personal activities as well as political meetings.) Another interesting finding is that more female than male users rate the mobile at ten, although the differences are small. One vivid example of how important the mobile is considered to be in modern society comes from a sixteen-year-old high school boy, who claimed that he would feel half-naked without it—you need to have your mobile with you, just like you need to wear pants.

These statistics give us an impression of the importance of the mobile among young Danes, but they obviously don't reveal what lies behind the numbers. Why is it considered important or why is it not? And why do many of the young users evaluate the mobile as very important, yet at the same time express concerns about the impact of this? We do know, of course, from previous research what the main uses and meanings of the mobile are. The interviews, however, put the attitudes toward the importance of the mobile into young people's own words, albeit more or less enthusiastically expressed. The following quote from twenty-two-year-old Freja is brief, but clearly demonstrates why the mobile is important to so many: "I can't believe how much there is in such a small thing like this, right. If I throw this away it is simply the contact to everything—all and everyone—I am throwing away. It is damned scary."

It seems that there are two main arguments for the importance of the mobile. First, there is its immediate and ubiquitous use for social coordination and updating. Secondly, and related to this, the mobile—combined in some cases with the laptop—is a personal medium which liberates the user from the constraints of physical proximity and spatial immobility. Twenty-year-old Danny says: "It is incredibly good to be mobile—when I put my mobile in my pocket and my laptop under my arm I have my office, my life, my work and my education with me—I carry everything I need with me, and the flexibility of that is totally fantastic." Danny has started his own small firm and mobility and flexibility are the key words to him because he needs to be available not only socially, but also professionally, and in relation to his continuing education. Danny's story is somewhat extreme compared to those of average young mobile users in Denmark. Even so, he is a relevant example of a young person whose self-identity is closely related to his professional activity and the appearance he gives of the young professional who is always on the move. His use of various digital communication and information media in combination reflects the state of flux that exists between different spheres of modern life, between working time and leisure time, between private space and public space, and between physical and virtual grounding that is independent of time and space.

Use and Adaptation

The common mobile is a kind of Swiss Army knife, which holds a number of useful tools—even if people almost always tend to use the same ones. The use of the mobile can be seen as either practical (instrumental) or related to content (expressive).[18] Aspects of the meaning of content are discussed in some of the following sections: my immediate focus here is on the range of different uses.

Young Danes use the mobile mainly for communication—it is primarily still a telephone with text messaging and additional services. However, the practical facilities such as the alarm clock, notebook, and diary are also used by many. Internet, MMS, games, and music/radio are the least-used services, even if increasing numbers of adolescents have advanced mobiles with the software and subscriptions that facilitate these more advanced uses. The usual arguments for not using one of these services are that the price is too high and the quality too low, but for example when it comes to radio and music (MP3) this is no longer the case, and we do see a significant increase in interest in these uses between our 2004 and 2006 surveys. The young users like to take photos with their mobiles, but rather than sending them, they show them to one another on the physical devices or save them on their computer via infrared or Bluetooth and share them via email, Messenger or chat rooms. Games and the mobile Internet are not popular possibilities among the young people we studied—the most common argument being that the mobile phone user has a much better computer a few minutes away at home, at work, at school or college. In this context the mobile must be seen as one of a broader ensemble of media.[19]

Another explanation for the generally mundane and nonadvanced uses of mobile technologies is the low levels of technological literacy, which themselves reflect low levels of interest in the potential of mobile technologies and software. Many do think that the advanced services would be smart, fun, and helpful, but they haven't bothered to check out how to set them up and use them. Due to their potential access to other kinds of digital media, the inclination to explore these potential uses and make them work is not strong enough. Young people may also prefer a larger screen, a better keyboard, and faster connection speeds than the mobile provides at present. Some find it too complicated to set up the software and to use the advanced services. However, many of those who claim to be technological illiterates turn out during the interviews to demonstrate quite substantial knowledge about potential services, functions, solutions, and the qualities of desirable or unwanted content. More young people in 2006 than in 2004 said that they used Bluetooth, infrared, and usb ports to transfer data (photos, videos, music) from their mobile to the PC and vice versa. It is likely that the mobile Internet will become more popular when prices fall, the speed and quality increase, and the interest in services such as email, Messenger, news, and entertainment on the mobile matures. As this implies, the mobile is increasingly the focus of a convergence of technologies, media formats, and content which have previously been available through other platforms; and mobiles are in turn much more easily combined with other media through different forms of wireless and wired connections.

The long-term impact of these possibilities is not easily predicted, as the same technologies seem to be adapted and integrated in different ways and with different meanings in different countries. Across the globe, we can identify a number of basic uses and meanings of the mobile (with communication and information as the lowest common denominator). However, several sets of conditions affect the adaptation rate and the common as well as unexpected uses in different national and cultural contexts: these include cultural factors (traditions, norms, trends), social aspects (legislation/regulation, needs, norms), and practical constraints (access, economy, infrastructure, work/study/home distance). Some of the best examples of the similarities and differences here are represented in Katz and Aakhus's edited book *Perpetual Contact,*[20] which analyzes mobile phone uses in ten countries from different parts of the world, or in the five volumes edited by Kristof Nyiri, based on international conferences on mobile media research from 2001 to 2005.[21] Examples of studies which combine national approaches with general analysis are Rich Ling's *The Mobile Connection,*[22] Ito et al.'s *Personal, Portable, Pedestrian: Mobile Phones in Japanese Life,*[23] and the outcomes from the research project *Mobile Media, Mobile Youth*[24] on which this chapter is based.

The variety of uses and forms of adaptation is not simply determined by usability, functionality, and needs. The choice of the mobile and use of services also indicate the mobility and fleeting inconsistency of trends[25] in youth cultures. Is it trendy to display the smartest phone or is it trendy to be extremely discreet, while owning the hottest brand and new services and while being an intensive user, or is it more trendy to be laid-back or to prefer a primitive "retro" model?[26] Young people in this age group seem to be divided into two large categories, but internally for quite different reasons. Our studies show that many of the participants have quite advanced mobiles, but still, few claim to be interested in the most advanced and expensive devices. Others do in fact like to have the newest technologies, although, according to some of the boys, this is less about functions than about showing off, flashing the new device, maybe also demonstrating the functions as part of the show. As Jacob puts it, "You know, among friends, you show off the new gear you bought. You do that when you're a boy: 'Hey, take at a look at this, I guarantee it's better than yours.' Two weeks later he has bought a new one and then he says: 'Take a look at this!' Jacob claims that boys grow out of this inclination to show off when they grow older, although some might see that as an open question.

To some of the young users, the quality of the mobile is also important. It is seldom, though, that having a "wrong" or somehow untrendy mobile leads to such drastic solutions as chosen by the sixteen-year-old girl who in a satirical way talks about the childhood traumas she suffered due to her huge brick-like mobile with only call and text-message services: "That's why I got rid of it again and decided to go into 'mobile-celibacy,' I simply boycotted mobiles for years." At the time of the interview, however, she did have a new, advanced mobile and could not imagine life without it.

Some informants claim they do not care much about the look of the mobile as long is it works, while others say that they like to have a mobile with a good design. Some of the girls decorate their mobile with various covers, holsters from Gucci and other designers, or with fun stickers. They modify the set up, the screen picture, and the ringtone, partly according to the image of themselves they like to display, but primarily according to the perception of the mobile as a kind of "shell" which encloses their social life and networks, emotional experiences, personal information and so forth. The metaphorical meaning of "shell" is a protecting case or layer, in this context, the physical device which contains and represents the sensitive, personal content relating to personal identity.

However, a small group of adolescents simply do not prioritize the mobile, as something completely indispensable. During our empirical work we didn't meet anyone who didn't have a mobile, although there were a few who had very old, simple models and who very rarely made calls and exchanged very few text-messages. They simply didn't care and didn't mind not being part of the intense hyperactive social communication pattern which is the reality for the majority of girls as well as boys.

Another group of young boys also demonstrated a laid-back attitude, but did so quite consciously. They sometimes left the phone at home and openly cultivated the attitude of not being dependent on it. Even so, compared to the first group of laid-back users they still had a rather intensive and extensive pattern of use, and combined the use of the mobile with Messenger and other digital services. They could not risk being completely "out of sync," because mobile communication is primarily carried on with people whom you see often or every day. This laid-back attitude does not necessarily express resistance to peer-group culture, even if it may arise from a wish to distinguish oneself from the group.[27] Part of the attitude is about demonstrating that you are in control, that you are cool about youth culture, including media use, and not part of the visibly hectic text-message culture. These different attitudes and to some degree diverse patterns of use reflect the fact that personal needs and interests do contribute to the social shaping of mobile phones, even if common patterns of social use and meaning can be distinguished, the social networks, individual interests, contextual factors (background, access, norms in family and peer group), and attitudes all have an effect on how the technology is adopted and defined.

Interestingly, most of the students who wrote high school essays about *My Mobile and Me* and the participants in the two qualitative studies discussed the dichotomy between actual and ideal uses of the mobile. Again and again, they discussed on the one hand their almost uncontrollable use of the mobile, their fear of being without it, and of being disconnected from their social network, and on the other hand, their experience of being unable to control the information flow and their need for face-to-face social exchange and for periods of free time. The majority of users were divided between experiencing the instant need for communication and updating, and a more distanced reflection upon the pace, stress and greater or lesser dependency on the mobile as a social tool. In conclusion, however, almost all agreed that the mobile, both in itself and combined with other communication media, is extremely useful, necessary, and good for maintaining all kinds of relationships. (Susan Herring in her chapter also comments on the schism between ideal and actual uses, reminding us that youth also participate in "moral panics" about media effects.)

Having discussed the range of ways in which mobile communication is perceived and used within contemporary youth culture, I want now to move on and consider four broad themes that relate more specifically to the question of identity: availability, presence, the personal log, and social learning.

Availability

With the mobile you don't miss much. You have your friends right at your hand and you do more spontaneous things. (Marie, twenty years)

One essential aspect of mobile phone use is the fact that the phone, and following this, the personal user, is always on. Our 2006 survey showed that 80 percent of the informants never turned off their mobile phone and that 20 percent turned it off for between four and twelve hours. The qualitative data indicate that the mobile in these latter cases was turned off at night to allow undisturbed sleep, at work when required, and in cinemas. Adolescents very seldom completely turn off their mobiles, even at school, in restaurants, silent compartments on trains, at the dinner table, and so forth—they simply put the phone on "mute" and are able to check the display for incoming messages when the mobile vibrates.

This means that users—in particular the adolescents who never turn their phone off—are always available for communication, information, entertainment, or, in short, for other people. One nineteen-year-old girl says that even if she sometimes turns off her mobile when she really needs to relax, it isn't for long—"I can't be without it for too long. What if I miss something? [laughs]." "Missing something" refers to the constant updating of the social network, while the laugh indicates her self-conscious collusion with this practice. On the one hand, the girl openly tells about the reality of her life with the mobile and how she depends on it. Yet on the other hand, she takes a more reflexive, distanced—even ironic—stance toward such extensive uses, needs, and attitudes.

Time off or mobile-free zones are a luxury,[28] which only the few who are so secure in their position in their social network can dare to enjoy. Such users like to demonstrate that they are in control by leaving the mobile at home or turning it off every now and then. However, the absence of the mobile—either by choice or as a result of lack of money or stolen or broken devices—is a threat to the important updating of the social network, and hence also to one's own position, one's ability to take part in social activities, and ultimately to one's self-perception or identity.

Several of our informants said that they would keep the mobile on at night and even have it next to their head on the pillow, not only because the mobile functioned as an alarm clock,[29] but also because they did not want to miss any messages or calls. Some stated that it may be important to your friends that you are available around the clock, if they need support, comfort, someone to talk to, or laugh with. In that case, sleep is less important. One example is twenty-year-old Marie who says: "It is next to the pillow so you can hear it if someone calls at night, because you wouldn't like to miss a call.... If someone is sad or drunk or has had some bad experiences and needs to talk to me I would feel terribly bad if they couldn't get hold of me." In these cases the mobile is a line to instant friendly support and emotional presence. Nineteen-year-old Jacob says the same: "Your true friends—those with the label 'real good friends' in the address book—they're the ones you call or text at 2 a.m. and say: 'Hey, I'm in trouble. You've got to help me!'" Being always on and available expresses confirmation of trust which is fundamental for true relationships.[30] The unwanted calls of all kinds which are a consequence of this are the inevitable price to pay for constant availability in one's intimate social relationships. (These examples of the importance of the mobile have an equivalent in the case of the British immigrant girl, Walia, in Sandra Weber and Claudia Mitchell's chapter in this volume. Just like the participants in the Danish study, Walia cannot imagine being without her mobile, not least because of its role as a mediator or link between social and personal identity.)

Phatic Communication

Many young users send messages to one another that ask "Hey, what are you doing?" or calls with the same intention: to be in contact means being correctly "tuned in," or "in phase."[31] A reply to these phatic messages is not expected quite as fast as it usually is to other messages, but not answering a message like this at some point still amounts to a rejection of the relationship.

A phenomenon that is not known as such among Danish youth is *pilaris*, which is familiar, for example, in Finland and Italy. *Pilaris* is a kind of "no-call," where you ring once and then hang up just to indicate that you are thinking of the receiver.[32] Mathilde, 19, has met this phenomenon during a stay in Italy and compares it to text-message-use in Denmark: "Well, I think it is really nice to receive messages. . . . It may just be the fact that someone is thinking of me and just writes me something. In Italy I had a somewhat different experience . . . that is, if you think of someone you call just once and hang up . . . and then, suddenly you have a lot of unanswered calls." It appears that Mathilde prefers to receive a message with some kind of content, no matter how void of apparent meaning it is. As the meaning of phatic communication is created by the context of the message, it ought not to make any difference how the message looks, but there may be some cultural aspects that influence how such messages are understood. In Finland, it appears that the unanswered calls may be of a more informative kind, understood only through the codes the group agrees upon, for example, a call may mean "goodnight" in the evening or "I'm ready to go" in the morning (Kasesniemi 2003). A similar phenomenon is beeping, described by Jonathan Donner based on his studies of mobile phone culture in Rwanda.[33] He divides beeping into beeps for the receiver to call the caller, relational ("hey, I am here") and prenegotiated (based on a shared code) calls. Even if young Danes seldom use pilaris or beeping just as a form of greeting, a number of the "hello, where are you?" calls or text messages have similar intentions. Fifteen-year-old Salem explains how it works: "Well, if I haven't got anything to do, right, then I ask all my friends: 'What are you doing?' right? That's how a conversation starts. You send 'what are you doing?' and then they begin to send: Playing a computer game, playing soccer, playing basketball. . . . I just want them to know what I am doing." A negative variation of void calls or messages is "bombing," that is, calling or texting someone either endlessly or at odd times to get them in trouble or to harass them. The mobile can be an effective tool for mobbing and harassment, although it has not been not frequently mentioned in this way in our studies.

Learning the codes, the unwritten rules for meaning, language, and normative behavior[34] is essential in order to make the communication meaningful, at the level of actual content and at the level of phatic communication, when the meaning must be interpreted by the contextual situation of the exchange. Therefore a beep may mean something different in Denmark, or Finland or Rwanda, but also between much more locally rooted groups. Signe Bloch identifies maintaining social contact as a superior motive for phatic mobile communication along with other general uses. The superior motive can be seen as the glue between other motives for maintaining contact: belonging to a group, confirmation, status, presence, entertainment.[35] These motives are closely related to the importance of being able to mirror, reflect, and test one's own personal identity in relation to the group identity.

No Free Moments Another relevant aspect here is that with the phone (along with Messenger, email, and chat) always on there are no free moments, no time off except in very rare situations.[36] The ideal is to be in control of life in general, symbolized by the ambition of being able to control the use of the mobile phone: "It is nice that you have a small rubber button which simply has to be pushed down for a few seconds, and then you are ok again." However, the reality of the immense amount of work and effort it would take to exist without the mobile phone, not to mention the "sacrifices" in the form of loss of social interaction, is illustrated by the sentence which recurred in different forms throughout our interviews: "I guess I could choose to turn it off . . . but I can't."

Young users in particular therefore have constant reminders of the presence of others, either through the mechanical expressions of the mobile—sounds, vibrations, visual effects—or through meaningful content,[37] both from their own and from other mobiles. The qualitative data indicate that many adolescents are in fact constantly being interrupted—in their private situations and in public spaces—by one or more digital media like the phone, Messenger, Internet, email, or other people's mobile phone use. And in addition to this comes the ordinary use of television, Internet, music, and games. This raises significant questions about the cognitive abilities that are needed to focus, concentrate, multitask, and deal with large amounts of information of all kinds, although these are beyond the scope of this article.

Stress Even if young users almost unanimously agree that it is de facto not possible to manage without the mobile, critical reflections are aired. Stress—used in its popular sense—is a repeated topic in our studies as well as in other research: how is it possible to deal with the pace and pervasiveness of information and the built-in expectations of rapid replies and the constant negotiation of context and meaning that are required by mobile communication?[38]

For example, one sixteen-year-old girl writes: "I believe that in order to have a healthy mobile phone culture we need to find out how we can avoid the demand of being publicly present around the clock. To have some clear restrictions when people have time to turn off their mobile, the computer, and log off completely—to prevent stress from being a national disease." This opinion was more or less shared by several of our informants, and it exemplifies the gap that often seems to arise between practice and reflection. It is, however, remarkable that the absence of the mobile also causes symptoms of stress. It is worrying not to be in contact, not to be updated on one's social networks. Marie, twenty years old, lost her phone for a few hours and thought: "'Oh no, everybody is trying to reach me and I can't reach anyone and now I have lost all these phone numbers and how can I get them back?' The friends whom I don't talk to often would simply disappear from my life, I thought. Well, I found the mobile again and since then I have never left it anywhere. I really don't know what I would do without it." Likewise, another sixteen-year-old girl says: "What if you don't get to answer the phone in time? Then you aren't there around the clock and then at least I would have broken many promises to friends; I have more than once said: 'You can always call me!' or 'I'll always be here for you.' You can't just withdraw from these promises of eternal loyalty."

Sometimes it becomes quite obvious that this experience of confusion, pressure, and stress is not always strictly connected to mobile phone use but is a more general condition of being young in modern society. In this sense, the mobile can be seen merely to reinforce tendencies that already exist. Nevertheless, the mobile can become the catalyst for broader frustrations: "It is also a stress factor that your friends can always reach you. This means that you constantly have to consider a lot of things. For example what you are going to do on Friday and so forth. . . . " Thinking about social activities on Friday shouldn't be too difficult to think about for a teenage girl; here the statement is a good example of how remarks about the mobile express more general frustrations. Adolescents are dealing with the constant coordination of everyday activities, and the fact that time has become flexible[39] and that all arrangements can be negotiated or changed on the run. This makes the microcoordination of everyday life fluid and constantly open to question. In principle, the liberation from very fixed times and appointments should lessen the stress of needing to be on time for everything. But some adolescents become frustrated, and feel that they waste time waiting, and this in turn is seen to reflect back on the quality of relationships themselves, which are also seen to be constantly in flux.

Presence The second theme to be discussed here is the question of presence. Presence in this context relates to three mutually related understandings: the perception of presence in a shared space, whether physical or virtual (or indeed psychological); the potential for being simultaneously present in more than one space; and the potential disturbance caused by the mobile in social situations.

It seems that modern people, in particular young people, are often potentially somewhere else mentally than in their present physical location. This can be due to the MP3 device, which makes it possible to shut off the surroundings and establish a private space where one's psychological presence is transferred to another symbolic place of experience. It can be due to the mobile, which is always nearby and potentially disrupting the full experience of presence in the situation, or it can be due to the mobile's ability to add to the users' experience of being in a shared, virtual space. Even if young people also tend to develop ideals of normative behavior regarding mobile talking or texting, for example, when they are with friends or family, it is more common than not that the mobile phone "takes away" the people you are with in a social situation because they have to check their mobile or reply to a call. It simply is not possible to be equally present in two places at the same time.

The Perception of Presence in a Shared Space

Biocca et al. make a useful distinction here between physical presence and social presence. Their point is that social presence is a state "that varies with medium, knowledge of the other, content of the communication, environment, and social context."[40] This means that the experience of presence in the same shared space depends on what information you get, whom you are talking to, what you are talking about, and what distractions you may experience in the physical location. Lombard and Ditton[41] define presence as the perceptual illusion of nonmediation. That is, if we perceive ourselves to be in another space than the physical space, the mediated situation is experienced as real. The feeling of presence is not as such bound to a specific medium. Lombard and Ditton talk about high presence and low presence media and suggest (along with other theorists like Biocca et al.) that the more modalities a medium uses (for example, images and sounds), the more senses are activated and the more effective is the feeling of presence.

Young people who are growing up with digital communication media are in a position to explore the potentials—and limitations—of different media for various personal communication purposes, and this often entails developing a strong notion of usefulness that is practical as well as social. Most have rather strong feelings about what can be said or written on the phone, and what must necessarily be communicated face-to-face. Most young users, however, are able to establish intimate spaces for shared presence when they talk on the phone or have a text-message conversation. The physical space is shut out, no matter if it is the bus, the crowded street, or the bedroom.

The experience of presence is important in most interpersonal communication situations in order to establish a feeling of trust and social bonding. The experience of presence may, however, vary a lot, especially depending on knowledge of the other people and the content, the characteristics of the situation, and the intentions of the communication. Very good friends or lovers may be able to have intimate conversations with a strong feeling of mutual presence via text messaging, while a telephone call to a teacher or a trainer or a less-close peer may appear distanced and formal. In short, the use of the mobile may add to the creation of a feeling of copresence, nearness, intimacy, or it may be perceived as an alienating medium, depending on the context of the communication.

Phatic communication of the kind described above may also include strong feelings of presence, because of the psychological experience of being close, or caring. For example, Marie, aged twenty-two, refers to the way in which monkeys socialize when they pick lice from one another: "That is just one way to keep in contact, to tap each other's shoulder and say that you are still here. Like monkeys picking lice from each other, you send text-messages just because it is cosy and to demonstrate that you are still here. So, I guess I pick lice from my friends. Yes. (Laughs)." Ling describes these "grooming" messages as rituals[42] that are important to sustaining relationships,[43] while Geser also compares this use of phatic calls with face-to-face "grooming talk"[44] and concludes that there is a close similarity between grooming communication offline and online. Beyond the "simple" maintaining of relations, grooming may also—as it does among grooming monkeys—express codes of dominance, levels of interconnectedness, types of relationship, and so on. It can serve as an important means of mutual social confirmation and expressing trust in each other. Thus, a sixteen-year-old girl talks about "grooming" over time, the experience of being constantly connected: "Even the experts tell us that we become lonelier by being present 24/7. But I don't see it that way—at least not in my case. I feel closer to all my friends when I can just call or write a message. It makes it easier to have the same contact in places where you can't see your friends."

Communication about intimate or deep issues is, therefore, possible on the mobile with good friends. But our young users agree that in order to deal with serious problems you need to be present in the same physical space. A fifteen-year-old girl says: "If I am at home lying down alone in my bedroom, well, then I can talk about anything [on the phone]. But not problems. Then you have to be face-to-face. It is too easy to misunderstand something if you can't read the body language and the faces—a single word can easily be misunderstood." Text messaging is too noncommittal, and over the phone you can simply hang up. Text messaging about important or problematic issues is an easy way out. Almost all the respondents in our research agreed, although their perceptions of text messaging and phone talk varied. However, others said that they found text messages easier to use, for example, if they were feeling sad; by contrast, the direct connection and the sensual use of voice in a call may create an intimacy that makes it difficult to open up and to keep control. As Dea, seventeen years old, says: "Well, I think... when you text you say things you wouldn't say on the phone. You know... you don't gibber along and if you meet again it isn't completely embarrassing. If it is your close friend and something about her irritates you it is difficult to say it directly. Or with a text-message you can write and simply say 'Listen, I am sad about this or that.' Because then you have that distance and still talk it out but without being completely hysterical and girlish."

However, the general perception is that serious topics must be dealt with face-to-face, with the visual information provided by facial expressions and body language to support what is said and to reveal one's emotional responses. Even so, none of the participants like video calls very much. Some do use webcams when they communicate with close friends on Messenger or various chat channels. But—at least thus far—most young users think that video calls are disturbing. A shared feeling of intimacy and trust can be better established through talk on the phone or even through a text-message conversation between friends. Young people are generally such skilled mobile phone users that they learn how to read meanings, moods and emotions "between the lines" of what is said. Interestingly some of the young informants mentioned that they have photos of those with whom they communicate most, and when a text message is received or a call is answered, the information on the screen is supplemented with a still photo of the person calling. As twenty-one-year-old Jacob says about talking to his girlfriend: "Then you can look at her photo while you're talking."

Being Simultaneously Present in Several Spaces

Erving Goffman describes the human ability to divide one's attention while interacting between main and side activities.[45] The main activity completely engages the individual's attention and it clearly determines action at a given time, although a side activity can often be maintained simultaneously without disturbing it. However, a sixteen-year-old girl complains that it is not possible to be present in two communicative situations at the same time: "When we were together and tried to have a conversation, she wasn't present at all. We weren't two friends talking but a third one was present: her mobile and whoever it represented at the given time. This created a distance in our friendship when we were together but on the other hand you felt close as soon as you were the one writing or calling with her. Fundamentally a mobile represents a person you are in contact with without being at the same location." In this situation, the partner in the physical location is excluded and becomes the audience to an interpersonal exchange. Gergen makes a useful distinction here between the inside conversation, among those who are talking, and the outside conversation, among those who are present but prevented from participating, because they aren't "invited" to the inside conversation.[46] For those in the outside position, this may provoke a strong feeling of being excluded from a community. On the other hand, the situation may also cause frustration for those in the inside position. Thus, twenty-four-year-old Anna expresses her experience of the opposite situation, where she is the one who communicates, as equally frustrating: "It can be very disturbing that you can be in *one* room and communicate with someone who is in another room at the same time. Then you can't be present in the company or the room you are in."

Gergen describes this phenomenon of being physically present in one space and mentally present in another as "absent presence."[47] Twenty-one-year-old Benjamin, for example, uses the mobile as a helper in social situations when he feels excluded or at least not part of the community, for instance, at a party with people with whom he has nothing in common: "Well, if you are at a party and you are bored or don't find anyone to talk to then obviously you become a little restless, and then of course you bring out your mobile and maybe you text someone who is coming downtown later." By using his mobile in this way, he demonstrates that he—apparently—has nothing in common with the people present but also that he doesn't need to have, since he is connected to someone out there, in another place. The mobile becomes the practical social savior and face saver in one. It is not good—in some youth terminologies it may be labeled "slack"—to be visibly excluded from a fun, intensive, social situation. Another boy says that he sometimes catches himself looking through his mobile address book or reading text messages in order not to look as if he isn't having a great time. This demonstrative use parallels the way girls in particular use the mobile to demonstrate that they are connected, that is, not alone and just a second from potentially alerting someone, when they are moving in unfriendly or lonely places. The presence of the mobile phone may not actually prevent something bad from happening, but it does create some feeling of nearness and safety in the situation.[48] Hans Geser describes this use of the mobile as a "symbolic bodyguard,"[49] whereby the user fends off threats to their minimal private space by monitoring the mobile's screen, signalling that even if they are alone in the local, physical setting, they are virtually somewhere else in the company of others.[50]

The Mobile as Personal Log

All my stuff is on my mobile, I mean my diary and like everything is simply on my mobile. My entire phone numbers, everything. Nothing could be worse. Because all my things are on my mobile, really. (Girl, nineteen years)

The third theme I discuss here is the function of mobile phones as personal mobile logs—that is, as a kind of life diary that saves experiences, memories, thoughts, or moments in a visual and textual form. The sim card in your phone could be seen to contain the story of your life (at least at the present time): not just text messages, photos and videos, but also chosen or given tokens such as icons, ring tones, music lists; and the diary, address book, alarm clock all save and display the experiences and activities of the user as they have been mediated and captured by the mobile. As one of the sixteen-year-old boys says: "Actually I would ten times rather lose my mobile than my sim card because that is where you have all the important stuff."

Moblogging is not so far very popular in its developed form, but all kinds of representations in (or on) the mobile phone function as a private moblog which may be shared with friends, and sharing can itself be seen as a means of exposing your personal life to a more public gaze.[51] The mobile phone documents your immediate story, as logs have to be erased with a frequency, depending on the extent of use and limitations of data capacity. Alternatively, you may choose to save parts of your story by uploading it to your PC. Users can also transfer these compressed stories when they change mobile phones. Generally, however, the capacity of smart mobiles in combination with the possibility of transferring data to the PC, the mobile memory, and "life log" seems to be sufficient for what is important to save at the moment.

The documentation of personal experiences in sound, photo or video proves that the mobile user himself or herself has been on the location when something happened, which may include special occasions, accidents, criminal activities, funny or interesting happenings. Not many people carry their digital camera with them, but as the mobile is always there it becomes the key tool for capturing moments, storing information, and documenting experiences. Even if the mobile camera and video recorder do play a role as potential tools for the citizen reporter and for capturing remarkable content for the scrapbook of one's life, the mobile is used primarily to document more everyday happenings and experiences. Twenty-three-year-old Freja says: "You usually just have photos from special occasions, right. And the pictures that really mean the most are everyday pictures, those you remember in your head right? Sound memories would be fun. That thing about documenting life, that's what I am thinking of."

Jacob, 19, has taken photos of his dog growing up from when it was a puppy and shows the photos to his colleagues in the army where he is serving for four months. He also sends his mother MMSes of himself from the army, for example saying: "Look mom, I am green in the face." Like many other young people in our research, Jacob primarily documents everyday situations and sorts them through over time. He saves the funniest pictures on his computer, and likes to look at "old" photos of things he did with friends some time ago—festivals, parties, and activities with friends and family. Fifteen-year-old Clara prefers to photograph unusual, funny, atypical situations and to relive the situation when she edits the photos and videos on her laptop. In this context, documentation is also used to include others within one's private sphere; sharing insights into everyday little events, moods, emotions is much more intimate and personal than sharing photos of sensations experienced in the street, of a rock star at a concert, or collectively distributed jokes or icons. It reveals something about the "owner's" self-perception, and the adequate reception of this insight is important to the "owner" as it confirms his or her personal identity. The mobile or digital log may not be fundamentally different from traditional photo albums or other kinds of personal storytelling. However, the data in the digital log are always ready, it is easy to edit, and it is personal, which means it can only be shared by invitation from the owner. Friends look through the picture galleries together and comment on them, either reliving shared past experiences or getting insight into one another's personal lives and experiences. The images trigger collective memories or provide insights into each other's personal histories.

Not only photos and videos, but also text messages are memorable, however, and not all of this documentation is necessarily shared. Marie, aged 20, uses the phone to have happy thoughts at night: "Before I go to sleep and if I am alone I lie there reading old, happy messages." This use is similar to the exchange of text messages between friends or lovers before going to sleep, although reading old messages also exploits the bittersweet sentimentality of memory by reviving the moods and sentiments of earlier experiences.

The Mobile as the Data Double

The mobile is a kind of digital diary which is gladly shared with friends, but it may also be perceived as a "data double," a mobile extension of the body and mind, even a kind of "additional self." As I have noted, the mobile is always close at hand, ear, or eye: it represents a lifeline to self-perception, a means of documenting of social life, expressing preferences, creating networks, and sharing experiences. To this extent, one could argue that the mobile user is becoming a kind of cyborg. The young users in our research do not use the term "data double," but it seems that they experience a kind of symbiosis with their mobiles, in which the physical devices come to be understood as a representation of personal meanings and identities.

One example is the young woman who puts her phone on her pillow beside her at night. She doesn't do it just in order to be able to monitor activities, even if that is considered to be important around the clock, but also because she doesn't have the heart to put it on the table or floor, as it represents her social life, her intimate experiences, and her social network.[52] But even if the mobile at one level is the physical, immediate representation of the user, it is also simply a representation and a useful tool. To the users, the shell, the device itself, holds no or little affective value—it may be exchanged for a newer model. It is primarily the content and the representations it contains which establish the meaning of the mobile. Even if the mobile phone is regarded as a *personal* device, it is simply a *device*. The devices in themselves do not appear to be substitutes so much as conduits for affective and social bonds between people.

The user identification with the mobile at some level extends to the mobile phone number as such. The mobile phone number is very important to the young users—almost all informants in the two studies say that they would definitely keep their old number when they exchange the old mobile for a newer model, even if it would be easier to buy a new phone with a new license and number. Telephone numbers are the codes for social and intimate relations, the code to access social networks. Twenty-year-old Marie, for example, suggests that "it gives you a kind of safe and good feeling that people you haven't talked to for a long time and someone you probably shall never talk to again anyway have your number." Danny, aged twenty, considers the meaning of the phone number as an alias that facilitates the transcendence between the physical and the represented "you." Danes are already digitized as citizens through a civil registration number, but to him the mobile phone number is the code that gives access to his world and makes possible interaction and communication across time, space, and physical borders.

Social Learning

My fourth and last theme is social learning. This may be understood in two ways: as learning through social interaction and, related to this, learning about social norms.[53] The first of these has been indirectly discussed throughout the article, so the focus here is on the latter, learning about social norms.

Our research clearly shows that the rules and norms for social behavior with the mobile phone are constantly tested and modified by young people.[54] The modification takes place as the patterns of use and the meaning of the mobile in everyday life change and develop. This means that norms are constantly changing and also that they are not the same for all social groups. Most of the informants we have talked to reflect on issues of normative behavior, disturbance in public places, and the interruption of interpersonal situations. Their observations in the study do not, however, necessarily correspond to their own behavior at all times. Furthermore, it is important to note that the adolescents we have talked to represent a broad average of young Danes but are not in any way radical, subcultural, marginal, or provocative. If we had sought out angry young boys and girls in the southern suburbs of Copenhagen or frustrated rich kids to the north, we may have found a somewhat different picture of the mobile as an identity marker and a means of social provocation, and different perceptions of normative behavior with the mobile.

One of the key questions for the informants in our research is about mobile phone use in the company of others, which is closely related to the themes discussed in the two previous sections of this chapter. As we have seen, the mobile is often perceived as a potential disturbance or rival intrusion in situations of face-to-face communication. Our young users were particularly disturbed by talk and texting in cinemas,[55] a little less in restaurants and cafes, and on public transportation and least of all in the streets. Even the use of headsets in public places is disturbing to many, particularly when the music in the headset is very loud and yet not audible, and when others talk too loud into the tiny mic on their headset while glancing absentmindedly toward the horizon. Another quite significant disturbance of public space caused by mobile phone use is the ways in which personal, sometimes intimate content, is presented in excessively loud voices, particularly in public spaces. The young informants complain about not being able to avoid eavesdropping unless you turn up your iPod to the threshold of pain. The young users are on the one hand used to communicating and being visible in public space, especially when they are in a group. Yet on the other hand, they do not want to be included in other people's intimate exchanges without having the choice. This is perhaps a typically Danish attitude: in some cultures it is not acceptable to be loud and visible in public spaces, while this is not a problem in other cultures.

It may seem to adults of older generations that young people do not moderate their behavior with their mobiles in public places. But two significant points must be made here: whether we believe it or not, young people's social norms largely mirror the norms for social behavior they were brought up with, both personally and institutionally. Secondly there is a lot of moderation and teaching each other "good behavior" going on in young people's social networks. Every communicative exchange involves negotiating social norms and hence group identities. This is not usually a result of conscious reflection and interaction, although sometimes the behavior of a person or a group provokes a reaction or formulation of an attitude. For example, seventeen-year-old Dea gets really irritated when her friend talks continuously at the dinner table in Dea's home, where the norm is that there should be no mobiles at the table: "I think it is very annoying when someone talks on the mobile in my home. My friend does that a lot. I find it extremely rude—rrr, I get quite angry." Another example is twenty-year-old Marie who is usually with two or three very close friends who may answer their phones, although as they know each other well, they will ask "do you mind?" if it becomes too much. Others say that if you are with friends at a cafe you simply don't answer your phone because that would signal lack of respect and interest, and make deep or intimate or fun conversation impossible. Another example is the five friends who share a flat and who have decided that mobiles are not allowed during shared meals. They may have copied rules they know from other contexts, but it is remarkable that they agree on a mobile-free zone at an age when the mobile is widely perceived as indispensable at all times. Self-regulation is necessary and expected, although norms vary between groups and individual behavior mirrors the collective norms in a particular setting: personal behavior may change depending on whom you are with. Here again, behavior with the mobile is a signal of collective and individual identity.

Fifteen-year-old Salem underlines how seldom his mobile is turned off by saying: "I turn off my mobile for just about half an hour during the Ramadan, when we eat, that's the only time, then we must have peace, one has to respect that. I once received a text-message in such a situation and I told him off, that's over the limit." This may say more about Salem's self-identity as a Muslim, as he is otherwise quite loud and visible, and very fond of his mobile. By telling this story he demonstrates how important this culture is to him, even compared to the mobile and social networking. Still, he likes to relate that he has had to tell someone else off in order to make him behave according to the proper norms.

This mutual negotiation of social norms is a basic quality of group identity. In order to be included in the community, one must behave according to the normative codes. But the collective codes are also formed by individuals who test and mirror their individual identities in the group and vice versa, and so this is an ongoing process. This is certainly apparent in the use of mobile phones. The development from the portable telephone to the personal, handheld computer and the ubiquitous integration of the mobile has taken place within just a decade. The pace of the resulting changes in behavior, attitudes, and meanings, and their implications for identify formation, have potentially been enormous. Yet even if there is a gap between what young people say about their use of mobiles and what they actually do, they are increasingly reflexive about their uses of this technology. This may be a result of public debate and/or parental and institutional constraints. But it does seem that the extensive use, meaning, and impact of the mobile for young people have led to a considerable degree of spontaneous reflection and debate about broader social norms and values.

Conclusion

You never feel alone when you have your mobile, do you? (Grit, seventeen-year-old girl)

The four themes I have discussed in this article illustrate just some of the potential implications of new mobile communication devices for the formation of young people's identities in the contemporary world. The mobile has an immediate symbolic value to young users, not least through the technological possibilities and through the appearance of the device itself. Through its basic appearance, the decorative adaptations, the choice of ringtones and other alerts, and through the screen background, the mobile itself provides signals about the user's identity or at least their self-presentation. The use of language, spelling, their actual way of interacting in dialogues, and the use of additional communicative elements and services also reveal things about the user's "personal settings."

In the context of this article, however, I have focused primarily on the social meanings of the mobile. As we have seen, the mobile supports and enhances the maintenance of social groups and the feeling of belonging to a group. Young people live in a period of time—historically as well as in terms of age—which is characterized by a collectively and personally perceived sense of fragmentation and uncertainty. Many social theorists have argued that traditional resources for identity formation are no longer so easily available, and that the realization of personal expectations for "the good life" may seem increasingly difficult. Young people also have to deal with the sometimes conflicting expectations of parents, school, and friends. Social networks—the strong ties as well as the weak, ephemeral relations—offer possibilities for testing oneself in the light of shared values, norms and codes, for negotiating collective and personal identity, and for establishing a sense of belonging. The mobile is the glue that holds together various nodes in these social networks: it serves as the predominant personal tool for the coordination of everyday life, for updating oneself on social relations, and for the collective sharing of experiences. It is therefore the mediator of meanings and emotions that may be extremely important in the ongoing formation of young people's identities.

The need to learn how to manage and to develop personal identity and the importance of social networks in this process are strongly facilitated by mobiles; and this makes it possible to talk about "mobile identity." The constant negotiation of values and representations and the need to identify with others result in a fluidity of identity which goes beyond the ongoing process of identity formation, to encompass the constant negotiation of norms and values and the processes of reflection that are characteristic of contemporary social life. The constant availability and presence associated with the mobile demonstrate how important it has become in all these arenas, even to those who use it only moderately. The mobile enforces an increasingly intense pace of communication and of intellectual and emotional experience. It, therefore, becomes both the cause and the potential solution to the frustrations of young people regarding the potential management of everyday life. The mobile is an important tool that allows one to be in control—which is an essential ability for adolescents in general—but simultaneously it is becoming more and more important to be able to control the mobile.

Notes

1. The quotes in the article are from the qualitative parts of the research project *Mobile Media, Mobile Youth*, 2004 and 2006 (see note 5). Quotes that refer to age and gender are from school essays, while quotes that refer to age and name (pseudonym) are from qualitative, individual interviews.

2. Rich Ling, *The Mobile Connection: The Cell Phone's Impact on Society* (San Francisco: Morgan Kaufmann Publishers, 2004).

3. See, for example, Kristof Nyiri, ed., *Mobile Learning: Essays on Philosophy, Psychology and Learning* (Vienna: Passagen Verlag, 2003); or James Katz, Mobile Phones in Educational Settings, in *A Sense of Place: The Global and the Local in Mobile Communication*, ed. Kristof Nyiri (Vienna, Austria: Passagen Verlag, 2005).

4. Social coordination and the coordination of everyday life is analyzed in a very useful way in Rich Ling (2004).

5. The analysis in this article builds on two studies of young Danes' uses of and attitudes toward the mobile, undertaken in a research and development project, *Mobile Media, Mobile Youth,* in fall 2004 and spring 2006 among fifteen- to twenty-four-year-old Danes. The 2004 study included a survey of 343 participants and individual, qualitative interviews with forty-eight in the age groups fifteen to seventeen, eighteen to twenty, and twenty-one to twenty-four. The 2006 study included a survey of 629 participants; twenty individual interviews divided between re-interviews of 2004 participants and new participants; observation studies of behavior with the mobile in public and semi-public places; and forty-three high school essays on *My Mobile and Me.* The quantitative data used in the article refers to the 2006 survey, while the qualitative data from both studies are used. The article is also informed by five re-interviews of informants from the 2004 study undertaken in spring 2005; by a previous study (2000) on young Danes' media uses; and by public statistics on media use in Denmark.

6. See e.g., Sonia Livingstone, *Young People and New Media: Childhood and the Changing Media Environment* (London: Sage, 2002) and Lin Prøitz, Intimacy Fiction: Intimate Discourses in Mobile Telephone Communication amongst Norwegian Youth, in *A Sense of Place: The Global and the Local in Mobile Communication,* ed. Kristof Nyiri (Vienna, Austria: Passagen Verlag, 2005).

7. See for example, Rich Ling (2004) and http://www.belllabs.com/history/75/gallery.html (accessed January 9, 2007).

8. Hans Geser, *Towards a Sociological Theory of the Mobile Phone,* Release 3.0. http://socio.ch/mobile/t_geser1.pdf (accessed December 12, 2006).

9. Rich Ling, 2004.

10. With reference to Mizuko Ito, Daisuke Okabe, and Misa Matsuda, *Personal, Portable, Pedestrian: Mobile Phones in Japanese Life* (Cambridge, MA: MIT Press, 2005).

11. Alexandra Weilenmann, *Doing Mobility* (Gothenburg: Gothenburg Studies in Informatics, 2003).

12. The English mode "nice" is used by young Danes in sentences in Danish. It enforces the meaning of "good" and adds to the level of "niceness" compared to use in English.

13. See Alex Taylor and Richard Harper, The Gift of the *Gab?*: A Design Oriented Sociology of Young People's Use of Mobiles. *Computer Supported Cooperative Work* 12 (2003): 267–296.

14. For example, almost 100 percent in the age group fifteen to twenty-four years old have their own mobile, 38 percent have their own laptops and 96 percent have Internet access, most of these in their home/bedroom. The data does not count ownership of PCs but other data indicates that almost 100 percent have either a laptop, a desktop PC or both. The mobile is cheap enough to make it the most accessible personal communication medium to everyone except a small group of very economically impoverished families.

15. See also the chapter by Sandra Weber and Claudia Mitchell in this volume for a short discussion of access to digital media on a global scale.

16. For a deeper analysis of the intimate and emotional meaning of the mobile see Leopoldina Fortunati, Italy: Stereotype, True and False, in *Perpetual Contact: Mobile Communication, Private Talk, Public Performance,* eds. James E. Katz and Mark A. Aakhus (Cambridge, UK: Cambridge University Press, 2002).

17. See note 5.

18. The concepts of instrumental and expressive uses are discussed in Signe Skovgaard and Anne Skov, Presence—følelsen af tilstedeværelse, in Gitte Stald: *Mobile Medier, Mobile Unge* (Report, University of Copenhagen, 2005). The distinction comes from U.S. social behavior theory in the early 1950s, but it has been transformed and used, for example by Rich Ling and Birgitte Yttri, Hypercoordination via Mobile Phones in Norway, in Katz and Aakhus (2002), op.cit.

19. All young Danes have access to computers and Internet, and many have their own laptop according to the 2006 survey: 50 percent of the fifteen- to seventeen-year-olds, 40 percent of the eighteen- to twenty-one-year-olds, 25 percent of the twenty-two to twenty-four-year-olds. Fully 80 percent across age bands have their own iPod or MP3 player—but 10 percent of these use their mobile instead.

20. James E. Katz and Mark A. Aakhus, eds., *Perpetual Contact: Mobile Communication, Private Talk, Public Performance* (Cambridge, UK: Cambridge University Press, 2005).

21. See for example Kristof Nyiri, 2005.

22. Rich Ling, 2004.

23. Mimi Ito et al., 2005.

24. For example Stald, 2007. Also the *Mobile Media and Cultural Seminar* at University of Copenhagen September 2006, with participation of Rich Ling, Norway; Shin Mizukoshi, Japan; Dafna Lemish, Israel; Rasmus Helles and Gitte Stald, Denmark.

25. "Trends" should be understood as the direction or tendency a phenomenon takes at a given time. There is a built-in necessity in cultures, including youth cultural groups, to constantly challenge and redirect the practical, aesthetic, and social uses and meanings of products, phenomena or attitudes. Advanced group members explore the potentials, which are then collectively adapted, formed and popularized. This is an ongoing process, closely related to the ways in which social and personal identity is constructed. Everett Rogers presents a theory of integration processes in *Diffusion of Innovation* (5th Edition, Free Press, 2003 [1962]), which frequently inspires discussions of adoption of digital media and meaning hereof in relation to trends and social identity—as for example in Sonia Livingstone and Moira Bovill, *Children and Their Changing Media Environment: A European Comparative Study* (London: Lawrence Erlbaum, 2001).

26. For further analysis of this based on the two studies, see e.g., Gitte Stald, Mobile Monitoring: Aspects of Risk and Surveillance and Questions of Democratic Perspectives in Young People's Uses of Mobile Phones, in *Young Citizens and New Media: Learning Democratic Engagement,* ed. Peter Dahlgren (London: Routledge, 2007).

27. See David Buckingham's discussion of identity politics in his Introduction to this volume, particularly in relation to the tension between separatism and integration.

28. Very interestingly discussed by Thomas Hylland Eriksen, in *Tyrannny of the Moment: Fast and Slow Time in the Information Age* (London: Pluto Press, 2001).

29. Even though most mobiles can do the alarm call when switched off—although many users do not seem to realize this.

30. With a reference to Anthony Giddens, *Modernity and Self-Identity: Self and Society in the Late Modern Age* (Stanford, CA: Stanford University Press, 1991).

31. A term that usually describes when a radio transmitter and receiver are tuned in correctly so there is a clear signal.

32. Eija-Liisa Kasesniemi, *Mobile Messages: Young People and a New Communication Culture* (Tampere, Finland: Tampere University Press, 2003).

33. See Jonathan Donner, What Can Be Said with a Missed Call? in *Seeing, Understanding, Learning in the Mobile Age,* ed. Kristof Nyiri, Vienna, Austria: Passagen Verlag, 2005.

34. See Rich Ling, 2004.

35. Signe Bloch, Postkort fra mobilen (Postcards from the mobile), *Mobile Media, Mobile Youth* (University of Copenhagen, Film & Media Studies, 2005).

36. Even in the cinema, at school or at work, the mobile is not turned off, just on "silent."

37. This distinction comes from Shannon and Weaver: "semantic noise and engineering noise," for example presented in John Fiske, *Introduction to Communication Studies* (London: Routledge, 1990).

38. A rather dystopian perspective on the consequences of information overload, pace of time and modernity is discussed by Zygmunt Baumann, *Liquid Modernity* (Cambridge, UK: Polity Press, 2000); Zygmunt Baumann, *Liquid Love: On the Frailty of Human Bonds* (Cambridge, UK: Polity Press, 2003); Thomas Hylland Eriksen (2001) also discusses consequences of pace of time and management of time in relation to media use. Rich Ling (2004) and Leslie Haddon (2005) both describe the meaning of time in relation to digital media (mobiles) in a social context.

39. See for example Leslie Haddon (2000, 2005), "Social Consequences of Mobile Telephony," and *Media in Everyday Life*, plus Rich Ling (2004).

40. Frank Biocca, Chad Harms, and Judee Burgoon, Towards a More Robust Theory and Measure of Social Presence: Review and Suggested Criteria, *Presence* 12, no. 5 (2003): 456–480.

41. Matthew Lombard and Theresa Ditton, At the Heart of it All: The Concept of Presence, *Journal of Mediated Communication* 3, no. 2 (1997).

42. See Rich Ling, 2004.

43. Rich Ling, 2004.

44. Hans Geser, 2004.

45. Erving Goffman, *Behaviour in Public Places: Notes on the Social Organization of Gathering* (New York: Free Press/Macmillan, 1963).

46. Kenneth J. Gergen, The Challenge of the Absent Presence, in *Perpetual Contact: Mobile Communication, Private Talk, Public Performance,* eds. James E. Katz and Mark A. Aakhus (Cambridge, UK: Cambridge University Press, 2002).

47. Kenneth J. Gergen, 2002.

48. See e.g. Rich Ling (2004) and Gitte Stald (2007).

49. Hans Geser, among others, describes this use of the mobile as a "symbolic bodyguard."

50. Hans Geser, 2004.

51. See Susannah Stern (this volume): Producing Sites, Exploring Identities: Youth Online Authorship and danah boyd, Why Youth ♥ Social Network Sites: The Role of Networked Publics in Teenage Social Life (this volume) for a discussion of young people's uses of blogs.

52. Jane Vincent and Richard Harper, The Social Shaping of UMTS: Preparing the 3G Customer. Report, University of Surrey Digital World Research Centre. http://www.dwrc.surrey.ac.uk/portals/0/SocialShaping.pdf (accessed May 31, 2007).

53. In their paper "Reconsideration of Media Literacy with Mobile Media" Shin Mizukoshi et al. (2005) discuss the clash between the idea that correct normative behavior (with the mobile) copies existing ideals while the mobile itself "undermines and reconstitutes such cultural norms." That is, mobile behavior mirrors and challenges existing norms at the same time. http://www.mode-prj.org/document/HongKong2005_1.pdf (accessed May 31, 2007).

54. See David Buckingham's reference to Erving Goffman's theory of front-stage and back-stage behavior in the Introduction to this volume.

55. The cinema is one of the last resorts for young people for immersive experience, undisturbed by incoming alerts.

PART III: LEARNING

Leisure Is Hard Work: Digital Practices and Future Competencies

Kirsten Drotner

University of Southern Denmark, Danish Research Centre on Education and Advanced Media Materials

This volume has provided numerous examples of the often innovative ways in which children and young people explore who they are by using new, digital media. We have also seen that adults tend to react to these explorations in rather normative ways, either by celebrating how creative, innovative and media savvy young users are or by ignoring their output as unimportant or trivial, not to mention the many parents, policy makers, and teachers who deplore the results as inferior in cultural quality or who focus on the perceived risks involved in going online or communicating on the go.

But what about adults' reactions in a more collected fashion? How can, and could, schools as well as public and private corporations handle young people's digital identity processes? Do they matter for these institutions? Should they matter? This chapter will attempt to answer these questions by focusing on education. The reason for this focus is simple: in many parts of the world, the impact of digital media on education has been one of the key issues in public debate and policymaking over the last two decades. Much has been made of the "information superhighway," of the wiring of classrooms, and of the technical training of teachers and pupils. Much less has been made of the challenges posed to education by the more varied and often more advanced communicative skills and creative media practices developed by young people in their leisure time—through texting and blogging; through the editing of visuals, graphics, and sound; through gaming; and through the circulation of images and text via cell phones.

Given the enormous expansion of these leisure activities, it seems timely that we begin to ask ourselves whether they should impact on educational priorities, and, if so, what these impacts and their implications might be. Let me state from the outset that I think they should, and the reason is this: young people's digital practices promote the formation of competencies that are absolutely vital to their future, in an economic, social, and cultural sense. Adults need to recognize the validity of these practices in the spirit of democratic participation, and acknowledge young people's right to have a voice and to be heard. However, societies also need to recognize and systematically develop these practices, because they are key to children's chances of survival in this century which is already now marked by intensified global, and often mediatized, interaction and mutual dependence—both with people with whom we agree and with people with whom we may disagree. School is still a key site for joint competence formation, and so this is another reason for discussing the challenges posed to education by these new digital practices.

In order to ground the discussion, I will describe a particular instance of youthful media production selected not for its spectacular results, but for its entirely mundane qualities that are repeated on a daily basis and through different means in children's bedrooms, in cyber cafés, and in youth clubs across the globe. The main difference is that this particular production process was documented and analyzed as part of an ongoing project on digital creativities where I was part of the research team.[1] I draw on this description and on the growing body of literature on digital expression, including chapters in the present volume, to discuss in more detail the challenges that these processes arguably pose to educational systems in many parts of the world. How do young people's experiences with digital media in their leisure-time impact on their attitudes to learning and to educational practices? How may they handle existing learning materials, and do these have to be modified? What about the social networks of learning, the distribution of roles, and power relations in schools? Last but not least, why should schools rise to these challenges and what are the dilemmas they face in doing so?

Obviously, children and young people who engage in digital practices in their leisure time rarely define their activities in terms of learning, in fact quite the opposite: when they are out of school, they want to do something different from the routines found when they are at school, and media are an obvious and popular choice. So, when I speak about learning processes in out-of-school contexts in this chapter, I inevitably apply an adult and not a youthful perspective. The point of departure for my deliberations is a belief that what seems least relevant for current school practice may, in fact, be highly relevant for the future of educational and social developments.

"Where do we want to go with this?" Digital Production and Joint Learning Processes

In the Danish provincial town of Viborg, known for its innovative policymaking on children's culture, two classes disbanded ordinary teaching in order to participate in a two-week digital animation project at a local media workshop. The young participants were aged twelve to thirteen and fifteen to sixteen, respectively. Facilitated by two professional animators and with little or no prior knowledge of the software applied, pupils and teachers met for what turned out to be a very intensive work process. All that was fixed beforehand was the pupils' group size (five or six) and composition; an agreement that for each class the workshop should result in four final productions to be shown to the entire school, including parents; and that the theme for these productions should be "mirrors." So, most of the pupils' work process was a matter of open-ended negotiation and social collaboration over their narratives, while at the same time learning how to use the software.

The teachers rapidly assumed a rather marginal role as managers of conflict and practical problems, while the professional animators, who did not know the children beforehand, took center stage as facilitators of learning, particularly in a technical sense. However, many technical challenges and most narrative choices were resolved by the young people themselves. Apparently without too much discussion, hierarchies of proficiency were established among the children, and bits of expertise readily exchanged. Although the four teams clearly competed to produce the best result in both a technical and a narrative sense, knowledge was shared and the often fierce conflicts over content and form were largely resolved within or between the groups, with girls often playing a mediating role. A few of the teachers clearly had difficulties in giving up their usual roles as directors of events, but most seemed to enjoy a bit of time off from their regular duties, with only a math teacher offering to be tutored along with the pupils in using the rather complex software through which moving and still images, graphics, music, and text could be combined and edited.

Not surprisingly, the common theme of "mirrors" resulted in different narratives, each lasting between two and four minutes. But these also shared some interesting features. For example, all participants drew on their existing knowledge of what a "real" animation narrative looks and sounds like. The Disney Corporation's animated cartoons had a decisive impact on their understanding of the genre, and most wanted to mimic or play with these understandings, while acknowledging their own limited technical resources. Moreover, through this tongue-in-cheek playfulness the young participants to varying degrees demonstrated an intimate knowledge about mainstream conventions drawn from their use of music and magazines, film and television.

Finally, particularly during the storyboarding phase, in which the narrative was decided upon and visualized graphically, their joint exploration and negotiation of aesthetic rules and conventions also made them more aware that such rules and conventions existed. It is evident that in order to break rules, one has to know the rules. As Thomas, aged fifteen, said: "This was when we began to ask questions: where do we want to go with this, and what do we mean by that, is there a 'how' and a 'why'?" The participants' individual and often unacknowledged abilities were illuminated as joint resources by being shared, and the young cultural producers moved from thinking in terms of what they wanted to tell to what audiences might want to know.

The animation project, although conducted mostly during school hours, was a time out from the ordinary division of the school day; it focused on themes that were not part of the regular curriculum, it took place in a professional media setting rather than in the classroom, and it facilitated other roles and different competencies from those normally nurtured between and amongst teachers and pupils. The animation project, like other creative media processes, therefore illuminates a number of features of learning that serve to question and challenge received notions of what knowledge formation is about in formal settings of education. What is knowledge in the first place? How does learning come about? Which means of learning are feasible, and in which contexts? And what are the roles, and the relations of power, between those who are in the know and those who want to learn? In discussing possible answers to these questions, we may begin to see how young people's self-directed, digital practices can help to highlight issues which are relevant for the future direction of education.

"You see things progress": Definitions of Knowledge

Few young producers of digital culture become interested in blogging, texting, or gaming because they are fascinated by the technology itself. Most enter the universe of digital production because they want to communicate on a simultaneous and ongoing basis with others, because they want to be entertained, or because they want to find out about things. Out-of-school media practices are therefore focused on processes and problems or interests, and not so much driven by systematic studies of particular facts or general issues.

The definition of school-based knowledge is different. Although teachers may use concrete examples and cases related to children's everyday experiences, a main goal of education is to develop conceptual knowledge. History lessons should train pupils to remember dates and events as mental props, so that they will acknowledge and recognize how these facts fit into larger, more general patterns of development and change. This means that pupils are trained to think about knowledge as discrete pieces of information that can be transmitted to them from their teacher or their textbook; and also as pieces that are compartmentalized into disciplines which, over time, may produce larger patterns, or concepts, that can be connected through abstract thinking. So, by grade ten, pupils should ideally recognize that revolutions in France and the United States could have had similar causes. Such an understanding of knowledge is clearly at odds with the interest-based and curiosity-driven approach to knowledge that digital forms of communication and production facilitate.

Moreover, young people's digital practices in out-of-school contexts are not only processual and problem-based, they are also based on immediate forms of communication and interaction. For example, one of the Danish animation groups worked with a stop-motion technique where clay figures and physical settings are constructed so that the camera can take single shots when participants move the figures. When re-playing little sequences of shots, the producers saw a very concrete, visual proof of their progress. As Katja, aged twelve, noted: "When we had worked for ten minutes, we could see that we had progressed, we could watch our progress." The here-and-now, hands-on character of the work process is rarely prioritized in ordinary school settings, where the ultimate proof of knowledge is a high score in a test or at an exam, not the immediate appreciation of the learning process itself.

In addition to being problem-based and tangible as a work process, leisure-time digital practices are also often focused on personal interests and experiences. As many popular and scholarly analyses have noted, the enormous expansion of today's media landscape in many parts of the world and the increase in personalized media technologies have meant that young people in particular have a more diversified, individualized use of media, that closely reflects their own priorities. This was also evident in the animation study. Most narrative themes revolved around personal issues that are of key importance to identity formation in (pre-)adolescence such as loneliness, romance, and appearance. Working on these themes gave the participants a chance not only to express problems of personal relevance, but also to do so in a symbolic form (sound, images, text) that could be communicated to others—both during the actual work process and in the results.

So, even if each participant contributed storylines that reflected their own interests, the themes found immediate resonance (if not always acceptance) with the others. This demonstrates the more general point that when we speak about individualization, including those forms that are spurred by digital technologies, we cannot define this concept as a simple process of personal choice; rather it is a social condition that is shared by people in many parts of the world, but which everyone has to tackle. "We seek biographical solutions to systemic contradictions," as the German sociologists Ulrich Beck and Elisabeth Gernsheim-Beck have cogently noted.[2] Like David Buckingham in the introduction to this volume, the Becks stress that individualization is a particular structural challenge of constructing identity in what they call late-modern risk societies, not an option that we can judge off-hand as either good and liberating or bad and repressive.

The forms of knowledge, then, that young people use and develop through their self-organized digital practices are clearly at odds with the definitions of knowledge on which most school curricula are based: they focus on the learning process rather than the resulting knowledge; they prioritize concrete issues over abstract concepts, experiences over facts and immediacy over delayed results. Also, they are motivated more by the sharing of personal problems than by the unraveling of wider social issues.

As long as both pupils and teachers accept the divide between school-based knowledge and leisure-based knowledge, these contradictions may not mean much. But if we begin to acknowledge that digital forms of communication nurture types of knowledge that are needed in forming future competencies, then these alternative types of knowledge do challenge prevalent ideals and curricular practices. Perhaps the most immediate question we need to answer is how these more processual and personalized forms of knowledge serve to restructure dominant educational thinking about knowledge—the view of knowledge as a set of discrete entities that may be handed down through the generations; that may be quantified, tested, and ranked; and whose validity exists beyond contextual boundaries and constraints.

Some of the most interesting debates on these issues can be found in the growing body of literature on science literacy. Spurred by young people's declining interest in many Western societies in taking up a science career, educationalists and scholars advocate a restructuring of science curricula to focus more on everyday cases and on the inductive explanations that may follow from these.[3] Still, advocates of these revisions are also aware of the possible losses in terms of conceptual reasoning and hard-science priorities. These attempts demonstrate the difficulties lying ahead as we begin to rethink dominant conceptions of knowledge and develop approaches that seek to balance the specific and the general, the personal and the principled, curiosity, and craft.

"I found it so chaotic": Means of Learning

If the very concept of knowledge is challenged by digital forms of identity performance, so is the learning process itself. Recent learning theories rightly stress that we learn on an individual basis, but that the learning process needs others in order to materialize. These sociocultural contexts are in unusual flux when it comes to creative digital production—with people milling around, with seemingly endless discussions alternating with spells of concentrated silence, and with testing out narrative and technical options only to ditch them because of disagreement or contraints of time and technical competence. Karen and Julie, both aged sixteen, found the preproduction of their group's animated narrative rather frustrating:

Karen: I just couldn't see why we needed so much storyboarding and in such detail.

Julie: Yes, I found it so chaotic, too.

Karen: I had thought perhaps it would be just one piece of paper, and you would quickly scribble a few drawings and stuff on it—just so that we knew where we were. And so when they started drawing everything in detail, with text and everything, and pasting it on the wall, I just thought: let's stop it here, right.

Even if not all everyday practices of gaming, texting, and speaking on the cell phone are creative processes in quite the same extensive manner as the animation project, they still to varying degrees display some of the same features of inconclusiveness, of making things up as you go along, and of taking decisions not knowing which options are the right ones. These are radical learning processes because they challenge everyday routines and taken-for-granted assumptions. As such, they can be frustrating to the point of anxiety, and they are often carried through only because the participants' personal investment, their curiosity, and drive overrule the obvious setbacks, the quarrels, and the disappointments also encountered along the way.

What is more, these processes develop the participants' ability to collect, select, and combine a wide variety of sound, image, graphics, and textual elements. This "collage creativity" is facilitated by the large array of mediatized symbols that are readily available to many children and young people; indeed, these symbols are offered by commercial enterprises as readymade packages to, for example, bloggers who want to spice up their sites on MySpace. Children playing around with these options clearly demonstrate an often-intimate knowledge of these symbolic repertoires—for example, the young animation producers knew and could argue for the "right" types of music that go with particular genres, and bloggers are very aware of the way in which particular visual styles promote their self-presentations, as Stern's chapter in this volume demonstrates.

Young people's recombinations of image, music, and text also nurture nonlinear forms of learning, where they move between rule acquisition and rule modification, between the familiar and the foreign—gaining knowledge about particular norms of communicative etiquette in a chat room or in responding to text messages on the mobile, acquiring insight about the technical and aesthetic elements that go into creating and managing a personal home page, and then being able to refashion and operate on those elements. Such forms of learning offer the young users immediate opportunities to reflect on the choices they make. This does not mean that they sit down and deliberate about these choices: rather, they intuitively modify their practices and often share good hints on best practice with their friends.

These self-styled digital practices are rather different from the processes of learning found in most classrooms. Here, learning is at best a result of teaching where pupils know what to learn, but not always why such knowledge matters. The teacher is in charge of creating the parameters for learning and of dividing the learning process into neatly defined steps that challenge the pupils, but hopefully not so much that they lose heart or interest. This so-called scaffolding of the learning process is most easily accomplished in a school environment in which activities and their outcomes can be planned and coordinated by the teacher. By contrast, anyone who has witnessed the intense interaction that goes on at a game session or during an Internet chat session will know that scaffolding is difficult, and, when it happens, peers are in charge of the process. Learning is perhaps never a linear process, but this becomes particularly evident at such instances. Through their engagements with digital media in their leisure time, young people experience the fact that learning can be different from being taught at school. It can be driven by curiosity, which serves to overcome set-backs and frustrations; it can be a playful process of training and breaking rules and conventions; and its results can be immediately shared and appreciated by peers.

Many proponents of innovation and of the so-called knowledge society emphasize some of the same elements, noting that they are fundamental to creative processes and to life-long learning. One need not embrace all of the underlying assumptions of these arguments in order to acknowledge that dynamic, globalized societies need people who can and will modify and develop existing competencies, who may think and act "outside the box," and who can do so in practice-based environments providing immediate feedback. These competencies apply most readily to the employment profile of the well educated, but in more general terms flexibility and reflexivity are needed by most people living in dynamic late-modern societies. A concept of learning as neatly compartmentalized bits of information that can be scaffolded and taught through intense and repeated training called "education" is clearly challenged by the demands made by these societies. Naturally, this prospect does not invalidate schools, but it does change the basis on which they may define their teaching and hence the learning obtained by their students. In this process of redefinition, considering the means of learning involved in young people's digital engagements offers an obvious route to follow.

"The expression is all that matters": Modes of Literacy

Equally challenging, of course, is the debate on *what* children should learn. This is not a new question; in fact it has existed since the origin of modern, dynamic societies and the "invention" of childhood. For in dynamic societies the demands made on people's competencies change over time, and children are a particular focus of adult concern, since adults are in a position of power to shape these competencies. Two hundred years ago, public debate on education often focused upon whether or not children should learn to calculate and read—and especially whether or not they should also learn to write (since writing is much more difficult to control). In Western societies, the book was the technology of literacy, and Arabic numerals were the basis of numeracy.

Today, public debate in many societies displays similar concerns about children's future competencies—only now the debate has become even more complex, because the book is surrounded by live and still images, by sound and graphics, and by intricate, and often mediatized, mixtures of all of these. Clearly, print literacy is not an adequate term to cover all of these modes of expression, and so we see an upsurge of hyphenated forms of literacy, mostly defined in relation to particular technologies, such as media literacy, information literacy, visual literacy, teleliteracy, metamedia literacy, computer literacy, digital literacy, internet literacy, and so on.[4] Information, computer, and Internet literacy were prevalent terms through the 1990s when the personal computer and Internet communication were taken up in a big way in most Western societies. Currently, no single term seems predominant, perhaps because no single technology may be seen as the most prevalent; rather, it is the often complex constellations of old and new media, and the combinations of text and sound, live and still images that stand out as the main trend in today's media culture.

Based on this current trend, some scholars speak about multimodal literacies, others prefer multimedia literacy, while still others offer the concept of multimodal interactions.[5] Whatever the terms, this volume testifies to the fact that young people avidly engage with most or all of these new media forms, and with their recombinations—they take and send pictures with their mobiles, they produce websites and personal blogs, they use camcorders for filmmaking and go on the net for gaming, they edit music and refashion avatars downloaded from the net. All these activities implicitly require and develop new competencies or new forms of "literacy."

The "collage creativity" that I mentioned above surfaces with particular clarity when young cultural producers manipulate images, sound, and text. In the animation project, one group made an animated narrative that was clearly inspired by *Help, I'm a Fish* (2000) and *Finding Nemo* (2003). The group had intense debates about whether to rip music from existing sound tracks, to remix and edit sound bites to suit the visuals, or to create their own music. In the end, time set the limits and provoked choices. Fifteen-year-old Jonah and sixteen-year-old Adam agreed that the most interesting part of the process was using the software program Flash to make the figures come alive—in quite concrete terms, to animate them (from the Latin *animus* = soul):

Jonah: I thought the best thing was making the movements—well, the figures and all.

Adam: What I liked the best was structuring the figures, because that's what brought it all to life.

Jonah: For example, when you make a fish, you give it an expression. If you think about an ordinary fish, it has no expressions, right.

Adam: No. But [in animation] the expression is all that matters.

When the group manipulated visuals, sound, and text through software, their identity work materialized in quite concrete ways. Speaking along similar lines, the British cultural theorist Stuart Hall defines cultural identity as a form of *symbolic articulation* that operates as a bridge between inner feelings and external surroundings.[6] We have no direct access to other people's thoughts and emotions, but symbols, such as words and text, image and sound, offer a means of expressing inner states so that they may be shared by others. Hall's term "articulation" encapsulates this important duality of expression (as in an articulate person) and connection (as in an articulated lorry) that is key to the way in which symbols operate in the formation of cultural identities. In performing identity work through digital practices, young people can gain a new perspective upon ordinary media products; as one of the pupils said during the animation project: "I watch TV commercials now in terms of Flash" (the software program her group was using). At the same time, they can get a new perspective upon themselves because they enter new cultural and social terrains.

Why are these multimodal articulations of identity relevant to learning and schooling, one may well ask. One answer is because such articulations are tangible and visible, and so they may be shared, critiqued, and possibly changed through interaction with others. This was exactly what happened during the animation project, when participants' ideas and products were up for discussion, evaluation, and appreciation or dismissal: issues that mattered to them could be tackled not as personal issues, but as aesthetic and technical issues. Such an approach has obvious advantages in educating young people to whom issues of identity are pertinent, but who rarely, and for very good reasons, lay themselves open to scrutiny in the classroom. For both pupils and teachers, it is much easier to handle issues of identity as differences of opinion about color grading or sound than it is to handle them as personal problems.

Of course, it may be debated whether the often complex digital practices performed by children and young people in their leisure time involve real competencies at all. What we may say with confidence at this stage is that these practices involve the use of important cultural resources that reflect back on formal schooling and, in doing so, point to limitations in the current emphasis on print and oral literacies as primary competencies. The tangible nature of many digital practices, mixing visuals, sound, and text, offer an important means to tackle matters of cultural identity, if only because they may be stored, shared, and reflected upon. Such reflections have obvious relevance for contemporary societies whose members need to be able to handle complexities across a range of sites and settings—being able to shape and refashion an often complex constellation of aspects of identity within structural parameters that are not up to individual selection. While this situation is not new, the constitutive role now played by media in this process makes it imperative that educators and policy makers begin to reorient their educational priorities and practices toward a broader understanding of literacy.

As Buckingham notes in the introduction to this volume, such a broader understanding immediately raises key questions about the aims of literacy. Should young people simply learn how to use media technologies, or do they also need to know about the social, cultural, and historical dimensions of those technologies? Do we define media as tools of information processing, which users need to apply effectively, or do we define media as social forms of communication, which users need to appropriate critically? So far, most educational debate and reform has focused upon introducing computers as information-processing tools, a focus that may be due to the novelty and the rapid, if uneven, take-up of the technology. Whatever the reasons, this functional focus fits more easily with the forms and organization of learning on which most schools are based than does a critical focus on media that emphasizes shifting contexts of use and evaluation of the social function of media. As the animation project and many similar studies demonstrate, young people harbor more diverse and advanced resources concerning the media than the merely functional approach suggests, and, importantly, these resources are key to their chances of developing relevant competencies for the future. But as is also evident from the examples given in this chapter, there are clear limits to the young cultural producers' ability to develop their skills of evaluation and reflection on their own. They were not helped in this by the professional animators, who explicitly prioritized training in production skills, and the insights gained from the project were not developed further by their regular teachers or integrated into the school curriculum. To do so would require a redefinition of literacy that Denmark and most other countries have not yet prioritized. It would also require a redefinition of what counts as legitimate learning resources.

Today, textbooks combined with oral presentations are still the main teaching materials in most schools in Western societies, while in other parts of the world even textbooks are sought-after commodities. Children who grow up with a plethora of multimedia forms, and who in many cases create their own digital productions and interactions, are developing aesthetic sensibilities and insights that few ordinary schoolbooks can match. If it is true that one of the main challenges facing traditional schooling is to retain and develop children's curiosity and craving to learn, then this challenge is certainly even more pronounced when children encounter teaching materials in schools that rarely meet their expectations in terms of multimodal presentation, selection, and interaction. The current mismatch between teaching materials found at school and the often highly sophisticated digital expressions found at home makes it very difficult for teachers to systematically develop the cultural resources that children bring from their out-of-school contexts. A key challenge in developing multimodal literacies at school is therefore to create and use multimodal teaching materials to underpin those learning processes.

"Like a roller coaster": Learning as a Social Practice

Identity performances are clearly involved in most of the leisure-time engagements that children and young people have with digital media. To the uninformed adult eye, teenagers blogging in their bedrooms or playing online games may, indeed, appear engaged, but these also seem to be individual, even lonely, activities. However, as this volume has amply demonstrated, these engagements are fundamentally social in nature. Since many of the recent media technologies afford and demand interaction and dialogue, young users are collaboratively developing their abilities in personal expression and dialogue, in handling disagreement and questioning decisions. They get used to operating in relation to teams and through open-ended processes of negotiation.

Such processes are not always easy to sustain, let alone to master. Anne, aged twelve, described her participation in one of the Danish animation groups as a painstaking process, where she moved between elation and exhaustion: "I felt like a roller coaster, going up and down." Anne was often unsure about what would happen next, and how she could position herself within the shifting working relationships. Even for participants who clearly thrived on being "let loose" to engage in ad hoc networking, the continuous dialogues and negotiations demanded extra efforts, which were accepted if not always liked. In one group, for example, the young producers agreed that each of them should have one theme or idea included in their joint narrative. Following well-known gender preferences, girls tended to argue in favor of girl-meets-boy ideas, while boys preferred more action-based elements. The result was a mainly romantic plot into which a red "joy car" (a car used in funfairs and tivolis) raced into the final scene—the boys' humorous send-up of a happy ending.

Digital practices offer children and young people experiences of learning that are malleable and collaborative, and where nearly everything can be questioned and debated. Through these processes, the young participants learn how to tackle rather complex issues and to find workable, if not perfect, solutions. Most participants take responsibility for their actions and they invest all, or at least most, of themselves. This inclusiveness is part of the thrill but also a potential pitfall, because critique may be taken to reveal personal flaws. This duality is evident when Anne speaks about herself as being on an emotional roller coaster, but it is also seen when young people go online with their own homepages or blogs; as Stern's chapter indicates, they perform various forms of self-presentation, but they also lay themselves open to comments from unknown audiences. In a similar vein, boyd in this volume notes how teenagers use their social networking sites to develop an outsider's view of themselves while at the same time seeking acceptance within the group.

Prevalent notions of learning in schools are clearly challenged by digital forms of learning—they are joint sites of action which train participants in handling complexity, and whose success depends upon the young users investing most of themselves and being validated accordingly. By contrast, in many societies, educational policy favors individual training for explicit ends, which are often particular tests or exams. Here, learning is less open-ended, less dialogic and team-based, and, in the short term, less risky for pupils' self-perceptions, because their learning processes seem to have few implications for their everyday lives and personal priorities.

Recent educational theories have begun to question these prevalent policies. For example, Jean Lave and Etienne Wenger speak about learning as a process that is situated within "communities of practice."[7] Their account draws on the learning processes found in traditions of apprenticeship, where the gradual acquisition of skills learned by emulating the masters was the entry point to social acceptance at the center of the professional group. Scholars have seen parallels to these learning routes in current game communities, and, indeed, computer games have been offered as one of the main alternatives to standard forms of learning, precisely because gaming is perceived to be in tune with future demands of collaboration, strategic thinking, and hit-and-run decision making.[8]

While this promotion is understandable in terms of the tremendous impact of the games industry on contemporary media output, much less is made of the fact that gaming remains the most gendered media practice amongst young people.[9] Some researchers have claimed that girls' relative lack of interest in gaming can be overcome by designing different types of games that fit girls' genre preferences for relationships over action and construction over combat.[10] However, this claim contradicts contextualized studies of media uses which demonstrate that girls often prioritize being with friends rather than doing things with friends (like gaming) and hence play computer games more on an individual basis as diversion and less as a collective pursuit. As Karen Vered states: "Contrary to dominant research trends which emphasize the narrative analysis of computer games, I suggest that girls and boys approach computer play differently, irrespective of the software content, including genre and specific elements of narrative such as character and setting."[11] Given the complexity of contemporary media culture and the potential diversities of youthful uses, we should be careful not to single out specific genres or media as particularly relevant for innovative learning. Rather, the important challenge seems to be to develop inclusive contexts of learning at school, contexts that balance dialogue and monologue, security and risk, communal and individual aspects of learning.

Children's digital engagements outside school not only nurture other learning processes and learning contexts; they also help develop different notions of *time* involved in such processes. Much popular and academic literature has focused on the so-called heavy users of digital media. Gamers in particular have been subject to critical scrutiny on the grounds of their "excessive" time-use, in a manner that mirrors earlier concerns over magazine-reading, film-going, and TV-viewing.[12] Less has been made of the ways in which many digital practices engage their young users so intensively that they refashion their usual sense of time. In fact, this refashioning resembles what is known from more professional working practices in areas such as art and science—only here the sheer abandonment and self-absorption is seen as a sure sign that something original is brewing. Whatever the verdict, it seems as if intensive creative engagements go together with at least a certain reorganization of one's sense of time. So, in the Danish animation project, teachers had to urge the young participants to leave the premises at particularly intensive work periods, while the participants would fill up slacker work spells with texting or gaming on their mobiles and had little incentive to stay around after school hours.

What we see in many Western societies today is a generation of children whose digital leisure activities entail learning through negotiations in online and offline networks; who expect to be heard and to listen with respect to other views; and who often have extensive experiences with restructuring time according to their personal investments in particular projects or issues. If schools want to elaborate on and develop those resources, they need to create new contexts of learning that facilitate both spatial and temporal flexibilities, for example by extending sites of learning to include virtual spaces and the local community and by modifying existing time slots called lessons. But in doing so they also need to heed other lessons learned from studies of digital practices. Some children, such as Anne in the Danish animation group, find the open-ended character of learning and its personal investments very provoking or too scary, and so they opt out or disengage themselves from the ongoing activities. These children need added, professional scaffolding in order to develop a sense of security about the process and trust in the other participants. Among other things, this means scrutinizing the position of teachers in relation to pupils.

"We all made decisions": Social Roles and Rules of Power

As we noted earlier, mobile texting, online gaming, and blogging as well as digital editing of visuals and sound are all embedded within youthful communities of practice. Even when these practices seem to be individual affairs, they are surrounded by social envelopes of peer learning—which may include the sharing of basic "know how," such as tips on how to get cheap ring tones, tricks on little-known links, and warnings about useless, or risky, characters online. Both online and offline networks operate through intricate processes of social inclusion and exclusion, but the hierarchies spurred by digital practices are often different from the ones found at school since they adopt different markers of success. An experienced gamer may not score very highly in the hierarchy of schooling, just as successful pupils can be ranked very near the bottom in their digital networks.

In the animation project, most of these reorganizations of roles and status were conducted by the young participants themselves as part of their work process. Conflicts were managed through discussions that often seemed endless from an adult perspective, but whose merit according to some participants was that "instead of one person making the decisions, we all did," as thirteen-year-old Chris put it. In some cases, new alliances were formed. For example, a girl and a boy who constantly disagreed during lessons found themselves working together in the editing phase of the animation project, not because they agreed to do so, but because their competencies turned out to be complementary—the boy was an expert on rap music, which was to be used in the narrative, while the girl had experience with graphic design.

Likewise, the young participants in the animation project mainly turned to one another for help during the production process—a clear sign that they defined their work in relation to out-of-school contexts rather than school contexts. Only on a few occasions did they approach their teachers, and then it was mainly to get help to solve a conflict or for practical questions which they assumed the teachers could answer. The teachers, on their side, fit the part in that they rarely intervened in the creative process—this was left to the professional animators. They became facilitators of the pupils' work, a role that they mostly limited to resolving technical and narrative issues. Several of the young participants were very clear about what they considered to be appropriate limits of facilitation. Jonah and Adam, who were part of the group focusing upon a humorous plot about a fish, described the different approaches of the professional animators in this way:

Jonah: Well, Michael he wanted to change everything.

Adam: Yeah, adding spots to our fish and what not.

Jonah: Yeah, spots all of a sudden.

Adam: And so he changed our fish from a funny fish into a plaice [laughs].

Jonah: But with Jim it was different. One of the things I noticed was that, even if many wanted him to come, he finished what he was doing first. He did not disappear in the middle of everything, and I liked that.

The animation project offers just one example of the numerous ways in which children's digital practices challenge received roles in education. In most classrooms, both pupils and teachers know and perform their respective roles, and these are distributed along well-established hierarchies, with the teacher at the pinnacle. Even if pupils challenge these hierarchies, and this is an integral part of schooling, this is done from a knowledge of their existence. The forms of communication that the teacher instigates are mainly monologues, with the teacher in charge of distributing the right to ask and answer questions. Teaching is based on focusing upon one issue at a time, and this is a main reason why teachers find pupils' unwarranted interactions so disturbing. The teacher authorizes and monitors which media and materials should be used for learning, and in doing so certain types of information are also selected and deemed relevant before they are used for teaching.

If we compare these forms of classroom interaction with what goes on when young people engage with digital media, the differences stand out. Users will often perform several tasks at a time, they do not focus on one particular issue, and they mix media and modes of expression. These modes are shaped, selected, and assembled while they are being used. What is more, the social relations involved in these activities are often as important, or more important, than the tasks or technologies at hand. For example, boys will spend a long time debating the "proper" rules of conduct before playing a computer game, or they will interrupt the game in order to discuss different interpretations of such rules.

If schools begin to build on and integrate some of these unacknowledged learning processes, will that make teachers superfluous? Quite the opposite, I would say. Teachers will be as necessary for learning as ever, but their roles will have to be modified from information authorities into knowledge facilitators. Moreover, their roles of authority will become more complex. Insights based on textbook sources may be challenged by pupils gathering the latest information on gene modification or cultural conflicts from wikis or net portals, and so teachers will have to constantly prove their authority in concrete action, rather than assuming a given status. Even so, teachers will also need to act as gatekeepers of information, for example in teaching which sources and content to trust on the Internet. In performing these roles, teachers will not only be facilitators of social networks, but, just as importantly, they will be facilitators of knowledge validation and acceptance. Just as we saw how digital production processes afford and demand a constant movement between expression and reflection, so teachers will have to master such dynamic movements if digital media are to be incorporated more extensively into existing frameworks of education.

From Resources to Competencies

It may well be argued that identity work and media have always gone together. Indeed, since the advent of mass literacy, children and young people have been some of the first to take up and explore new media, and through much of the previous century youth cultures in Western societies have centrally been articulated in relation to music, film, and television—being a Clara Bow fan, an Elvis enthusiast, a Trekkie. What is new are the implications following from those processes in terms of learning and the formation of competencies.

As I have argued in this chapter, one of the key global challenges of the twenty-first century is to develop the human capacities that are needed to deal with increasing complexities of an economic, political, and cultural nature. And, as we have seen, children's self-styled digital practices can particularly promote their handling of complexity. The often intricate interlacings of mass-mediated and interpersonal forms of communication, of reception and production, global and local interactions, operate as symbolic and social meeting grounds between the familiar and the foreign, inviting and demanding young people to position themselves in relation to new experiences and expressions. Children and young people have different resources for tackling such complexities, and they react in different ways—avoidance, negation, inclusion, and reflection are some of the reactions that we found in our animation study. Irrespective of their reactions, young people's digital practices are now one of the key areas of identity performance and creative learning. However, they are primarily exercised in out-of-school contexts and hence left open to individual differences of development rather than necessarily being characterized by equality of opportunities.

Viewed from this perspective, the dispersion of relevant learning sites and resources represents a key challenge for education. I have proposed that schools need to take on board in more systematic ways the insights gained from such out-of-school practices because they are vital to future competence formation. This does not mean that schools should abandon their existing strengths and forms of operation; indeed, any such proposal would be rather naive, given the fundamental role still played by education as a means of social selection and a definer of what is deemed proper knowledge. Nor do my suggestions imply that we embrace all digital practices performed by the young; indeed, I think we need to avoid easy oppositions between what is sometimes termed "informal" and "formal" learning. This is because such oppositions often operate on dichotomies that tend to obscure the complexities involved in school reform: school/leisure, hierarchical/democratic, teacher-centered/child-centered, monologue/dialogue, analysis/expression, serious/playful, emulative/innovative, dated/novel, and so on. Within this binary logic there is an imperceptible sliding toward a normative conclusion that schooling is bad because it is strictly based on rationalist forms of analytical inculcation as opposed to child-centered, autonomous, and playful leisure activities, which are good because they gear young people to the right future.

In addressing the implications of children's digital media practices for learning, concerted efforts should be made to heed results offered in the present volume as well as in empirical studies from school settings, all of which provide a depth of evidence about the complexities involved in working with digital media.[13] As we have seen, these results demonstrate how young media producers draw on existing genre conventions and stylistic repertoires culled from their experiences as media audiences, how analysis and expressiveness go together in production processes, and how self-propelled collaboration coexists with professional coaching. Rather than defining identity work per se as oppositional, and set informal leisure practices against mundane school routines, questions need to be asked about which forms generated by those engagements are relevant for education and may be developed into the kinds of competencies children will need as they grow up in more dispersed learning environments and more complex societies.

For it is evident that the digital practices carried out in out-of-school contexts do not automatically develop into competencies in and of themselves. To do so, young people need systematic training and development, so that insights gained from one particular experience or problem may be transferred and applied to other issues and situations. These forms of joint training can only be performed through formal education. This is because school is the central social institution in which individuals come together with the specific purpose and possibility of pursuing sustained, joint learning processes. Also, schooling affords and demands learning processes that develop concrete forms of knowledge into more conceptual forms of knowledge. These forms of knowledge are needed in order to make abstractions—a key competence that is required to handle complexities and that is therefore in great demand in late-modern societies. Abstractions are also at the core of critique, which is to do with making connections between different problems and with drawing conclusions across seemingly different discourses and practices. Finally, competencies ultimately need to be subject to some form of institutional selection, evaluation, and approval. We need to map more systematically the scale and scope of children's self-defined media practices, and we need to determine which of these practices are relevant resources for their future and thus merit educational attention.

In doing so, there are some key oppositions that we need to acknowledge and tackle. As I have mentioned, the education system in all known societies operates as one of the main mechanisms of social selection. How can this function be balanced against the obvious resources for democratic participation and involvement that today's generation of children develop through their digital engagements? Schools traditionally privilege abstract and discrete forms of knowledge. How can these forms be mixed with the more problem- and context-based skills that young people develop through their out-of-school digital practices? Moreover, schools are social institutions that serve to select and organize disparate bits of information into coherent bodies of approved knowledge. How can this function be combined with the dynamic changes in knowledge formation that are brought about by Internet and mobile communication, and which are appropriated by many youngsters as second nature? How can schools in the future train pupils in trusting some forms of knowledge over others and in acknowledging the validity of knowledge whose usefulness cannot be determined on the spot? Similarly, schools are hierarchical organizations operating on continuity rather than change. How can schools build on these continuities to scaffold pupils' learning processes without forfeiting their opportunities to think and work "outside the box"?

Last, but not least, we need to discuss our definition of schooling in view of the digitization of learning. For example, in 1999 poor children in one of New Delhi's slum areas with little or no access to formal education were provided with computers in public spaces to be used with minimal adult intervention, as part of the so-called hole in the wall project. According to the project director, Sugata Mitra, the results demonstrated that users intuitively developed computer skills.[14] Such experiments invite debate about whether educational interventions are needed in order to develop literacies at all—and if so, of what kind. In Western societies, discussions of literacy and competence formation focus on equity of access and use in formalized educational settings, which are set against individualized, domestic uses that tend to reinforce existing differences across boundaries of age, gender, and ethnicity. How do these notions play out under widely different circumstances? Is it possible to conceive of other ways of gaining systematic training and other forms of validation of the outcomes?

Different societies offer different answers to these questions, which are partly dependent upon their educational traditions. For example, Singapore is currently reforming its school system to allow for more differentiated and creative work processes, while in Northern Europe and the United States, the pendulum is swinging in the opposite direction: here policy makers put increasing emphasis on national tests and on evidence-based learning along well-defined lines, in order to counter what are perceived as the unduly permissive tendencies of the past.

Whatever the educational policies favored, it seems clear that in their leisure time many children and young people are already busily rehearsing for a future in which the handling of mediatized complexities is key. Such processes involve identity performances that are more diverse and wide ranging than the specific training in technological skills that is emphasized within most schools in Western societies. If these educational priorities remain unchanged, the obvious result will be a widening not only of social, ethnic and gender divides within particular societies, but also a widening of divides between societies. This process is typically referred to as a matter of "digital divides," which reflects the fact that media in general, and digital technologies in particular, are constitutive elements of contemporary societies, of social positionings, political power, and cultural practices. However, as the Spanish sociologist Manuel Castells emphasizes, digital divides are basically *social* divides, and education plays a key role both in the formation and in the potential dissolution of these divides.[15] For it is through education that some learn to handle mediatized symbols in both work and leisure, and others do not. In debating and attempting to tackle the challenges to education posed by digital practices, it is vital that we keep these wider perspectives in mind.

Conclusion: Unity in Diversity?

Several conclusions may be drawn from the present chapter, in terms of both future policy and research. Most importantly for educational policy, our results and discussions demonstrate that formalized schooling is vital for the formation of digital competencies. This is because in school, pupils' individual resources are harnessed for joint processes of learning that push the boundaries of these resources in ways that leisure-time and ad hoc communities of practice cannot do, at least without similar levels of societal legitimation. And while education involves, and will continue to involve, organized selection through evaluation, it is equally one of the few social institutions in which both learners and teachers can and must interact beyond themselves and their own choices: it is a joint meeting ground for encounters with others—with what seems strange, difficult to comprehend, and accept. Hence, education is also the place in which very real divisions of access to and use of digital resources may be minimized.

In training pupils to handle the complexities of a heavily mediatized world, and the forms of identity work that it entails, educators will need to draw on children's out-of-school experiences, which increasingly involve complex negotiations between self and others. They will also inevitably be doing so within school settings that are still characterized by diversity and divergence. There are important questions here about how educational policy makers and practitioners will define and handle such encounters with "otherness." One way forward is to follow a route of cosmopolitanism, where mutual tolerance and dialogue are seen as leading to consensus and where such processes are perceived as individual choices that can be followed at will.[16] Another option is to follow a route of critique, in which mutual respect and dialogue are defined as joint conditions of living together in one world, including with people whose outlook on life may not be shared, but without whom no life is feasible.

We may also ask questions about the organization of various educational institutions. The dispersal of learning sites and the key importance of young people's digital practices potentially reframe the relations between statutory and voluntary sectors in advancing digital learning. Here, the chapter has pointed to prevalent oppositions between formal and informal learning that seem to constrain cooperation—an issue which needs to be more directly addressed in future policy developments. Such issues of organization are also related to issues of substance—should digital media practices be for all or should they be relegated to specific "creative" sectors, subjects, or individuals? Should digital, or multimodal, literacy be defined as a functional tool or as a critical resource?

In terms of research, this chapter raises core issues about the future organization of media studies relating to children and young people. As we have seen, young people live in an increasingly complex media culture, and one of the key challenges for scholars is to match this empirical complexity with the requisite theoretical and methodological complexity. One of the best ways forward is to develop comparative studies, across several dimensions. First, it is obvious that to analyze and understand an interlaced media culture, researchers need to address not single media, but entire media ensembles. Second, these media are embedded in a range of settings, and so studies need to cross boundaries, for example, of home and school, or online and offline practices. Third, young people in many parts of the world interlace processes of production and reception in unprecedented ways, and these interlacings may be investigated in their own right as means of handling complexity. Finally, the crossing of boundaries in terms of media, genres, settings, and appropriations takes place not in one, but multiple, locations around the world. The increasingly global reach of contemporary media technologies makes it imperative to conduct multidisciplinary, cross-national studies in order to address the selective take-up, the divergent uses, and the resulting divides that are bound to set the conditions for future learning and literacy.

Notes

1. The study formed part of a larger project carried out in 2005–2006, which also involved storytelling, drama, and digital museum productions in addition to the animation workshop described in this chapter. The project was funded by the Danish Ministry of Culture and the animation project was studied by a research team from the University of Southern Denmark. The research team undertook observation of the production process, individual, and focus-group interviews with pupils, teachers, and animators,

and analyses of the final products. Thanks are due to my coresearchers, assistant professor Lotte Nyboe, and research assistant Heidi Jørgensen.

2. Ulrich Beck and Elisabeth Gernsheim-Beck, *Individualization: Institutionalized Individualism and Its Social and Political Consequences* (London: Sage, 2001), xxii.

3. See e.g., Rodger W. Bybee, *Achieving Scientific Literacy: From Purposes to Practices* (Portsmouth, NH: Heinemann, 1997) and Morris H. Shamos, *The Myth of Scientific Literacy* (New Brunswick, NJ: Rutgers University Press, 1995).

4. David Bianculli, *Teleliteracy: Taking Television Seriously* (New York: Continuum, 1992); Richard Sinatra, *Visual Literacy: Connections to Thinking, Reading and Writing* (Springfield, IL: Charles C Thomas, 1986); Lyn Elizabeth M Martin, ed. *The Challenge of Internet Literacy: The Instruction-Web Convergence* (New York: Haworth Press, 1997); Jay L. Lemke, Metamedia Literacy: Transforming Meanings and Media, in *Handbook of Literacy and Technology: Transformations in a Post-Typographic World,* eds. Michael C. McKenna et al. (Mahwah, NJ: Lawrence Erlbaum, 1998); John M. Nevison, Computing in the Liberal Arts College, *Science,* 22 (1976): 396–402; Paul Gilster, *Digital Literacy* (Indianapolis, IN: Wiley Publishing, 1998). For a useful overview of media literacy research and policy issues, see David Buckingham et al., *The Media Literacy of Children and Young People: A Review of the Research Literature on Behalf of Ofcom* (London: Ofcom). http://www.ofcom.org.uk/advice/media_literacy/medlitpub/medlitpubrss/ml_children.pdf (accessed August 2006).

5. Carey Jewitt and Gunther Kress, eds., *Multimodal Literacy* (New York: Peter Lang, 2003); Fred T. Hofstetter, *Multimedia Literacy* (New York: McGraw-Hill, 1995); Sigrid Norris, *Analysing Multimodal Interaction: A Methodological Framework* (London: Routledge, 2004).

6. Stuart Hall, Introduction: Who Needs Identity? in *Questions of Cultural Identity,* eds. Stuart Hall and Paul DuGay (London: Sage, 1996).

7. Jean Lave and Etienne Wenger, *Situated Learning: Legitimate Peripheral Participation* (Cambridge, UK: Cambridge University Press, 1991).

8. See e.g., Stephen J. Ceci and Antonio Roazzi, The Effects of Context on Cognition: Postcards from Brazil, in *Mind in Context: Interactionist Perspectives on Human Intelligence,* eds. Robert J. Sternberg and Richard K. Wagner (Cambridge, UK: Cambridge University Press, 1994); James Paul Gee, *What Video Games Have to Teach Us About Learning and Literacy* (New York: Palgrave Macmillan, 2003); John Kirriemuir and Angela McFarlane, *Literature Review in Games and Learning* (Bristol, UK: Nesta Futurelab series, Report 8, 2004).

9. Sonia Livingstone and Moira Bovill, eds., *Children and their Changing Media Environment: A European Comparative Study* (New York: Erlbaum, 2001).

10. See e.g., Kaveri Subrahmanyam and Patricia Marks Greenfield, Computer Games for Girls: What Makes Them Play? in *From Barbie to Mortal Combat: Gender and Computer Games,* eds. Justine Cassell and Henry Jenkins (Cambridge, MA: MIT Press, 1998); and discussion in Jo Bryce and Jason Rutter, Digital Games and Gender, in Jason Rutter and Jo Bryce, *Understanding Digital Games* (London: Sage, 2006), 186–204.

11. Karen Orr Vered, Blue Group Boys Play Incredible Machine, Girls Play Hopscotsch: Social Discourse and Gendered Play at the Computer, in *Digital Diversions: Youth Culture in the Age of Multimedia,* ed. Julian Sefton-Green (London: Taylor & Francis Group/UCL Press, 1998), 57.

12. Kirsten Drotner, Dangerous Media? Panic Discourses and Dilemmas of Modernity, *Paedagogica Historica,* 35, no. 3 (1999): 593–619.

13. See e.g., Julian Sefton-Green, ed., *Young People, Creativity and New Technologies: The Challenge of Digital Arts* (London: Routledge, 1999); Glynda Hull and Kathrine Schultz, *School's Out! Bridging*

Out-of-school Literacies with Classroom Practice (New York: Teachers' College Press, 2001). For a reasoned analysis of the ways in which mediatized identity work is integral to students' everyday lives at school, see Dominique Pasquier, *Cultures lycéennes: la tyrannie de la majorité* (Paris: Autrement, 2005).

14. Sugata Mitra, Minimally Invasive Education: A Progress Report on the "Hole-in-the-Wall" Experiments, *British Journal of Educational Technology*, 34, no. 3 (2003): 367–371; Ritu Dangwall, Public Computing, Computer Literacy and Educational Outcome: Children and Computers in Rural India. http://www.hole-in-the-wall.com/docs/Paper10.pdf (accessed August 2006).

15. Manuel Castells, *The End of the Millennium. The Information Age: Economy, Society and Culture* (Oxford: Blackwell, 1998), vol. III.

16. See e.g., Nick Stevenson, *Cultural Citizenship: Cosmopolitan Questions* (Milton Keynes: Open University Press, 2003).

Mixing the Digital, Social, and Cultural: Learning, Identity, and Agency in Youth Participation

Shelley Goldman and Angela Booker

Stanford University, School of Education

Meghan McDermott

Global Action Project, New York

Innovations in technology are, once again, shaping how adults and youth interact with each other in school, at home, and at large. Our focus in this chapter is on how youth use multiple forms of media and technology, in concert with their commitments to community dialogue and social justice, as they learn to be participants in civic and democratic practices. We share two case studies that revolve around youth–adult interactions in learning environments that offer youth real opportunities to be influential in their respective communities. We look firstly at youth media production in the context of a community-based media arts project, and secondly at how young people use technology in the course of their work as student representatives on their local school board.

Our aim in this context is to understand how digital media are used in relation to what we shall call *social and cultural technologies*, those tools that organize social participation in particular settings.[1] Our definition of the word technology is consistent with Raymond Williams's view:

> A technology . . . is, first, the body of knowledge appropriate to the development of such skills and applications and, second, a body of knowledge and conditions for the practical use and application of a range of devices. . . . What matters in each stage, is that a technology is always, in a full sense, social. It is necessarily in complex and variable connection with other social relations and institutions. . . .[2]

As we have seen in the earlier chapters in this volume, youth are using a wide range of digital media that facilitate social interaction, from MySpace.com and instant messenger systems to video production and editing equipment, to organize access to and production of digital output such as the texts of online debate, Internet data (audio, visual, and textual), and text messages. Our goal here is to spotlight the intertwined ways in which youth are engaging with multiple types of digital media as a feature of their learning. We also consider how digital media combine and mix with social and cultural technologies.

Social technologies are tools that organize social activities. They intentionally focus the attention of participants. A key element of social technologies is the flexibility in form and in content. For instance, brainstorming is a technique used broadly to generate a list of ideas (and to define an area of focus), but it can be implemented in a variety of ways, using various and adjustable conventions (for example, providing a time limit, starting with an opening question and with any content). Cultural technologies, on the other hand, are formal tools that organize processes for communication in specific settings. They structure participation in standard ways that are consistent in form, but not necessarily in content. The standardization of form is a key element of these technologies, while the flexibility of content allows for appropriation of the tool to achieve unanticipated outcomes. Examples of cultural technologies are legal resolutions, standard notation in musical composition, and so on.[3]

The notion of social, cultural, and digital tools being mutually constitutive of learning experiences also finds support in the work of John Dewey: "It is possible to isolate . . . several types and levels of tools, as well as several levels of functions performed. Plans of action at their various levels are tools, as is the hardware utilized in their realization."[4] The idea here is that beyond what the media art forms and technology tools allow, their application and impact on learning and identity are mediated by the social positions and community contexts that organize participation.

Our view of learning is therefore very participatory.[5] Whenever people are engaged in activities with each other, the potential for learning is there. In both the case studies we discuss, the practice of participating—that is, being a youth media producer or a student representative to the School Board—gives youth a chance to learn in a way that would be difficult to achieve in a classroom. The learning contexts are about constructing opportunities for youth to experience authentically how to participate in a community dialogue or in decision making. Mullahey et al. define participation in its extension into the broader community:

> Young people's work that focuses on individual learning and development, rather than on changing their surrounding, is not real participation—participation should not only give young people more control over their own lives and experiences but should also grant them real influence over issues that are crucial to the quality of life and justice in their communities.[6]

Through such experiences, students learn how to use the technologies, but they also learn to understand the power relationships, to be critical about the assumptions, to speak the language (i.e., to use the discourse of the organizing systems), and generally, how to get things done. In these learning environments, identity and agency are thus intertwined.[7]

Our two case studies feature youth learning how to have leadership voices in their communities. The cases are comparable in their prioritizing of learning goals, the importance of technologies in supporting both participation and learning, the presence of adult guidance and intervention, and youth-led attempts to steer community discourse. They contrast in their uses of digital media, the pedagogical approaches, and how these engagements enhance young people's participatory capacities. In the first case, digital media are front and center, yet dependent on the social technologies brought into the learning process. In the second case, youth are deeply immersed in cultural technologies and default to the use of everyday digital media to make progress. In both cases there are multiple channels through which these interactions happen, some with and facilitated by adults, and some through "back channels" that are created and negotiated by youth. We describe how youth and adults establish learning environments for each other, negotiate the grounds for participation, and explore the possibilities and limitations of the various technologies in the process. Both cases support the idea that this learning is something that young people do actively as agents in their own development.[8]

Education of the next generation of youth in the areas of youth leadership, civic activism, and social justice is proliferating worldwide in formal and informal learning settings.[9] The idea of youth as agents who shape society stands in contradiction, at some level, with having their voice and agency managed by adults. Current attempts to promote positive youth development entail a range of participation opportunities, including public policy advocacy, community organizing, and organizational decision making.[10] They emphasize youth voice, and push toward reallocating systemic access to positions of power for setting agendas, taking actions, and making decisions in partnership with adult decision makers. While both the settings we describe are explicitly trying to engage youth in learning to participate in civic leadership, the use of technology differs in each case. While the media organization engages digital media forms as a function of its social justice work, the student board illustrates the use of *everyday* media that youth access as a means of organizing their participation in the policy-making process. Yet, as we shall argue, it is precisely in the combination or mixture of social, cultural, and digital technologies that the possibilities for learning and identity reside.

Identity and Youth Media: Learning to Change the Discourse

I make media because it's important to me . . . not everyone gets the chance to voice their opinion through media. Just because we're teenagers doesn't mean that we don't care about social issues. Many of us do care and it's time for the world to hear our voice. —Youth producer, age fifteen

Working Together and Coming Apart: Adultism

The young people had spent weeks getting to know each other, but now they were at a crossroads. Twelve ethnically diverse youth from New York City's public schools and low-income communities were in a group at Global Action Project (G.A.P.),[11] a social justice youth media arts organization. They were debating intensely what their collaborative documentary video would be about, and were starting to feel the pressure of the production deadline—they were running out of time. Frustrated by each other, the process, and their facilitators, the youth had to reach a collective decision quickly. Guided by Shreya and Max, two media educators new to G.A.P., the youth agreed on a compromise: they would make a video about their common experience with "adultism," the practice of adults' systematic discrimination against young people.

The topic of "adultism" had emerged from a series of preproduction media workshops on identity and power designed by the media educators in which the youth had visually charted social relationships and questions about identity (e.g., how many people connect with a "subordinate" identity as the one that is most important to them? Why do you think that is? There are many dimensions of our identities we don't always think of—was there any privilege or power you had taken for granted?). In employing the organization's social justice framework for media production, which critiques systemic social issues by exploring identity, community, power and social action through a collaborative team work model, the educators had been hoping to cultivate common ground among the youth by having them generate shared experiences from their daily interactions with adults. What materialized was a raw, if limited, picture of urban youth being searched, followed, monitored, disrespected, and silenced.

Although they had spent workshop time brainstorming an array of topics for their documentary, such as abortion and substance abuse, the group had already generated footage on the theme of "adultism" in their practice camera shoots and "vox pop" interviewing exercises (to investigate how media shape identity, identity workshops are paired with technical training exercises). Team building efforts such as generating safe space rules and expectations for working with each other (e.g., be respectful, listen) had created a functioning group dynamic, but ongoing and conflicting opinion in the room about "adultism" as a topic was having a negative effect. Shreya reflected, "We had a contingent of youth who wanted the topic . . . then we had some who picked it because it would enable them to start editing

Figure 1
Youth slavery at the Harvard Club. ©Global Action Project, 2005.

and get to an advanced skills stage sooner, and then we had some who didn't want it, and eventually compromised but felt badly about it later." Amanda, a youth leader within the program, agreed, "It was really tricky to work on, because half of the group didn't like the topic. After lots of debate, it was the only thing more than three people could agree on, and so we went with that. I wouldn't really say that we 'chose' it." Adultism, by default and design, had chosen them.

With the deadline for the public screening of their video at a community-wide winter celebration fast approaching, the group dived into a frenzy of hands-on production work, shooting first-person narratives, editing, and sound scoring. Visually and conceptually addressing the topic remained problematic. They decided to have peers speak directly to the camera and recount their experiences with adultism, and one after another, they described being victimized, tokenized and put down. One story features Tati, a young woman who attended a conference on youth slavery at the Harvard Club as part of a school-based human rights community service project. Sharply recalling how conference organizers made the youth wear humiliating baseball caps and sit in the corner of the room, denying them food, and ignoring their questions, she says, "It was like youth slavery at the youth slavery conference!" (see Figure 1). Outraged by her own powerlessness, she admits to rebelliously swiping a coffee cup from the club to make a point, albeit one she suspects went unnoticed by the adults.

To prepare for the public presentation of their video at the screening, the group discussed their concerns about the project. Although they had moved forward on the topic, the "us versus them" framing of youth/adult relationships was still a concern. What about loving parents and grandparents, favorite teachers, their staff facilitators? some asked. How would that be addressed? What about talking down to younger youth? others argued. Weren't older teens just as guilty of adultism? With Max and Shreya, the youth discussed new questions about power—"how does this experience of power over-impact interactions with fellow youth and with adult allies? And how does it impact your self-image? How can you resist various levels of adultism?"—and created a pre-screening audience activity called *Please Stand Up If*. They entitled their video *The Missing -Ism,* to underscore the absence of adultism in a "canon" of inequalities (i.e., racism, classism, sexism), and wrote an artist statement to explain their intent:

> Adultism is the oppression of young people, through attitudinal, cultural, and systematic discrimination. We wanted to look at an issue that is ingrained in societies across the globe . . . that everyone faces at

one time or another, often without recognizing what it is. It is an overlooked -ism that many take as part of the norm in society, and therefore, internalize it. Especially in media, youth are portrayed as ignorant and apathetic—as a youth video group, this is our way of countering that. —Youth producers, 2005

The winter celebration was a packed community affair with youth, staff, family, friends and others. Two youth led the group's *Please Stand Up If* exercise. To allow all in the room to observe who else had experienced adultism and have people reflect on their own, they asked the audience to "please stand up if":

- You have ever been called a name by an older person (e.g., stupid, ugly)
- Your dress, appearance, body size, height, shape or looks were ever made fun of or criticized by an adult
- You ever put down someone else for his or her dress or appearance, body size, height, shape, or looks
- Adults have ever ignored you, served you last, or watched you suspiciously in a store
- An adult or someone your age ever stood up for you.

The room moved up and down as waves of adults and youth stood together in response to the prompts. After watching the video, youth in the audience had overwhelmingly positive feedback. Their questions revealed how engaged they were by the topic—"I'm really glad you did this," "teachers disrespect us all the time," "why did you make this?" The group, although pleased, was surprised and some members spoke directly about the disagreements that were such a difficult part of the process, from representing adult–youth relationships, to feeling forced to choose the topic, to not even being sure what "adultism" meant. Yet presenting *The Missing -Ism* had become an occasion for the transformation of the group, enabling its members to see how their struggles could generate dialogue. It also challenged them to take on a greater level of ownership when it came to choosing the next documentary topic, regardless of the production timeline or staff-generated activities. They had experienced that "power is the ability to take one's place in whatever discourse is essential to action and the right to have one's part matter."[12]

Critique and Questions: What Did They Learn?

Nevertheless, for the media educators and adult staff, *The Missing -Ism* was problematic. Featuring short pointed cuts of youth naming how they had been oppressed, the video was honest but overly simplistic. It lacked technical or aesthetic accomplishment, relied on "talking heads," and focused solely on the issue of victimhood. Staff raised questions about why the video did not portray the disagreements youth had about the roles adults play in their lives, did not feature instances of youth who are organizing and responding to pervasive forms of adultism (e.g., against military recruitment actions, youth-led educational reform efforts), or present an analysis of "adultism" as a social justice issue. Significantly, some staff felt the topic was misleading as a "stand-alone category" and should not be equated with historical and institutional oppressions such as racism and classism. One member of staff asserted, "I don't think rich straight white kids are oppressed. This country and its culture fetishize its youth population."

The video also raised questions about the organization's curriculum, the professional development of media educators, and the deep challenges of engaging youth and adults in a collaborative process—a process that should, as education philosopher Maxine Greene has written, enable youth to discover the power of their voices through making media, when they "find themselves able to 'name' and imagine how they might change their worlds for the first time as they capture it through a scene or narrative, a gesture or dialogue."[13]

Taking Charge: Producing "Set Up"

The youth and staff moved to the spring production cycle with renewed energy, focus and attendance. Staff encouraged youth to develop their topic further, and to ground it in specific daily life and community concerns rather than solely identity-focused ones. Other important elements were in place: the youth were working as a group, had completed a challenging project, and had developed their media making skills (e.g., camera work, editing). They had moved from being peripheral players to more central ones: the group was now positioned to increase the quality of their collaboration, production and analysis.

During topic selection it became clear that almost everyone in the room had, at some point, seriously considered leaving high school before graduation, and that two of the twelve were considering the Navy, in a time of war, as their only alternative. They saw that education affected them individually, as a cohort, and in relation to the political, economic, and social well being of their families and communities. This time the group agreed quickly on addressing the issue of "dropping out," but with a twist. The youth felt, or had seen others, "pushed out" from completing high school by being discouraged, criminalized, punished for being pregnant, or having special needs. They planned a different kind of documentary, one that reflected their new skills as media makers. Through workshops and research, the group identified who and what they wanted to represent, from in-depth interviews with community activists and scholars who had studied the issue to young people directly affected by discriminatory school policies. They hosted advocacy group workshops on the legal rights of minors (with a special focus on mental health and reproductive rights, which have an impact on graduation rates) and attended youth media and activist conferences to interview peers about dropouts and pushouts in their schools. They brainstormed segments to produce or research. Shreya recounted, "we tried to get each young person to commit to something they wanted to do . . . for example, Gabriel wanted to do music and interview his brother who left high school and is still successful. Amanda wanted to add narrative elements and interview someone with a General Equivalency Diploma. Corina wanted to find a documentary she had seen on the history of education."

Demonstrating greater visual storytelling, cinematography, and editing skills, the youth developed and shot dramatic reenactments of a young pregnant woman who believes she will be forbidden from graduating, and of a parent struggling with a confusing contract that waives her rights to keep her son in school. They also creatively represented educational statistics, and concluded with a powerful personal story told by Jessica, a participating youth, who tells of three generations of her family being pushed out of school and of her own determination to be the first to make it through to graduation and beyond. Reflecting an informed frustration with the NYC public school system's policies and a belief that youths' attempts to get the education they deserved were being routinely thwarted, they entitled the video *Set Up*. Again in an artistic statement, they explain:

> This video questions why people leave school or fail to graduate. Rather than focusing on the more commonly held problem of "drop outs," the video examines the trends of push outs, and the many ways that young people feel discouraged by the educational system. Interviewing educational researchers, students, and the young people in our group, we try to present the stories behind the statistics.

Figure 2
Screen shots from *Set Up*. ©Global Action Project, 2005.

For the final screening, the group produced a viewing sheet, which offered structured discussion ideas for audiences, and explained why they had chosen to address this particular issue:

> This was a topic that was important to all of us in group. We all knew someone who had left school, or had struggled with that decision ourselves. During our research on why people leave school, we started looking at school policies, laws, funding, and realizing that the reasons why people leave aren't just personal. Students can be pushed out, literally, or *feel* pushed out in a subtle way. We focused on push outs, because it's something that people don't really talk about in mainstream media, and something that even people who *are* pushed out don't really realize what has occurred to them. We wanted to make a movie that showed some of the real reasons people leave school, and that would spur people to action.

The viewing sheet included prescreening suggestions: "How would you define a drop out? How would you define a push out? Does anything in this video relate to your life or personal experiences?" They also offered resources for learning more about the topic, from websites for groups such as the Drum Major Institute for Public Policy and Advocates for Children to the Civil Rights Project at Harvard University (see *Set Up* shots in Figure 2).

From conception to completion, *Set Up* reflected the active learning and participation that enabled the group to reach its potential for producing compelling media, in collaboration with peers and with the support of adults. Publicly presented and emceed by the youth at the organization's end-of-year screening celebration to an audience of over 200 people, *Set Up* generated an intense viewer discussion, from personal reflections by adults who shared their own experiences with dropping out and appreciated seeing the issue framed in a new way, to youth who were being pushed out, to those who wanted to know what organizing work the young people were doing along with media making.

Set Up was not without challenges or limits. From the media educator perspective, it was clear that this video documentary went much farther than *The Missing -Ism* in terms of both group process and final product. Critiques of the piece focused on its potential to be used by youth as a teaching tool, the need for a more diverse range of experts (e.g. community-based, of color, young), and a suggestion for youth to offer strategies for solutions from their perspectives. The production reflects ongoing struggles to locate and define "youth voices" and to promote young people's participation in the wider social structures that influence their lives. At its best, this kind of participatory media production work reflects a "ladder of participation—from token representation to active self-determination"[14] that the youth, the adults who worked and learned with them, and the organization itself were able to climb.

Digital Media, Social Technology, and Learning: The Broader Youth Media Context

Only by engaging in society—and working to make it better—can youth come to terms with who are, what they believe, and how they relate to others and to society as a whole. —Nicholas Winter.[15]

The number of programs in the United States that use digital media to engage young people in positive activities outside of school settings has grown tremendously during the last decade.[16] What began as a small community-based arts movement is defining itself as a field, encompassing a variety of communicative art forms such as audio/radio, film/video, print, web and media production. From digital storytelling to documentary production, programs range broadly in their missions, methods, audiences, and media forms.[17] Many focus exclusively on creative expression, while others actively use media as a vehicle for leadership development and civic engagement. The learning practice used by these kinds of programs is typically hands-on, experiential, and focuses primarily on production.[18] Core challenges facing youth media practitioners include managing the delicate balance of process versus product, and defining "youth voice" in the context of making digital media.[19] Those particular challenges are clearly reflected in the case above, where the most important decisions and experiences of the youth were responsively shaped—and contested—by production timelines, group dynamics, demands of adult educators, and young people's own developing skills and sensibilities as social issue media makers, as youth "with a voice."

The Missing -Ism and *Set Up* were produced in an organization that has spent years crafting a curriculum and methodology that aims to engage young people in creatively representing themselves and their communities, in making media that respond to the social, cultural, economic, and political forces that affect them daily, and in using media for dialogue and positive social change. These goals are not easy to attain, and their accomplishment requires ongoing questioning and negotiation by staff and youth, while meeting the demands of the production process.

Informed by approaches drawn from social justice campaigns, community media, youth development, and popular education movements, the organization has designed a critical literacy framework to engage young people in the collective examination and production of media. The term "critical literacy" is gaining more traction within the youth media field as a way of describing a pedagogy that teaches multiple literacies, continuous inquiry, and reflection.[20] In this social justice youth media arts organization, it also refers to an intentional process supported by curriculum, teaching methods, staff training, media production/analysis activities, outreach efforts, and assessment practices that strive to be intergenerational and dialogic (as it explicitly acknowledges the role of adults in the mix). It also describes an intentional outcome, the goal of which is to enable youth to "read," "write," and "rewrite" the world through making media, and to encourage them to see themselves as active agents, able to shape their own identities, experiences and histories—what educators Paulo Freire and Donaldo Macedo have described as a "relationship of learners to the world" shaped through an interpretation, reflection, and a "rewriting of what is read."[21] In this sense critical literacy is more than a set of thinking strategies: it should enable youth to produce media that, as the staff describe, use "the power of storytelling to challenge dominant narratives and write new histories." Steve Goodman, a leading US media educator, argues that this necessarily entails developing an awareness of one's identity and agency, in which "learning about the world is directly linked to the possibility of changing it."[22] It also approaches the learning of youth and staff as a social endeavor that supports youth as coconstructors of knowledge and values creating a responsive setting in which young people can enter "a community with a level of expertise on which to build deeper understanding."[23]

Clearly, these are guiding principles on which practice is based, and it is in practice that the greatest tensions and possibility are seen. The developmental arc that young people experienced in the process of making media reflects the context and the intent of learning that was actively shaped, pushed, and at times limited by the critical literacy framework. Often critical pedagogies claim to empower young people through developing new knowledge, but they are also criticized for being directive and agenda driven, ultimately the work of an adult-initiated vision of justice or social change.[24] In this story, we saw adults and youth both struggling and working together to find their place in the process, sometimes successfully and sometimes not. Through production and public screenings that involved their reflection on identity, not least on what it means to "speak" as a young person or to represent young people, youth were organized and compelled to identify issues of importance to their lives and communities, and adults scaffolded access to working relationships, new skills, and meaningful opportunities for youth participation in reshaping social conditions that affected them. The social technologies of curriculum, activities, debate, public presentation, research, group dynamic rules, and organizational goals challenged youth to inquire, reflect, and apply their knowledge to connecting with and negotiating the world, producing media and content that offer an informed perspective. It is through these practices and with a sense of agency that the youth might spark a conversation, create a new understanding, or educate communities, peers, and organizers. Critical literacy, then, is the outcome of such participation. As one of the youth, Amanda, explains:

> That is what youth leadership is about, having confidence in yourself to stand up and speak about your work, your beliefs and not be intimidated . . . youth are equipped to lead not only workshops but also entire movements if we wanted to. This is important because young people grow up and if they have the skills, tools and knowledge, changing the world is not impossible.

The key point of this case is that the process of developing young people's leadership and active participation in the world around them does not come about simply as a result of having access to the technology, or even to training in the analysis and production skills they need to use it. It is a complex, iterative process that involves identifying and thinking through what it is they want to say; interacting with adults, who play a key role in setting parameters, offering possibilities and challenges; collaborating with peers in new ways; and taking account of the audiences that they are seeking to address and to influence. Taken together, these "social technologies" embody particular social relationships, expectations of producing media together, and ways of working that engage young people in dialogue, and support and challenge them to recognize their own capacity for inquiry and action. Learning doesn't necessarily happen instantly, but develops over time as youth have the structured opportunity to reflect on and critique what they have done, with the goal of improving the next time around. "Social technologies" give digital media purpose as a means for youth to craft new identities as learners, and potentially as social leaders.

Mixing It Up: Everyday Digital Media and the Cultural Technology of Policy-Making

I think it just comes into our lives because we're a technology-based age anyway. We've all grown up with computers, so it just kinda comes naturally to us. It's not like we have to do any struggle to work with any, um, technology. —Interview with Eliza, junior, January 2, 2006.

Eliza was a representative for her school on the Student Advisory Board (SAB)—an officially recognized organization of a large, urban school district in northern California. Seventeen high schools in the district could elect and send student representatives to the SAB, which presented student perspectives on policy issues to the School Board and the Superintendent. In an interview about her experience as a student representative, Eliza argued that technology was simply a given in her experience. It was just a part of how she and other students lived in the world, and as such, it became a part of how they fulfilled their representative duties. Here, we will talk about shifts in the students' use of digital media as they learned more about what it took to be responsible for raising "student voice."

Like the youth filmmakers in New York, SAB representatives were part of an intentional learning process supported by adult facilitators, and they were committed to bringing a youth perspective into view. However, their use of digital media was not the primary focus in organizing their opportunities to learn. Instead, the SAB illustrates ways in which student representatives incorporated their use of "everyday digital media" into their work. By the term *everyday*, we are referring to digital media tools and electronics—mobile phones, instant messenger tools, websites, etc.—that students were using as a matter of course in their daily lives. These everyday media were appropriated for unanticipated or unintended uses (for example, using a text message on a mobile phone to spontaneously convene hundreds of people in a designated location). Yet activity on the SAB was dominated by youth learning to use the *cultural technologies* that made up their district's policy making mechanisms, such as bylaws, parliamentary procedures, public notices, and resolutions. These cultural technologies organized specific forms of activity (for example, using a resolution to fuel public scrutiny of a contested decision). Taken together, the cultural and digital technologies became mutually constitutive of youth participation on the SAB (for example, using email to urge other students to react to a document or using a resolution to introduce a policy recommendation), and it is the combination that is of interest in understanding how students participated and learned.

As the student representatives on the SAB learned how to use the district's cultural technologies while managing their own communication needs, the everyday and the formal gradually became intertwined, a process which had its challenges:

Over the phone and instant messenger, we could multitask with our homework and talk to people. . . . In the beginning . . . we tried to do instant messenger group meetings, like if we can't meet, just to talk about certain topics online. But that really didn't go so well because people were just joking around and stuff like that. That's an informal kind of thing that came into play. It was kind of hard to mix both worlds. [We're] supposed to be formal about something, but it's hard. —Interview with Chris, senior, February 11, 2006.

Chris's assessment of early attempts to combine their formal responsibilities with their everyday, informal online communication points out an instance where identities appeared separate and competitive—where what they were "supposed" to be doing as representatives was in conflict with what they *were* doing as students. The story of two events illustrates how competing identities were organized and reconciled between student and adult participants.

Meet the New SAB: Knowing and Showing How to "Represent" with a Cultural Technology

The goal was to emphasize how the whole group participated in developing and/or approving the bylaws. The group decided that Jack, Chris, Milton, and Janel would make the presentation at the board meeting... [and] that each SAB member present at the board meeting would come to the podium and introduce themselves (name, school, and grade). —Field note, SAB Meeting February 23, 2004.

Nine students were present at a February 23 SAB meeting to prepare for their upcoming presentation at a public meeting of the School Board, and they were concerned about demonstrating full representation in the face of declining participation. During the previous school year, the SAB had temporarily lost their sanction after a series of public disagreements with the Superintendent that resulted in the removal of one of their representatives from his position as a student delegate to the School Board. Following the suspension, the Superintendent required that the students update their bylaws before resuming their roles as official student representatives. The youth learned that the district required its official boards to maintain bylaws that defined the group's purpose and the rules governing its functions. They had been working toward presenting their revised bylaws for two-thirds of the school year, meeting biweekly as a whole group and in additional subcommittee meetings:

I just remember the bylaws because that's what our goal was. The first meetings were just an introduction to what we were doing... we were laying out the foundation of the [SAB] for the next year so it's stable. From my understanding, the Superintendent fired the old people who were working with us, so everything had to be rearranged and fixed. I wasn't really sure what happened... the superintendent wanted to us to have bylaws before we could represent the students. It took us almost the whole school year because there'd be something wrong. Then we'd have to go to a subcommittee. It was a back and forth thing until it was perfect for us. —Interview with Chris, senior, February 11, 2006.

Regaining the official sanction would ultimately require approval by the district's legal department, the Superintendent, and a majority of the School Board. In short, the youth were disenfranchised from their advisory roles, and the task of bylaw writing had consigned them to the periphery until it was completed.

Early in the rebuilding process, the students' use of digital media was very much an everyday matter. They used e-mail to set meetings and share updated drafts of the bylaws. They used their mobile phones during meetings to confirm their whereabouts with their families and for their usual social commitments. Milton attested to this, stating, "It's also an organizing tool, so students can get rides home. I get calls from my parents during meetings. Sometimes I don't take it right away to avoid being rude" (Junior, Interview, August 21, 2005). Their digital media use was secondary to and mostly separate from their focus on learning to use the cultural tools required by the district for participation. At this stage, digital media were useful but not necessary to develop their intended identity as respected participants in district policy making.

The SAB members were primarily concerned with meeting high standards of conduct and professionalism. Issues of representation dominated the writing of the bylaws, particularly regarding the issue of quorum—the minimum number of representatives who must be present before the group can conduct business. Without the bylaws assignment occupying them, they would have been contributing to the district's debates about how to improve school safety and addressing student concerns with the nutrition policy. Instead, they were tackling the issue of quorum from all angles (How do you count it? When do you need it? What can you do if you don't have it? What is a high-enough standard?). They were regularly responding to recommendations for change from the Superintendent's office and the legal department, and they were not quite sure what the quorum requirements were for voting on the incremental changes. Minutes of the meeting showed the quorum deliberations:

The group discussed what action could be taken about the revisions to the bylaws without a quorum . . . Could the smaller group simply accept the recommended changes, or was a quorum required for this as well?

Pro [Decide without quorum]	Con [Wait until we have quorum]
▪ If these are required recs, then a quorum isn't necessary ▪ The [SAB] has already passed the bylaws ▪ Avoid re-doing the subcommittee process	▪ Complete [SAB] voice isn't represented ▪ It's the right thing to get a full vote ▪ This meeting's attendees can act as a subcommittee and make recs to full [SAB] ▪ Concern over legality of decision without a quorum

Decision: Work on bylaws at this meeting. Unofficial vote on recommendations. Bring recommendations to next [SAB] meeting for final discussion and vote. Work hard to make sure [SAB] has a quorum at the next meeting.

The youth had been working on the bylaws for four months when they had this discussion, and attendance had dropped to roughly one third of the group. They were concerned about leaving themselves open to attacks on their process that might further hamper their ability to function as representatives of the student voice. So, for the public record, they agreed to wait two more weeks for a vote on the recommended changes. They put the word out by phone and e-mail that they were ready for a final vote and managed to double attendance to achieve quorum.

Their concern with appearing thorough and professional was unmistakable, and it extended into every discussion that followed. This event clarified an early intersection of the students' representative and youth identities. Their identities as representatives were beginning to be expressed through their use of the cultural technologies for "official" participation, in this instance, bylaws and quorum. Their identities as youth were being expressed through their use of everyday digital media for managing the constraints on their physical presence (i.e., being distributed in neighborhoods across the city and grappling with transportation challenges).

Formality Gets Familiar: Using Everyday Digital Media to Assert Powerful Identities

My committee had chats on AIM [AOL Instant Messenger] about stuff. We debated a lot over AIM. I remember long chats debating stuff like the Superintendent's raise with four or five people in a chat.

There were pretty much two sides. We had things we all could agree on, but different opinions about how to do it. —Interview with Vince, sophomore, September 17, 2005.

Over a year after rewriting their bylaws, the SAB was back on track. They focused on rebuilding relationships with adult decision makers in the district, and they refined their processes for accomplishing work. Attendance was up, and they rarely worried about achieving quorum. They also had the cultural technologies well in hand. Meetings ran smoothly on parliamentary procedure with two or three students chiming in to second a motion they supported. They successfully wrote, revised and passed formal resolutions addressing curriculum needs and equitable access to extracurricular activities that were endorsed by the Board of Education, and they successfully convened a summit on safety and sexual harassment drawing hundreds of students across the district to boot. As a result, their attention was no longer focused on how to become representatives but on *being* representatives. Milton, a three-year veteran of the SAB, put it this way:

I think another big challenge is training. If you're going to get a bunch of new members, you need to get them to a point where they can start thinking about these issues by themselves . . . Once I understood the ropes and the processes, I got more comfortable understanding what I could contribute. —Interview with Milton, junior, August 21, 2005.

SAB representatives refocused their attention on issues rather than processes, and their identities as both representatives and youth began to meld. Their abilities to take action and need to involve many students affected their use of digital media tools. Vince offered the practical perspective, saying, "On a phone you can get three-way, but on AIM you can get as many people as you want to talk, and you won't run up a phone bill." Students consistently reported using web tools to communicate and conduct research, and using mobile phones to convene youth-only meetings. Their resolutions contained lists of citations with URLs to support their claims. What was originally experienced as unfamiliar formality became absorbed into students' everyday practices. So, at the end of the 2004–05 school year when the students tackled two of the most controversial issues in their district, their combined use of cultural technologies and digital media was nearly seamless.

In the wake of budget cuts and school closures, members of the SAB drafted two resolutions that directly challenged the Superintendent's decisions. The first and most controversial called for the renegotiation of her contract after a recently approved pay increase and renegotiated severance plan. The second opposed "reconstitution,"[25] a feature of one of her signature reform programs. These were contested issues among a wide range of communities connected with the school district: the teachers' union, parent groups, youth activist and governance organizations, and inside the School Board itself. The youth faced pressure from all sides. Students contacted the local media, and the Superintendent's office responded with a 30-page press release suggesting that adult-driven interests were co-opting a student group and drawing them into a political debate that was not appropriate territory for the SAB. At the same time, other groups such as the Teachers' Union mobilized to support the resolutions.

During this storm of activity, representatives used their access to digital media to bring the formal world of policy-making into the "youth-only" spaces they had created in their everyday lives. The intensity of the moment gave them a formal purpose inside their typically informal world of digital communication. It also allowed them to express themselves more freely: as Eliza put it, "You can display emotions on e-mail!"

Based on accounts in interviews, by the time the resolutions were introduced for the first time at an SAB meeting, most of the representatives were already familiar with them and had spent significant time debating their merits in online discussions and phone calls. This was evident during a heated public meeting where some members were pushing for an immediate vote on the resolutions:

> Eleanor said she hoped the group would not vote on the resolutions tonight because they needed to hear both sides first. Manny asked if there was anyone there who could speak from the other side. Katherine, the SAB's staff person, responded that the group would need to invite someone else to speak. Shannon encouraged the group to vote tonight because, "you should trust yourself and your thoughts about it because you've already heard about it before." —Field Note, SAB Meeting, May 23, 2005.

Shannon, a junior, spoke about the group's use of mobile phones, although she did not own one herself, explaining how they used them "to schedule the secret meetings and not-secret meetings . . . Eliza and I sat at [a pizza place] and called everyone, passing Eliza's cell phone back and forth and checking our numbers against each other."

At the last regularly scheduled meeting of the school year, tensions ran high. Adults accused each other of trying to manipulate the students. Students accused adults, on all sides, of pressuring them and stepping into what they felt should have been a youth-led decision. Still, the students managed to run their meeting according to parliamentary standards. Members of the public complimented the SAB for their efforts to conduct a professional meeting, and the district's legal counsel congratulated them on "navigating a difficult meeting very well." Still, a decision on the resolutions had not been made, and the students opted to schedule a special meeting for the following week—a date that came after the completion of the school year.

At this point, the Superintendent asserted her legal authority to postpone the meeting due to her inability to attend. Attempts to negotiate alternative solutions failed. Student representatives anticipated that summer break would make it difficult to get a quorum, and they resisted the attempt to postpone. They tried a novel approach to beating the system by resigning their positions, via e-mail, to reduce the quorum requirement. After the first four attempted resignations were sent, Milton responded with this message:

> . . . quorum was established for a reason: that we would have at least a MINIMAL amount of all [schools in the district] represented when we make decisions, so when we lower quorum, we are lowering membership represented, which is the strength of our voice because we are representatives . . . It's a weighty responsibility, to be a representative, so even if it is just because you can't make the meeting doesn't mean you should give up. Try to get an alternate. If all else fails, at least we all would be doing our jobs in trying to get the most represented out of all the schools in the district, cause it's more than us bringing ourselves, it's bringing our schools' representation. —E-mail to SAB and staff, Milton, June 11, 2006.

As it turned out, the resignations were not necessary because the group reached a quorum on the night of the meeting. It is noteworthy that representatives used their understanding of the resignation policy in their bylaws and their access to e-mail to formalize their strategy. The integration of cultural technology (in the form of bylaws and quorum) with digital media (in the form of e-mail communication) indicates that the students had developed a degree of confidence in their identities, to the point where they felt able to resign in service of the student body. They had developed a *collective* identity as a student group with the right to be heard and had moved beyond their *individual* identities as representatives. Meanwhile,

Milton made a plea to their shared identities as representatives to challenge the resignation maneuver, reminding them of their strength as a group.

Ultimately, the students chose to hold the meeting in opposition to the Superintendent. Eliza wrote this email to the Superintendent in defense of their decision:

> We believe it is important to have this vote. In accordance with the Brown Act we could not legally vote on these resolutions Monday the 6th because we did not notice it 72 hours in advance, hence the meeting being called this Monday. We cannot postpone the meeting, nor does anything [you say] have the legal right to do so. We have checked with lawyers on this matter, to make sure that we are not over stepping our bounds in keep the meeting as is, as well as parliamentarian procedures. Everything I have read and everyone I have talked to has stated the same thing: (1) that the only people with the power to [cancel] or postpone the meetings are the members, and (2) that it says nowhere that the superintendent, nor any other staff, has the power to postpone the meetings. Even I, the president, do [not] have the power to postpone the meetings . . . the students want us to speak on it, and our first concern is to the students. Though we would like you to attend the meeting, it is unnecessary seeing [as] we are talking for the students. We speak for them, not for the adult[s] of the district.

The SAB had come full circle. They were back to focusing on process, but in a qualitatively different and unanticipated way. Eliza's e-mail to the Superintendent is an instance of student-representative agency, though it did not focus on the issues directly. She asserted her view of what processes were legitimate to a leading authority in the district. After hearing public comment from lawyers, parents, teachers, and students and choosing to hold the meeting in direct resistance to the Superintendent's postponement, the SAB passed both resolutions.

Once student representatives had an opportunity to reflect on the events, they spoke with pride about their abilities to stand up for student voice in the face of intense opposition. In interviews, they spoke of having real power, and how their views of their abilities to make change were bolstered by the standoff with the Superintendent. Still, at the end of the day, their resolutions did not achieve their stated goals as they did not prevent the Superintendent from obtaining her compensation package or from engaging in school reconstitution. This fact did not dissuade the student leaders. One of the group's long time members put it this way:

> We all came together and were so united. Initially, we were all over the place, we had a lot of media attention and our principals calling and threatening us. We still came together because we knew it was right for the students . . . The Superintendent was screaming at me and making accusations, and she's at the top of the whole district. I had to stand up to her, and I think she was taken aback that I could handle things like an adult . . . Sometimes all you need is your peers saying, "Yes, you can do it." —Interview with Eliza, January 2, 2006.

Combining Social and Digital Technologies: Comments on the SAB Case The cultural technologies and digital media played an integral role for SAB representatives in relation to their learning and their developing sense of agency. This, in turn, promoted the growth of a participant identity that was both supported and contested in the broader community. For the SAB, the cultural technologies were imperative for participation. In order to operate in an official capacity, they were required to have approved bylaws and to carefully follow state regulations for public meetings. When they intended to make an advisory statement to the Board of Education, they were compelled to produce formal documents called resolutions written in a format that was distinctive in its language and unfamiliar to most high school students. During their public meetings, they learned to use parliamentary procedure to work through the agendas in order to convey a professional and thoughtful approach. As they became more confident, they developed their own protocols to be used in conjunction with these formalized procedures. These were the technologies that lent them legitimacy and, more importantly, opened up opportunities to influence school policies and to become active agents on behalf of the students in their district.

These cultural technologies resided in the deliberation space of adults, but through communication facilitated by digital media, the students appropriated these technologies and used them to their own advantage in public meetings that were open to scrutiny and regulation by powerful adults. For student representatives, digital media became a key element in making those adopted cultural technologies their own. It was in the youth controlled spaces of instant messenger chats, text messages, and "secret" face-to-face meetings that students more freely considered strategies, priorities, and implications of various courses of action. The digital space was the site for students to consider creative ways of using the cultural technologies at their disposal to achieve their goals. It was also a place to create themselves as thoughtful and powerful participants—in a sense, to practice their agency before going public.

Digital media allowed students to learn as they moved forward, first testing ideas among peers before presenting those ideas to the district and the community at large. When they were wearily writing bylaws, they had not yet discovered ways to put the bylaws to work in service of their own goals. The same was true as they developed a process for deliberating about proposed resolutions. In the digital space, one student said it was difficult to accomplish much early on, because of the off-topic conversations and playfulness. Yet, as their facility with the District's tools increased, their learning became evident in their resolve to use digital communications for strategy, debate, and reflection. During the standoff with the Superintendent, the youth were required to be deftly improvisational in their use of bylaws, resolutions, and the local media.[26]

Their entrance into that political space was not welcomed by the Superintendent but was validated by some Board members, some adult staff, and members of the public. Still, tensions between youth and adults in all capacities ran high. The struggle for participation and the story of the SAB members' hard-won agency is important because it illustrates how youth can move beyond being token representatives in adult civic processes.[27] Still, students experienced even the adults who spoke in favor of their resolutions as politically opportunistic rather than as committed supporters of youth involvement and leadership. On one hand, the presence of so many different adults participating in this debate, fueled by student resolutions, gave the student representatives a sense of their own agency and ability to influence the public conversation. On the other hand, the actions of many adults—including the Superintendent, SAB staff, teachers' union representatives, and local journalists—disrupted the process students had diligently created to manage their own deliberations. Ultimately, the final vote was more about a show of solidarity in a struggle for student voice than it was about the content of the resolutions themselves. Relative to other decisions made by the SAB, the text of the resolutions that was passed received less scrutiny and revision during meetings. This was due in part to time pressure and intense public debate. Yet much of the concern over *how* the resolutions should be worded was addressed in the informal spaces of youth-only meetings and back channel communications rather than during formal public meetings where changes could legitimately be instituted.

The SAB members' use of both digital and cultural technologies developed significantly over the course of the debates we have described. During the early bylaws assignment, they did not yet understand their purpose or use and were acting solely on adult directives. Before they learned ways to appropriate the cultural technologies in conjunction with their everyday digital media, the Superintendent more successfully managed their involvement. However, that style of management did not work as effectively once the students learned to resist and apply their knowledge in the political arena of the School Board. Learning, identity, and agency were therefore tightly coupled in the SAB case. Without their learning experience, their representative identities—both individual and collective—would not have developed, and their agency as representatives in this policy-making environment would have been compromised.

Discussion

Our case studies of youth making documentaries and youth on the School Board provide powerful examples of young people learning to participate in their larger communities. Through their media productions and board resolutions, the youth learn to engage and lead in worlds where they previously had few participation rights, no access to power, and few skills for organizing.[28] The youth learned these lessons in intentional, yet informal, learning environments, and we believe that, as learning contexts, these settings offer youth a unique combination of problems to tackle, social relationships, and technologies that engage learning and identity development in seamless ways.

Each story alone is a complex one; yet taken together, we believe they have two major implications for educators who work with youth in an increasingly sophisticated technological world. The first is that social, cultural and digital technologies are in constant interplay in learning environments connected to larger community participation. The second is that in these intentional yet informal contexts, learning, identity development and the ability to act with agency are deeply connected. We discuss each of these points in turn.

Social, Cultural, and Digital: Supports for Learning and Participation

Examining these multiple and varied technologies and how they are put to use in interactions by and for youth is important to understanding how they encourage and support learning and open the door to many kinds of capacities. Curriculum, brainstorming processes, or specific activities such as *Please Stand Up If* are all versions of social technologies that provide process and content. Cultural technologies such as *Robert's Rules of Order* (for parliamentary procedures) or bylaws provide structure, and digital media such as film, cell phones, and Internet activity mediate dialogue and participation spaces with and for youth. While references to digital media are familiar and commonplace, the social and cultural are not typically considered as tools in the technology toolbox. What makes them technologies is their design and use: they intentionally organize activity and can be appropriated in novel and unexpected ways. In these learning environments, authentic participation opportunities are created through the shared appropriation of the multiple technologies.[29] The combinations of these technologies and their associated practices help youth and adults create something authentic in terms of engagement, identity development, and meaningful participation in democratic activity. We see digital, social, and cultural technologies as tools for crossing borders that make it possible to reveal, generate, or bridge "fault lines" of power and ownership between youth and adults and the institutions in which they participate.

The combination of technologies plays a vital role in these identity building experiences. In both cases, youth worked with technologies to help them get their messages across.

The work that they did to get to the point where they could exercise agency and have impact was substantial. In the case of the *Set Up* group, they spent a great deal of time working with facilitating adults to explore their identities, their relationships to each other, and what they had in common, and completing a great deal of creative planning, research, and production work. In the SAB, students spent nearly an entire school year agonizing over the minutiae of writing bylaws so they could eventually have a voice in School Board policies. The resistance from powerbrokers led them to use everyday digital media "behind the scenes" for brainstorming, planning, and establishing plans of action. In both cases, participation was increased and learning became evident as youths developed their voice through the interplay of technologies.

Learning with increased participation, engagement, commitment, and action changes both the youth themselves and the vision of the adults who work with them. In both our cases we see youth-allied adults envisioning what youth participation can and should be, scaffolding ways for youth to participate, working with them, and eventually enabling power shifts that allow youth to define participation on their own terms. We also see dynamics of regulation and resistance to aspects of youth participation that do not align with adult expectations. In the moments where misalignments are apparent, both digital and social mediating tools are used in an integrated fashion that makes democratic participation accessible, even while it may be contested.

Identity, Agency, Learning in Intergenerational Contexts

Identity development is an emergent process that comes with sustained participation in existing community structures and discourses.[30] Adults in these cases are intentionally guiding youth through learning processes that support them in intervening in the communities in which they seek to participate. Evidence of this process of identity emergence abounds when youth engaged in unfamiliar or newer forms of discourse collide with adult expectations, intervention or regulation. It is in these moments that we see youth assert their agency, while making use of the community's social and cultural technologies, as they put their everyday electronic media into action.[31]

The documentary-producing youth tell a promising story of critical pedagogy at work, yet it is also a story that illustrates some of the tensions between adults and youth. It exemplifies how youth and adults create knowledge, culture, and social action together, and how media production can foster young people's abilities to creatively communicate, alternatively represent, and impact others as they document and possibly change their lives. The collaborative video production was a medium through which young people developed "critical literacy" and recognized their potentials for leadership, for peer-to peer-mentorship, and for social change. This example illustrates how important it is to create and sustain intergenerational environments where youth can learn to lead in demonstrable and powerful ways.

By contrast, the youth on the Student Advisory Board were embroiled constantly in intergenerational tensions as they sought participatory rights to represent student issues to the School Board. After many months of slogging through a process of writing bylaws, and struggling with attrition of their membership, the students finally won back their participation rights. The adults representing the interests of the Superintendent and aligned board members still found ways to resist the students' participation, while the youth used "back channel" digital communications to organize in ways that kept their participation active, to the point, and youth-driven. This makes the point that, even in organizations that aim to engage youth in civic participation, there can be a reluctance to accept the participation of youth who fully and freely engage. When youth do things that violate expectations or move into areas thought to be off-limits, it often terrifies adults.

Taken together, the stories help us better understand the tensions, contradictions, and promises of educating youth for participation and leadership. Appropriating media for "back channel" communication is possibly subversive of adult power, yet it can assist in achieving youth development goals. At the same time, this is impossible in isolation: other mediating technologies become necessary to move the conversation into a public space for democratic participation. Youth use digital media to "convene" when other channels are adult monitored. They instant message, engage in-group dialogues, go on the web and pull down and share information. Sometimes they are experimenting with new identities or organizing for action. These back channels conjure images of traditional youth culture in its differentiation from adult culture, while at the same time exemplify the practices of leaders who operate behind the scenes to move practices in the more formal arenas forward.[32]

Both our case studies are about how the mix of social, cultural, and digital technologies brought youth to new levels of participation—levels that surprise, inspire, and even threaten the adults who support their democratic engagement. Technologies, as communicative vehicles, serve as platforms for dialogue, discourse, and connection. By using a mix of technologies educationally, youth learn to represent themselves without being confined to the structures that keep them out of the public debate, or tokenizing their "voices" as pure, and therefore either true or naïve. Youth in these kinds of intentional learning environments may in fact be able to join in developing what Jenkins et al. (2006)[33] have called an emerging "participatory culture" made possible by new media. Undoubtedly, significant challenges remain here—ranging from unequal access and the lack of critical understanding of how technologies shape perception to "the breakdown of traditional forms of professional training and socialization that might prepare young people for their increasingly public roles as media makers and community participants."[34] Yet well-practiced education with technology can allow for forms of participation that Miles Horton, an educator of social movement leaders, would recognize as truly significant and transformative:

> If we are to have democratic society, people must find or invent new channels through which decisions can be made... the problem is not that people will make irresponsible or wrong decisions. It is, rather, to convince people who have been ignored or excluded in the past that their involvement will have meaning and that their ideas will be respected. The danger is not too much, but too little participation.[35]

Notes

1. See Larry Hickman, *John Dewey's Pragmatic Technology* (Bloomington: Indiana University Press, 1990), 17–59, for a discussion of Dewey's theory of technology and inquiry that addresses the use of tools in context for the purpose of inquiry as a foundation for knowing.

2. Raymond Williams, *What I Came to Say* (London: Hutchinson Radius, 1981; 1989), 173.

3. For further explanation of these technologies and others such as philosophical technologies, see Angela Booker, Learning to Get Participation Right(s): An Analysis of Youth Participation in Authentic Civic Practice (Unpublished PhD dissertation, Stanford University, 2007).

4. Hickman (1990) interprets John Dewey on the role of technologies and inquiry.

5. Socio-cultural theory views learning as socially based in contexts and activities. See Buckingham, this volume, for an explanation of the perspective as viewed by authors in this volume. See Lev S.

Vygotsky, *Mind in Society: The Development of Higher Psychological Processes,* ed. Michael Cole (Cambridge, UK: Cambridge University Press, 1978); Jean Lave, *Cognition in Practice* (Cambridge, UK: Cambridge University Press, 1988); Jean Lave and Etienne Wenger, *Situated Learning: Legitimate Peripheral Participation* (Cambridge, UK: Cambridge University Press, 1991). For how this is treated in media arts programs see Meredith I. Honig and Moira A. McDonald, From Promise to Participation: Afterschool Programs through the Lens of Socio-Cultural Learning Theory, *Afterschool Matters* (No. 5. New York: Bowne & Co., 2005).

6. Romana Mullahey, Yve Susskind, and Barry Checkoway, *Youth Participation in Community Planning* (Chicago: American Planning Association, 1999).

7. See Dorothy Holland, William Lachicotte, Jr., Debra Skinner, and Carole Cain, *Identity and Agency in Cultural Worlds* (Cambridge, MA: Harvard University Press, 1998), for a discussion of how learning, identity and agency are reflexive.

8. Francisco Villarruel, Daniel Perkins, Lynne Borden, and Joanne Keith, *Community Youth Development: Programs, Policies, and Practices* (Thousand Oaks, CA: Sage, 2003), 397. They state: "Positive development is not something adults do to young people, but rather something that young people do for themselves with a lot of help from parents and others. They are agents of their own development."

9. Scholars increasingly acknowledge childhood as a socially constructed phenomenon shaped by economic, political and sociocultural forces that determine the extent to which young people can be assertive (have a sense of agency) and influence the adult world [Janet Finn and Lynn Nybell, Capitalizing on Concern: The Making of Troubled Children and Troubling Youth in Late Capitalism. Introduction, *Childhood: A Global Journal of Childhood Research,* 8, no. 2 (2001): 139–145; Sue Ruddick, The Politics of Aging: Globalization and the Restructuring of Youth and Childhood, *Antipode* 35, no. 2 (2003): 334–362]. Older conceptions of youth as merely acted upon in the world have given way to analyses that acknowledge young people as social actors with citizen rights [Mark Jans, Children as Citizens, *Childhood* 11, no. 1 (2004): 27–44]. See Sharon Sutton, Susan Kemp, Lorraine Gutierrez, and Susan Saegert, *Urban Youth Programs in America: A Study of Youth, Community, and Social Justice* (Seattle, WA: University of Washington Press, 2006), 16. Youth have been central to many major social movements around the world in the last forty years including but not limited to movements to protect the rights of indigenous people and human rights in general, as well as protests against war and occupation. In the United States, the historical mark of youth movements of the 1960s is present in the current dynamics of youth participation in social and political discourse. Such movements functioned to establish youth as powerful civic participants and opened a cultural space where youth could expand their roles as agents for change. Those same movements also brought with them a sense that youth participation in political and democratic practice must be managed in order to prevent the disorder that was a feature of those movements. See United Nations Department of Economic and Social Affairs, *World Youth Report,* ST/ESA/301, October 2005; Mark Kitchell, *Berkeley in the 60s* (Three-part documentary film, San Francisco: California Newsreel, 1990).

10. Assumptions in youth development models in the United States have shifted from viewing youth as passive recipients of intervention strategies to viewing them as active agents for change. These shifts have opened up opportunities for collaboration between youth development professionals and youth civic activism organizers as well as multiple avenues for youth participants to combat adultism and assert their participation rights. See Taj James, Empowerment Through Social Changes, *Bridges, a Publication of Health Initiatives for Youth* 3, no. 4 (1997): 6–7; Shawn Ginwright and Taj James, From Assets to Agents of Change: Social Justice, Organizing, and Youth Development, *New Directions for Youth Development* 96 (2002): 27–46; Inca Mohamed and Wendy Wheeler, Broadening the Bounds of Youth Development: Youth as Engaged Citizens (New York: The Ford Foundation, 2001); and Linda Camino and Shepherd Zeldin, From Periphery to Center: Pathways for Youth Civic Engagement in the Day-To-Day Life of Communities, *Applied Developmental Science* 6, no. 4 (2002): 213–220.

11. Co-founded by Diana Coryat and Susan Siegel in 1991, Global Action Project is nationally recognized for its synthesis of youth development principles with media arts and for its critical literacy framework, which helps youth recognize and act on their potential for making positive social change and engage in civic debate through media production. For more information, or to see excerpts of youth media produced at G.A.P., visit: http://www.global-action.org (accessed December 24, 2006).

12. Carolyn Heilburn, *Writing a Woman's Life* (New York: Ballantyne Books, 1998), 18.

13. See Maxine Greene's Foreword in Steve Goodman, *Teaching Youth Media: A Critical Guide to Literacy, Video Production, and Social Change* (New York: Teachers College Press, 2003), ix–x.

14. Sutton et al., 2006.

15. Nicholas Winter, *Social Capital, Civic Engagement, and Positive Youth Development Outcomes,* Paper prepared with support from the Edna McConnell Clark Foundation and City Year, Inc., 2003.

16. Youth media is also an international movement. See Sanjay Asthana, *Innovative Practices of Youth Participation in Media* (Paris: UNESCO, 2006).

17. For an overview of recent trends in the growth of youth media as a field, from its role in changing the nature of literacy to recent evaluation strategies to assess audience impact see: Kathleen Tyner, *Literacy in a Digital World: Teaching and Learning in the Age of Information* (Mahwah, NJ: Lawrence Erlbaum Associates, 1998); Kathleen Tyner and Rhea Mokund, Mapping the Field: A Survey of Youth Media Organizations in the United States, in *A Closer Look 2003: Case Studies from NAMAC's Youth Media Initiative* (San Francisco: National Alliance for Media Arts & Culture, 2003); and Traci Inouye, Johanna Lacoe, Jennifer Henderson-Frakes, and Rebekah Kebede, *Youth Media's Impact on Audience & Channels of Distribution: An Exploratory Study.* Prepared for The Open Society Institute and The Surdna Foundation (Oakland, CA: Social Policy Research Associates, 2004). Additionally the *Youth Learn* web site at Education Development Center provides a general overview of youth media as well as background on their collaborative research and evaluation work of the field, which generated an outcomes model. See http://www.youthlearn.org/youthmedia/evaluation/collaborative_research.asp (accessed December 24, 2006).

18. For a review of the history, qualities, and importance of hands-on production in youth media and learning see: David Buckingham, ed. *Watching Media Learning: Making Sense of Media Education (*London: Taylor & Francis, 1990); David Buckingham, Jenny Grahame, and Julian Sefton-Green, *Making Media: Practical Production in Media Education* (London: The English and Media Centre, 1995); Jenny Grahame, The Production Process, in *The Media Studies Book,* ed. David Lusted (London: Routledge, 1991), 146–170; and Tyner (1998).

19. For examination of role of youth voice in media learning, see: Steve Goodman, *Teaching Youth Media: A Critical Guide to Literacy, Video Production and Social Change* (New York: Teachers College Press, 2003).

20. Steve Goodman, The Practice and Principles of Teaching Critical Literacy at the Educational Video Center in *Media Literacy: Transforming Curriculum and Teaching,* eds. Gretchen Schwarz and Pamela U. Brown for the National Society for the Study of Education (Chicago: University of Chicago Press, 2005), Yearbook 104:1. Identifies three key practices and principles for the pedagogy of critical literacy within youth media. These are teaching multiple literacies, teaching continuous inquiry, and teaching reflection.

21. Donaldo Macedo, *Literacies of Power: What Americans are not Allowed to Know* (Boulder, CO: Westview Press, 2006); Paolo Freire, *Pedagogy of the Oppressed,* translated by Myra Bergman Ramos (New York: Herder and Herder, 1970); Paolo Freire, *Pedagogy of Freedom: Ethics, Democracy, and Civic Courage,* translated by Patrick Clark (Lanham, MD: Rowman & Littlefield, 1998).

22. Goodman, 2003.

23. Honig, 2005.

24. Allison Cook-Sather, *Authorizing Students' Perspectives: Toward Trust, Dialogue, and Change in Education*, Educational Researcher, (Washington, DC: American Educational Research Association, 2002), 31(4): 3–14.

25. Reconstitution is a process that can be applied in several ways. The form referenced here requires teachers in a school to reapply for their positions when their school becomes part of the reform program.

26. See Holland et al. (1998) for a discussion of agency and learning.

27. Discussions of the changing nature of youth development from tokenism to authentic participation can be found in Camino and Zeldin (2002); Ginwright and James (2002); and Mohammed and Wheeler (2001).

28. Renato Rosaldo, Cultural Citizenship, Inequality, and Multiculturalism, in *Latino Cultural Citizenship*, eds. William Flores and Rina Benmayor (Boston: Beacon Press, 1997), 27–38; Jonathan Zaff, Oksana Malanchuk, Erik Michelsen, and Jacquelynne Eccles, *Promoting Positive Citizenship: Priming Youth for Action* (Washington, DC: Report prepared for the Center for Information and Research on Civic Learning and Engagement, 2003).

29. Jody Berland, Angels Dancing: Cultural Technologies and the Production of Space, in *Cultural Studies*, eds. Lawrence Grossberg, Cary Nelson, and Paula A. Treichler (New York: Routledge, 1992), 38–55; Hickman, 1990; Raymond Williams, *Television: Technology and Cultural Form* (New York: Schocken Books, 1974).

30. For views of identity considering the role of social, community-based identity work is especially salient in the Buckingham's Introduction and the chapter by Weber and Mitchell. David Buckingham, Introduction: Fantasies of Empowerment? Radical Pedagogy and Popular Culture, in *Beyond Radical Pedagogy*, ed. David Buckingham (London: UCL Press Limited, 1998).

31. Our notions of identity trace back to those who consider the social in the conceptualization of identity. We consider George Herbert Mead as he describes the self. See George Herbert Mead, *Mind, Self and Society* (Chicago: University of Chicago Press, 1934). On the more recent front, these positions are represented and discussed in Holland et al. (1998), as they represent arguments by Pierre Bourdieu, *Outline of a Theory of Practice*, trans. Richard Nice. Cambridge, UK: Cambridge University Press, 1977) and Vygotsky (1978).

32. John Clarke, Stuart Hall, Tony Jefferson, and Brian Roberts, Subcultures, Cultures, and Class, in *Resistance Through Rituals: Youth Subcultures in Post-War Britain*, eds. Stuart Hall and Tony Jefferson (1975); Paul Willis, *Learning to Labour* (Farnborough, UK: Saxon House, 1977).

33. Henry Jenkins, Katherine Clinton, Ravi Purushotma, Alice J. Robinson, and Margaret Weigel, Confronting the Challenges of Participatory Culture: Media Education for the 21st Century. An occasional paper on digital media and learning prepared for The John D. and Catherine T. MacArthur Foundation (Chicago: The MacArthur Foundation, 2006), 3. They discuss the role of media literacy in building bridges to an emerging participatory culture made possible by new digital media forms. They define a participatory culture as one "with culture with relatively low barriers to artistic expression and civic engagement, strong support for creating and sharing one's creation, and some type of informal mentorship whereby what is known by the most experienced is passed along to novices" (p. 3). The paper identifies a growing "participation gap"—"unequal access to the opportunities, experiences, skills, and knowledge that will prepare youth for full participation in the world of tomorrow"—and makes recommendations for addressing it.

34. Jenkins et al., 2006.

35. Miles Horton, *The Long Haul: An Autobiography* (New York: Anchor Books, Doubleday, 1990), 134.